An Introduction to
Cultural
Anthropology

R.B. Chamberlain, PhD, ThD

*"Preservation of one's own culture does not require contempt
or disrespect for other cultures."*   *– Cesar Chavez*

"No culture can live if it attempts to be exclusive."
    – Mahatma Gandhi

An Introduction to
Cultural Anthropology
Copyright © 2013
Robert B. Chamberlain, PhD, ThD

Independently Published 2013
Charleston, South Carolina, USA
ISBN-13: 978-1490392301
ISBN-10: 1490392300

Other books by the author
(available from Amazon.com by ISBN or ASIN; or from bookstores by ISBN)
(also available directly from the publisher at CreateSpace.com/CS#)

An Introduction to World Religions
An introductory textbook on the great World Religions: Judaism, Islam, Christianity, Hinduism, Buddhism, and more than a dozen others.
ISBN: 978-1484891605   CS#: 4271647   ASIN: B00CSC1XD6

The Life of Christ
The Bible's life of Christ. Proposes possible explanations of the miraculous gospel accounts that do not require suspending the laws of nature.
ISBN: 978-1477552322   CS#: 3891742   ASIN: B00BIQGAHM

The Miracles of Christ
A review of more than 2-dozen miracles of Christ. Proposes possible explanations of each that does not require suspension of the laws of nature.
ISBN: 978-1478263654   CS#: 3940602   ASIN: B008RYT7NW

The Resurrection of Christ
An account of what reportedly happened at and after the crucifixion of Christ. Includes Persian and Kashmiri stories of His survival and later life
ISBN: 978-1479317806   CS#: 3996549   ASIN: B009OM3YNU

An Introduction to
Cultural Anthropology

Table of Contents

Table of Contents
[*continued*]

Foreword

At the outset of any course, there are several questions that should probably be asked:

- What the heck is it ?
- Why should I take it ?
- Will I ever actually use whatever knowledge I gain ?
- Who is the instructor, and what are his/her qualifications ?
- Does he/she have some bias of which I should be aware ?
- What book will be used in conjunction with the course ?
- How much does it cost, and is it worth the price ?

So, if those are valid questions, how do they apply to this course?

What the heck is Cultural Anthropology?
Cultural Anthropology is the study of human cultures and their idiosyncratic practices. It is a look at humanity as a social being that forms, and lives in, communities.

Why should I take it?
The world is, as the cliché says, getting smaller all the time. Not only individual people, but groups of people (*i.e.* communities) are coming into contact with one another on an increasingly frequent basis. Understanding something about these groups can make it a much more pleasant and productive experience for all concerned..

Will I ever actually use whatever knowledge I gain ?
Possibly. Nobody can guarantee that the opportunity will present itself, but the basic information is clearly of value in cross-cultural, inter-community contact situations.

Who is the instructor, and what are his/her qualifications ?
Instructors can vary. Every instructor should introduce him/herself at the outset, and contact prior to registering is always wise.

Does he/she have some bias of which I should be aware ?
Again, possibly. Evaluate the likelihood of bias during the introductory class to determine if there is anything you suspect might become an issue.

What book will be used in conjunction with the course ?
In the case of ANT-2410 at EFSC, you're holding it. The fact is that there are many texts that could be, and often are, used as the primary text for an introductory course in Cultural Anthropology. Some are very good; some, quite honestly, are not. This is complicated by the fact that the field is so broad that a different emphasis or focus can alter the nature of the course tremendously. Some texts are very good, but don't address the issues and areas that will be addressed in the EFSC version of the course very well. Finally, there is the issue of cost. Most of the better texts range in price from $90 to $150. That may be too heavy a burden for many of our EFSC students.

How much does it cost, and is it worth the price ?
Traditionally, cost (and production quality) have varied. This version of the text is produced by a professional publisher, and pricing has been stablized (so that it won't vary from semester to semester). Keeping the cost this low is accomplished by writing the text here at EFSC, and printing it at an On-Demand publisher. As for value, it would be difficult to have anything at this price that would not be worth the cost; and, the text has been designed to present material in lock step with the course presentation. Each chapter aligns with one class meeting throughout the semester.

Will I ever actually use whatever knowledge I gain?
This is entirely up to you. Knowledge of the wide variety of ways which are considered "the norm" in different cultures, and by different people, has value commercially, politically, and personally. Whether or not you opt to take advantage of that is a very personal decision.

Student input
Many of the changes that occurred over the history of this text have occurred as a result of student input. Major revisions will be kept to an absolute minimum, so a new edition may not appear for quite some time (if at all). Nevertheless, if you, as a student, have suggestions how this text might have served you better at EFSC, the author would like to hear from you. All serious suggestions will be considered prior to any future edition of this work.

Section I
Introductory Material

This course is what is commonly known as a *Survey Course*. As such, the goal of the course is to provide a very broad overview of the material. Students who major in Cultural Anthropology (at any educational level – BS, MS, or PhD) might spend a full semester or more on any of the numerous topics covered in this course. Clearly, in this course, the opportunity to spend that amount of time on any specific topic is simply not available. So, all of the material covered here will be presented in very 'broad strokes'.

This material will be presented grouped into Sections that take a similar approach, but not necessarily topical areas that share any specific attributes. The purpose in a course such as this is primarily to acquaint the student with the tremendous degree of diversity that exists in common social functions. In many areas, the student just assumes that the 'way they do something' is the most logical, most natural, and most obvious way to do it. Frequently, however, they discover that most of the world does whatever it is in a completely different way. The student is not 'doing it wrong'; but, neither are those who do it differently.

A good example of this is the American-German-French practice of driving on the right hand side of the road. This isn't something that one even thinks about; it just occurs naturally (after having observed for decades that "everyone" does it that way). But, everyone doesn't do it that way: British-Australian-Indian drivers all drive on the left hand side of the road. Are they wrong? No. Are we wrong? No. We're just doing it differently. Historically, there were reasons why those countries that drive on the right elected to do that; and, similarly, there were reasons why those that opted to drive on the left decided to do that. Different history, different environment, different circumstances – different result.

So, what are these "Sections", and what do they cover? The course will be divided into six sections. These are:

- o Section I – Introductory Material
- o Section II – Socio-Cultural Markers
- o Section III – Ethnic and Cultural Systems
- o Section IV – Otherness
- o Section V – Applied Anthropology Research
- o Section VI – Applied Anthropology

Each of these sections will be briefly outlined prior to presenting the chapters included in them. For this section (*Section I*), the following four chapters are all concerned with establishing a common understanding of what the course is designed to accomplish, how the field of anthropology developed and is constructed, where *culture* comes from (*i.e.* what are the sources for it), and finally a look at genetics and a sub-field known as Sociobiology.

Chapter 1
Course Overview

Anthropology is one of the younger entries into the science field; and, Cultural Anthropology covers an extremely broad area within that science. As a result, an introductory course in Cultural Anthropology often tends to appear scattered and unfocused. The reason for this is the tremendous amount of material that needs to be introduced, into none of which is there time to delve very deeply. Be aware that this course is an overview of a topic which many colleges and universities offer as a full four-year baccalaureate program. Ideally, each topic area will be introduced sufficiently for the student to appreciate how it fits under the Cultural Anthropology umbrella, while also leaving the student with an interest in further pursuing the specific topic in their own studies.

This text consists of the materials to be covered in ANT.2410, the Cultural Anthropology course offered at Eastern Florida State College. In keeping with what is likely to be the typical school calendar in the upcoming years, this edition is divided into 28 chapters – each corresponding to one of the class meetings. It is expected that, if the school adheres to a 15+1 schedule each semester (15 weeks of instruction + 1 week of Finals) with 2 class meetings each week, that there will usually be 28 instructional meetings (assuming that one will be used for a mid-term exam, and there will be at least 1 legal holiday). Should weather (*e.g.* a hurricane), medical (*e.g.* a flu epidemic), or other emergency (*e.g.* a fire or power outage) reduce the number of class meetings, some material may either be dropped from the schedule or streamlined and consolidated with another class to enable the course to complete in the time allotted.

Although there are a number of very good Cultural Anthropology textbooks, this course does not use a typical commercial text. The cost for most of these texts is most often in the one hundred dollar range (or higher); and, none appear to add enough additional information to warrant this level of expenditure. If you are interested in a more formal treatment of any of the subjects, a list of recommended texts is included in *Appendix A: Suggested Further Reading*.

Our goals in this course are: (1) to determine the nature of "culture", and explore how it varies across the globe; (2) to develop an enhanced cultural sensitivity to varied cultural norms, and recognize the inherent validity they possess for their host cultures; and, (3) to develop ways in which we can apply this heightened sensitivity to make the world a safer, more harmonious, and more productive place.

There are six specific *course labs* (exercises) that will be conducted in class. These will be done on specific class dates identified in the Syllabus and Course Schedule, and will contribute to the final grade. The intent of each lab is to reinforce the material presented in the corresponding chapter/meeting.

There is also a *Course Project* that is required and contributes to the final grade for the course. Although you may read ahead in the Syllabus to see what is required, it is mandatory that you not actually undertake to begin work on the Project prior to the point where it is outlined and reviewed in class. The project introduces the *field work* concept; and, field work within the Anthropology discipline follows very strict professional constraints on what is done, and how it is conducted. These will be discussed in that class meeting, and work on the project should not begin until after that discussion.

Detailed information regarding grading and other issues will be discussed in the first face-to-face meeting.

Approach

We will begin this section with an overview of the field of anthropology, all of its sub-fields, and a review of the historical development of the field. This will be followed with a look specifically at *Cultural Anthropology* (the focus of this course), and an overview of the potential sources of culture. Finally, a quick look at genetics and a field known as *Sociobiology*. The student may have philosophical or religious views that object to what genetics tells us about evolution; but, there is significant scientific evidence in support of it. Has it been absolutely, incontrovertibly proven beyond a doubt? No. Does the evidence, however, establish the likelihood of evolution beyond a *reasonable* doubt? Absolutely. So, we'll take a look at where evolution tells us that humanity comes from, and who our closest relatives probably are. We do this because we can determine quite a bit about human behavior by looking at similar behavior amongst our "family".

The second part of that chapter will take a very quick look at a field known as *sociobiology*. This is a very controversial area within the field of anthropology. Although supported rather convincingly by Harvard professor E. O. Wilson, it has been soundly rejected by most (not all) of the traditional respected experts in mainstream anthropology (*e.g.* the late Dr. Marvin Harris of the University of Florida).

The Second Section of this text will take a cursory look at a number of areas where the social membership that a person has often provides an indication as to their behavior or preferences within a particular area. In general, these are stereotypes, and may even be seen to border on 'profiling'; but, there is a statistically significant likelihood that a random member of that social group will exhibit these behaviors or preferences. They do not serve a serious analysis of cultural issues for that group, but they do give some insight into what that group might 'look like' to an outsider. Areas that will be considered include: language, religion, art, music, humor, food, and clothing.

The Third Secion is more critical to the study of Cultural Anthropology, and takes a look at several of the *social systems* that are found in virtually every society around the globe – often in very different form, but present nonetheless. Systems to be covered will include: the Economy, Marriage, Domestic Arrangements, Kinship Conventions, Legal Systems, Political Systems, and the most widely recognized Causes of War.

In Section Four, the concept of *otherness* will be explored. What makes someone "one of us" as opposed to being "one of them"? There are many factors which occasionally get used to answer this question, but we'll take a look at what are perhaps the six most common: Race, Ethnicity, Class, Caste, Nationality, and Legal Status.

Sections Five and Six will focus on what is commonly known as *Applied Anthropology*. Although some colleges teach this as a separate and distinct field of Anthropology, the majority do not. It is the practical application of what is learned in the academic study of anthropology; and, this may apply to any of the four principal fields of anthropology. Here, we will review how Cultural Anthropology is appied in "the real world" (*i.e.* the world beyond the *walls of academia*). Section Five will focus on research – particularly that of two of the most important applied anthropologists in history, and Section Six will show how this research can aid in understanding the world around us. In other words, once we have data, how do we use it effectively? This includes discussion of motivation, conflict resolution, commercial application, charitable application, and even governmental application.

Chapter 2
Anthropology Overview

What is Anthropology, and how did it all begin ?

Anthropology is a combination of the Greek *anthopos* and *logos*, and literally translates as "the study of man". This can take many forms, and cover many areas. There are four, however, that are generally seen to comprise *Anthropology*.

The Four-Field Model

Anthropology is generally subdivided into 4 related, but distinct, parts. This process yields what is usually called the *four field model*. This identifies those areas that are usually included today in the science of anthropology, and divides the study of man into four distinct categories:

- *Archæology* — the recovery and study of evidence of past human life and culture;
- *Physical anthropology* — the collection and study of biological and physical human data;
- *Linguistics* — the study of human languages and communication; and,
- *Cultural anthropology* — the study of current and recent human communities.

Each of these four categories is, in turn, further divided into sub-categories. It is typically these sub-categories that best describe what any specific anthropologist studies (and, to which professional organizations they likely belong). Examples include:

Archæology
- Historical archæology (past cultures and communities);
- Industrial archæology (past industrial facilities, processes and products);
- Contract archæology (environmental impact, historic preservation); and,
- Legal archæology (legal development, forensic accounting, *et cetera*).

Physical anthropology
- Forensic anthropology (victims, criminals);
- Population genetics (human genetic variation, *e.g.* the human genome project);
- Ergonomics (a predominantly British term; more often known as *human factors engineering* in the United States – describing the interaction between humans and the physical world); and,
- Human paleontology (human fossil remains, which may also be viewed as a sub-category of archæology)

Linguistics
- Historical linguistics (the origins and relationships of languages);
- Symbology (the study of non-verbal communication methodologies);
- Descriptive linguistics (the structure, grammar, syntax, *et cetera.* of language); and,
- Sociolinguistics (language as a culturally determined communication system).

Cultural anthropology
- Ethnography (the study of contemporary cultures);
- Medical anthropology (cultural factors in health, disease and treatment);
- Urban anthropology (city life, urban communities, redevelopment); and,
- Development anthropology (community development characteristics).

Literally, anthropology is the "study of man", and yet there are many who consider primatology to be a sub-set of anthropology. Technically, they're wrong; and, in fact, it should probably be the other way around. Anthropology (the study of man) should – technically – be a sub-set of primatology (the study of primates, of which humans are but one example). The problem is that the recognition of man as "one of the primates" occurred largely after the field had become well established. Now, nobody wants to turn the whole field upside down just to be more precise semantically.

Some texts and colleges also include *Applied Anthropology* as a separate field, making it into a *five field model*; but, properly, Applied Anthropology is simply the <u>practical</u> <u>application</u> of one of the four fields previously mentioned – nearly always defined as an application "outside academia". Collectively, the four fields comprise the full extent of Anthropology, and Applied Anthropology spans the entire composite field 'in practice'.

Primatology

We have seen that Anthropology is comprised of the four fields of Linguistics, Physical Anthropology, Archæology, and Cultural Anthropology. There are related fields of study, however, that are sometimes grouped under this Anthropology rubric. They probably should not be; but, they are. So, where should they be? That depends on the field involved. The field most often incorrectly placed under Anthropology is Primatology. Where should it be?

Primatology – the study of primates – has become a popular field of study in recent years. Most often, this is taken to mean the study of the so-called *great apes*. These are not humans; they are gorillas, orangutans, chimpanzees, and bonobos. It may surprise many students, but these great apes are not seen the same way universally.

- To most of the world, they are "animals". And, they are treated no differently, and no better, than other animals.

- Although the US agrees with that definition, it did provide some differentiation by legally banning the importation of great apes into the US as pets back in 1975. This is something that very rarely ever occurs with other animals.

- Spain has gone so far as to agree with the GAP (the *Great Ape Project*) and, in a rare multi-party effort, granted them limited *personhood*. Being declared a person means, along with other things, that they can not be used for experimentation (of any kind) without their permission – which is more than a little difficult to get.

So, how does Primatology "fit" with the four-field model of Anthropology? To answer that, we need to do a little review of human paleontology (the "study of prehistoric human life").

Human Paleontology

You are a human being! Biologists and others with a prefer-ence for more technically precise terminology might call you a 'modern human', or even *homo sapiens sapiens*. But, what do these terms tell us?

Scientists recognize that there is always diversity within any group of closely related individuals. As that diversity expands, it is often advisable to consider the group to have actually split: to classify those individuals which differ the most from the rest to be a new, distinct grouping, while the rest continue on as a diverse, but still closely related group.

If we look at the history of primates, we have the problem that we (modern humans) were not there to observe these splits and classifications; and, none of them left written records of what they were like. Fortunately, archæology and paleontology provide us with a great deal of information we can use to hypothetically re-construct the process as it occurred. Although we can never be certain it is absolutely correct, all evidence indicates that it is ex-tremely likely to be highly accurate. Examining only those primates that are extant, this can also be presented in list form:

Timing*	Entity	Notes
~40 MYA	Monkeys	Simiformes split into New World Monkeys & Old World Monkeys
~25 MYA	Hominoids	Split from the Old World Monkeys
~20 MYA	Gibbons	Gibbons, or 'Lesser Apes' split from the other hominoids
~14 MYA	Orangutans	Orangutans split from the other Great Apes
~7.2 MYA	Gorillas	Gorillas split from the others
~4.5 MYA	Chimpanzees	The 'Common Chimp' split from the lineage
~4 MYA	Bonobos	Our closest living "cousins" split from the lineage

The so-called *Common Chimpanzee* shares 98.4% of its DNA with humans. The *Bonobos* (formerly called *Pygmy Chimps*) most likely split off roughly 500,000 years later (although possibly as late as just 1 million years ago), and are believed to share as much

---

* MYA is common shorthand for "millions of years ago". In the next listing, TYA similarly represents "thousands of years ago".

as 99.4% of our DNA.   Once the Bonobos have been separated from the *Hominoid* line, the remainder of the line is commonly known as *Hominids*. Branches of this group comprise what would have been our "closest" relatives – all of which, however, are extinct.

Timing	Name	Notes
3.9 to 3.0 MYA	*Homo Australopithecus*	stood about 4'4" tall
2.38 to 1.4 MYA	*Homo habilis*	Stood 4'6"; weighed ~100 lbs
1.8 to 1.25 MYA	*Homo ergaster*	Over 6' and 200 lbs
1.25 to 0.2 MYA	*Homo erectus*	5'11" & 130 lbs; probably looked & walked like us
600 to 350 TYA	*Homo heidelberg*	5'11" & 130 lbs
350 to 35 TYA	*Homo Neanderthal*	5'3" & 150 lbs
200 TYA to present	*Homo sapiens sapiens*	(you)
100 to 12 TYA	*Homo floresiensis*	3'4" & 55 lbs

Typically, this data is of more use to an archæologist or human paleontologist than to a cultural anthropologist; but, it also clearly shows that modern humans are one branch of primates, and not the other way around. So, *Primatology* should not be thought a field of Anthropology; but, Anthropology should be a field of Primatology. Nevertheless, Primatology is taught as one of the fields of Anthropology at many universities (?).

Chapter 3
Cultural Overview / Sources of Culture

What is Culture ?

So-called experts can not even agree on what the term *culture* means. One of the best definitions, however, has to be that provided by Dr. Geert Hofstede of the Netherlands. A psychologist by training, and a world renowned cultural researcher by profession[*], Dr. Hofstede wrote:

> Using the analogy of the way in which computers are programmed ... patterns of thinking, feeling and acting [are] *mental programs*, or ... *software of the mind*. ... A customary term for such mental software is *culture*.

Culture does not determine what you will think, how you will act, or why you are the way you are; but, it does predispose you to certain thought processes, responses, and life patterns. Some academics would simply define culture as 'the result of all learned behaviors'; but, this may be leaving out a great deal. Dr. Michael C. Howard, in <u>Contemporary Cultural Anthropology</u> defined culture as "the customary manner in which human groups learn to organize their behavior and thought in relation to their environment." This, a slightly more sensitive version of 'all learned behaviors', is one of the most common approaches to culture. Later in this chapter, we'll take a look at just what it is that may be getting "left out" by this traditional definition.

Why study Cultural Anthropology ?

What cultural anthropology does is to provide tools for evaluating, assessing and utilizing those "life patterns". There are many ways in which this can be done – from the most idealistic to the most profane. Some examples might be:

---

[*]   The research of Dr. Hofstede will be reviewed in Chapter 23.

o structuring negotiations to optimize the likelihood of gaining a peaceful agreement between two hostile parties;

Americans generally consider the "head of the table" to be the most powerful position at a conference table; but, Asians more often consider this power position to be at the center of the long side of the table. This is why the shape of the table, and the seating chart at a negotiation can set the tone for the conference before any opening remarks are ever made.

o leveraging cultural biases to maximize sales and profits;

Applied Cultural Anthropologists might have told General Motors not to sell a car in México called the "does not go"; but, GM never asked, and introduced the Chevy Nova — leading to the derisive Mexican chant: "¿Nova? ¡No va!"

o designing urban renewal projects in inner cities so that they result in "comfortable" living conditions for the people expected to reside there;

Although middle class Anglo-Americans are often attracted by the quietude of living on a "cul de sac", this is often seen as inherently limiting, restrictive, and undesirable in urban Latin-American and African-American communities. So, even if a Caucasian architect lives on a cul-de-sac, any urban renewal project she designs should minimize them as much as possible. Their very names indicate their social impact: in the suburbs, these may be known by the very continental (French) term "cul-de-sac"; but, in urban America, they are more often known simply as a "dead end". Potential residents may subconsciously interpret this phrase both physically and socially.

o designing political campaigns so that they are likely to be better received by the voting public.

On several historical occasions, presidential candidates who were millionaires, military leaders, or 'egg-heads' selected vice-presidential running mates perceived as self-made, peaceful, or an 'average Joe'. It is hoped by party leadership that these choices will make the ticket better received by middle-class America.

Technically, these ideas all fall within the domain of Applied Anthropology (since they all occur in the "world outside university walls") – an area to be covered in detail in Sections V and VI; however, the tools that are employed in their development all come from the various fields of the four field model.

Cultural Anthropology Development

In the field of science, Cultural Anthropology is a relatively new entry. The first professional anthropologists didn't arrive on the scene until close to the end of the nineteenth century (the late 1800s). But, amateurs had been increasingly active in what were known as local *ethnological societies* since before the middle of that century (Paris, 1839; New York, 1842; London, 1844; *et cetera*). The high number of amateurs created a problem for these groups in terms of scientific objectivity, for they often considered their own race and culture to be the only one worthy of study. When it came to the other races and cultures they encountered, their interest was comparable to that of Jane Goodall for the lowland gorilla – considering them to be somewhat intelligent and interesting, but clearly a lower-order primate. In other words, they doubted whether these other races and cultures should truly even be considered human – and, certainly not "civilized". The implied racism and ethnocentricity in these groups created an atmosphere that took more than a century to dispel – with anthropology being considered a largely white, male, European science until fairly recently.

Museum Anthropology

James Smithson, a wealthy British scientist, named his nephew as his beneficiary in his will. However, Smithson added that, if his nephew died without children, the entire estate went "to the United States of America, to found at Washington, under the name of the Smithsonian Institution, an establishment for the increase and diffusion of knowledge among men." Why Smithson did this is still unknown: he had never been to the United States, and no evidence can be found that he even knew anyone who had. It is thought that Smithson was using his will to thumb his nose at Great Britain, which he apparently felt had disrespected him personally.

In any case, his nephew died in 1835 – without children. The following year, on July 1, Congress accepted the legacy and established a charitable trust to manage it. Two years later (September 1838), the trust sent the funds (more than 100,000 gold sovereigns) to the US mint at Philadelphia. There, it was melted down and re-cast as U.S. currency: amounting to more than $500,000. [Note:

using the *share of the GDP* equivalency method, this 1838 sum is equivalent to 4.6 billion dollars today.] After eight years of Congressional debate, an Act of Congress signed by President Polk in 1846 established the Smithsonian Institution as a trust administered by a Board of Regents and a Secretary (Director).

Joseph Henry (left), one of the most respected American scientists of his time, was appointed as the first Director of the Smithsonian Institution. His early work in electricity and magnetism would help bring about the invention of the telegraph, the electric motor, and the telephone. At the Smithsonian, it was his vision that formed the outline of the unique research and cultural institution that it is today.

Under Henry, however, it was primarily a research institution. It was not until the second Director (Spencer Baird) that it would become primarily a museum – a natural history museum. There may be older natural history museums (such as Abraham Gesner's museum in Saint John, New Brunswick, Canada); but, the far superior financial resources of the Smithsonian and the leadership of Baird made the Smithsonian the first to have a real impact in the ethnological field. This was the first move away from living room, arm chair, discussion groups (*i.e.* the ethnological societies), and firmly established what has become known as *Museum Anthropology*. As natural history museums began to devote both space and funding to ethnologic collections, this brought public attention to the field; but, it also managed to focus the new science on *material culture*. If it wasn't something that could be bought, classified, and displayed by their museum, it had no real value to them. As a result, museum anthropology tended to concentrate on tools, clothing, paintings, and the like – and, to ignore many of the more dynamic aspects of culture, such as language, myth and music.

Unilineal Evolution

The next step in the evolution of Anthropology actually resulted largely from the work of someone with little interest in socio-cultural issues: Charles Darwin. (right). Until his contribution to science, the most common reason given for different primate species was that

God had simply created them that way. Darwin first published <u>On the Origin of Species</u> in 1859, and followed it 12 years later with <u>The Descent of Man</u>. These two books laid the foundation for a new theory of how the different species and races came to be – *natural selection*.

Darwin proposed that related groups of all species descended from common ancestors, and that it was natural selection that resulted in the differences – *i.e.* based on the differences encountered environmentally over many millennia. This was true, he maintained, regardless of whether the related groups under discussion were felines (lions, tigers, ocelots, *et cetera*) or humans (Caucasian, Negroid, Mongoloid, *et cetera*). Within anthropology, a descent from a common source became known as *unilineal evolution* or *classic social evolution*, and this provided the first scientific basis for the study of anthropology.

This was not without problems, however. Unilineal evolutionists believed that humanity naturally progressed along a path of steady cultural growth from the most savage, bestial state to that of modern, civilized (*i.e.* European) society. They therefore saw all other cultures as examples of defective growth — *i.e.* that something had kept them from reaching their potential to become *fully human*. Consequently, they were studied as a sort of living diorama of those earlier stages beyond which European humans had come. This blatantly Eurocentric attitude made the new science less than reliable in interpreting whatever data it did manage to collect. Early leaders in Unilineal Evolution included people such as Auguste Comte (right), Herbert Spencer, and William Graham Sumner.

Auguste Comte was a French philosopher whose primary contribution to anthropology was his *law of three stages*. Comte believed that all cultures, all societies, passed through three progressive stages: Theological, Metaphysical, and Scientific. The first of these was characterized by a society that attributed all inequalities in society to an 'act of God'. One man was a rich banker while another an abused slave because those were the roles they had been given by God. Gradually, societies evolve beyond this phase and begin to question and investigate the concept of universal rights, and evoke a culture which adheres to a more noble ethic. Societies finally evolve into the Scientific phase, where people discover solutions to the problems of the early phases, and bring them to fruition despite the obstructive restrictions of the earlier phases.

Herbert Spencer (below) was an extraordinarily respected English philosopher. Spencer believed, and proposed a comprehensive theory which promoted, that the physical world, all biological organisms, the human mind, and even human culture follow a progressive evolution that results in what they are. Although not a Darwinist, it was after reading Darwin's first book that Spencer coined the phrase *survival of the fittes*t to describe this irresistible drive. Spencer was a proponent of Lamarckism (named for founder Jean-Baptiste Lamarck), which proposed that a living organism passed learned lessons on to its offspring in just one generation. After Gregor Mendel published his findings (1866) in what would become the foundation for classic genetics, Lamarkism was relegated to relevance solely with regard to cultural evolution.

The third major figure in the development of Unilineal Evolution was William Graham Sumner (left). Sumner was an American philosopher, a long-time professor at Yale, and author of at least 40 published articles, papers or books. Sumner, who had been heavily influenced in the 1870s by Herbert Spencer, was a staunch proponent of *laissez-faire* politics – believing that survival of the fittest would weed out the weak, and lead to a natural evolution of a stronger society. Largely as a result of his many years at Yale, Sumner was highly influential in the United States (teaching the very first course in sociology offered by a college in the United States). Despite being an ordained Episcopal priest, Sumner saw conflict as an essential ingredient in social development; and, incorporating Spencer's survival of the fittest idea, wrote that "nothing but might has ever made right" (a rather brutish philosophy by modern standards).

Historical Particularism

The term "anthropology" was coined by combining the Greek *anthropos* (man, or human being) and *logos* (a discourse) to get *anthropology* (*i.e.* a "discourse on humanity"; or, "study of man"); and, it finally did develop into a discourse. Some early anthropologists (mostly German) found the unilineal evoltionist theory to be too confining; they believed that they were seeing far more variety and diversity than that theory could justify. This led to theories that recognized different peoples were not simply at different points on the same track, but might actually be on totally different paths. One such anthropologist was the German–trained Franz Boas [1858–1942]. Boas (right) emigrated to America and was largely responsible for spreading a radical idea at the time: that anthropologists should study each culture as a unique entity, and should stop trying to identify some underlying, universal law that dictated how cultural growth progressed.

Dr. Boas, unlike his earlier counterparts in anthropology, had been formally trained as a scientist (his doctorate was in physics). The result of this was that he refused to adopt any grand cultural theory woven around largely anecdotal evidence. He insisted on using the scientific method to formulate any cultural theory. As a consequence of this devotion to sound data and logic, modern anthropology is often dated to his involvement, and he is generally recognized as the "Father of Anthropology". It was in the 1880s that Boas insisted that environmental specifics had a great deal of impact on social evolution. Since different societies had experienced different environmental factors, he argued that one should expect that these societies would evolve differently. He was interested in the historical particulars of each cultural system, and this more comprehensive approach to understanding cultural variation thus became known as *historical particularism*.

Functionalism

Whether it was the old *ethnological societies*, the *unilineal evolutionists*, the *museum anthropologists*, or even the *historical particularists*, the question that was usually being asked was "what?". Then, early in the

1900s, the noted scientist Bronislaw Malinowski [1884–1942] began to ask the more important question "why?". He wanted to understand <u>why</u> a culture behaved in a certain way, what the function was that was served by a particular practice or development. This approach became known as *functionalism*. In pursuit of answers to these question, Malinowski made major strides in the realm of *fieldwork* (*i.e.* actually going out and observing another culture first hand). This was clearly different from the methods used by ethnological society amateurs, who apparently preferred to make their observations from the comfort of their living rooms.

Malinowski (above) argued that culture functioned to meet the needs of individuals rather than society as a whole. He reasoned that when the needs of individuals are met, the needs of society as a whole are met. To Malinowski, the feelings and motives of people were crucial to understanding the way their society functioned. Fortunately, circumstances forced him to discover this first hand.

Dr. Malinowski was a Polish citizen studying in England; but, after completing his PhD (his second) at the University of London in 1916, he left for the South Pacific (Australia, New Guinea, and Melanesia). While he was on the Trobriand Islands studying trade, kinship, and the practical value of ritual and religion, World War I intruded on his work. Great Britain instructed all of its territories to detain citizens of those countries with which it was at war. That included Poland; so, Malinowski was stranded on the Trobriand Islands, forbidden to return to Europe until after the end of the war.

The result of this predicament was that Malinowski gradually became increasingly integrated into the local population. He even ended up falling in love and living with a native girl.* He began to study the finer subtleties of the society – seeing how ritual, religion, and the cultural norms all impacted the daily lives of the people. These were observations that a "visiting academic" would never have made. Although he did not invent the concept of *fieldwork*, he clearly perfected it. It is from his work, also, that anthropology differentiates what they call *etic* and *emic*. An *etic* perspective is that of an outsider observing something of importance to

---

*   That was always his claim. When the war ended, he went home, but didn't take her with him.

others; an *emic* perspective is that of an active participant in the process. The appearance something has to an external observer and the meaning it has to the participant are often very different.

Collective Consciousness

Émile Durkheim [1858–1917] is often called the *Father of Sociology*. Nevertheless, this French sociologist had a profound effect on a number of Malinowski's peers in the field of anthropology. While adopting Malinowski's functionalism, they also applied Durkheim's sociological view that culture could be thought of as the engine that drives humanity. This combination had a profound effect on the field of anthropology: modifying *functionalism* to view society not as a collection of independent acts and practices, but as an integrated, functioning whole – a *collective consciousness*. Durkheim (above) was born into a distinguished religious family in France: his father, grandfather, and great-grandfather had all been prominent Jewish rabbis. Émile (actually David Émile Durkheim), however, decided to pursue a secular career; and, much of his sociological work was dedicated to showing that religion was largely a response to cultural and social stimuli, not the result of divine intervention or guidance.

Durkheim was primarily interested in how societies manage to maintain their integrity and coherence when key aspects of their culture (*e.g.* shared religious, racial, or ethnic background) were lost. He was one of the first to try to explain certain aspects of a society by referring to the function they served in making society work as a whole (proposing what might be called a *social gestalt*: society being greater than the sum of its parts). He wasn't particularly interested in what motivated individuals to act a certain way, but was more interested in those factors that appeared to have an existence all by themselves – concepts not directly tied to the actions of any specific individual. In his writing, Durkheim labeled these factors *social facts*, and argued that they exist separate from any individual in society. In fact, he held that they were greater and more influential than anything any individual might do.

It occurred to Durkheim that these social facts exist separately from individual people; and, that they might have a very powerful influence, or coercive power, over people. He saw this not only in formal laws and regulation, but also in the apparent force of tradition – in religious practices, family norms, neighborhood responsibilities, national duty, and so forth. He recognized that these social facts were virtually a separate category of phenomena – including ways of thinking, feeling, understanding, and acting. These were not individualistic traits, but they seemed to exert great influence over the individual. He saw these as cultural forces that could not be reduced to either biological or psychological facts.

Durkheim's students and supporters applied much of this view of *social facts* to the functionalist school of Cultural Anthropology founded by Malinowski. As a result, cultural anthropology became more of a study of group dynamics and social norms than an analysis of how it was influenced by individual participants.

Review

The evolution of the science of Cultural Anthropology can thus be seen as having progessed through 6 distinct steps to where it is today.

The Evolution of Cultural Anthropology		
Cultural Anthropology	Credited Founder(s)	Time
Ethnological Societies	John Russell Bartlett, Albert Gallatin	1840s
Museum Anthropology	James Smithson, Joseph Henry	1850s
Unilineal Evolution	Auguste Comte, Herbert Spencer, William Graham Sumner	1860s
Historical Particularism	Franz Boas	1880s
Collective Consciousness	Émile Durkheim	1890s
Functionalism	Bronislaw Malinowski	1910s

Where Does Culture Come From ?

In the most common definitions offered for the term *culture*, we saw before that it is usually thought of as *learned behaviors*. But, is that the only source for the cultural differences that we find all around the globe? If we are as open as possible to ideas that may seem strange to the typical westerner, we will quickly discover that there are, in fact, not one, but four possible sources for cultural traits.

Possible Sources of Culture

It is likely true that culture is overwhelmingly, exhaustively derived from what we learn. But, there are other potential sources: a total of four possible contributors to our cultural views. In addition to the environmental (that which we learn), there are the following (accepted by many, but not all, people): genetic (that which we inherit), biological (that which we experience and then encode biologically), and metempsychotic (that which results from karma as a result of past lives – *i.e.* reincarnation). You need not accept all 4 of these – most people don't; but, individually, each of these is accepted by hundreds of millions of people.

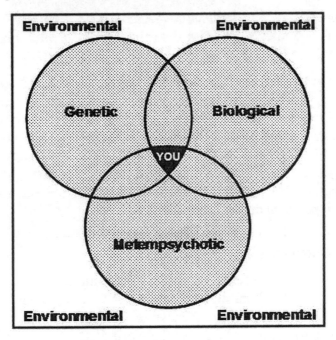

We'll come back to these sources in the next chapter (when *sociobiology* is introduced); but, since we have introduced them, we should at least define what each source is (box, next page). In addition, recognizing more than just environment (*i.e.* learned behavior) as the source of a community's culture makes it much easier to interpret some of the anomalies that have been discovered in the development of *cultural categories*.

Potential Sources of Culture

- **Environmental** — this is the traditional "learned behavior". There are numerous examples of learned cultural traits – ranging from the language you speak to the form of religion you practice to the brand of car you drive. All of these have been shown to be highly influenced by the attitudes of parents, friends and others close to you.

- **Biological** — scientists have shown that your brain grows new neural pathways at night while you sleep. This "biological wiring" apparently grows to enable you to perform repetitive acts more easily and automatically.

- **Genetic** — extensive research is now showing that there are many cultural traits that may, in fact, be highly influenced by some degree of genetic predisposition.

- **Metempsychotic** — Hindus, Buddhists, Jains, Sikhs, and millions of individual followers of other religions around the world believe in reincarnation – often incorporating some form of *karma*, where we 'ultimately must pay for our actions'. Although generally discredited in the US, at least ¼ of the world population (perhaps as much as ½) readily accepts this as a possible source of both physical and cultural attributes.

Cultural Categories

One of the primary reasons for wanting to categorize different types of cultural traits is to be able to apply them – to put them in a format where non-academic groups can make use of them. The best example of this is the work of Dr. Geert Hofstede. Working as a psychologist at IBM's European headquarters, he used his access to all of their European employees. This was the start of his cultural database. Later, colleges, universities and businesses who were using his findings provided additional data to him that had resulted from their work. The result is the single largest cultural database ever compiled.

Hofstede found 5 distinct categories of cultural variance (his initial work identified 4; the fifth resulted from later review of the ever expanding data). He termed these:

- Individualism (an ego-centered *vs.* society-centered continuum);
- Power Distance (cultural response continuum to perceived differences in authority, power and privilege across society);
- Masculinity (the cultural perception of a provider–nurturer continuum);
- Uncertainty Avoidance (the general range of cultural acceptability of uncertainty regarding future events); and,
- Confucian Dynamism (essentially, a cultural 'temporal horizon' continuum).

Using statistical correlation analyses, Hofstede found there was wide variation with each of these categories between cultural communities, but a high degree of consistency and predictability within cultural communities. Understanding where a culture falls on each of these continua has proven to be of tremendous practical value to commercial firms, government organizations, non-governmental organizations, supra-governmental organizations, *et cetera*. This will all be explored in detail in Sections V and VI.

Chapter 4
Genetics and Sociobiology

The Acceptability of the 4 Sources

Environmentally-induced Culture is not controversial, and is, in fact, the traditional explanation of cultural origination. Virtually everyone on earth, scientist or layman, would agree that most (if not all) of our cultural traits were learned – from our parents, our teachers, our elders, our friends, or from the community (often at the 'school of hard knocks').

Biologically-induced Culture is a newer idea; but, from recent physical research, appears almost certain to exist. In fact, biological encoding is often touted as the major reason why it isn't easy to alter our life-long cultural habits. It is often given as the explanation for why studies show that audio language tapes played during sleep appear to make foreign languages both easier and quicker to learn. But, many insist this is merely a biological "extension", or physical encoding, of learned behavior, and thus not a truly independent source of our cultural traits.

Metempsychosis-induced Culture (*i.e.* reincarnation) is unlikely to ever be proved (or disproved) materially. The physical, material world is simply not well situated to attempt a material proof of something nearly always considered a metaphysical activity. It is certainly beyond the scope of any introductory text on Cultural Anthropology, and will be left here to the world's religions to either accept or reject.

That brings us to the only remaining potential source for cultural traits: *genetics*. How much, if any, of our cultural make-up is either determined or predisposed by our genetic make-up? This is a highly controversial field; but, there are a great many anthropologists who ascribe at least <u>some</u> of our cultural traits to our genes. This view is known as *sociobiology*, and is sometimes used to help explain the *cultural take-off*.

The Cultural Take-off

For nearly a million years, the cultures of early, prehistoric hominids changed very little. Then, during a period that spans roughly 25,000 years, they simply exploded. Beginning around (or just after) 50,000 BCE, and lasting until about 25,000 BCE, cultures changed more than they had over the preceding million years.

- Technical skills increased with the introduction of new materials, tools, and methodologies.
- Artistic creativity increased: generating wall paintings, distinctive pottery styles, and non-utilitarian objects.
- Social organization increased: forging larger family units, formal hunting parties, and a division of labor.

This period, in fact, saw the first communities that modern humans would readily recognize as "fully human". Many anthropologists believe this resulted from a new-found human capacity for language and language-dependent thought and activities. But, it is far from certain that earlier hominids (*e.g.* Neanderthals) did not also have language skills. Another popular theory to explain this sudden explosion of cultural growth is that life spans reached a critical level – where the transmission of accumulated knowledge across generations finally became feasible.

Regardless of why this occurred, it is highly likely that this cultural explosion (and the new skills and tools that went with it) led directly to a concurrent extinction for the two other *hominids* alive at the time: Neanderthals (who went extinct about 30,000 BCE), and the so-called Hobbits (*Homo floresiensis*, who went extinct about 12,000 BCE).

So, exactly what did happen during this period about 25,000 to 50,000 years ago? Why did modern humans make such tremendous strides in cultural development – advances greater and faster than anything that had happened in the preceding years?

Humans suddenly and convincingly came into their own during this time frame. Most anthropologists seem to believe that humanity simply reached a level of "cultural capacity" that enabled cultural changes to occur without necessitating biological changes (a sort of *cultural critical mass*). Perhaps.

By contrast, some believe that it was a result of genetic mutation. Dr. Richard Klein (Anthropology professor at Stanford University) was quoted in <u>The Times</u>[*] (London) as stating that "a creativity gene that evolved about 50,000 years ago was the spark that kindled the development of the modern mind". He added that "recent breakthroughs in genetics, in particular the discovery of the first gene linked conclusively to language, suggest strongly that *Homo sapiens'* cultural revolution began with one or more genetic mutations that transformed the ability to communicate."

Dr. Klein said that "when you look at the archæological record before 50,000 years ago, it is remarkably homogeneous. There are no geographically delineated groups of artifacts. Suddenly, you see geographically and chronologically restricted groups of artifacts with a lot of style involved in the manufacturing, and the geographic distribution is very limited. Suddenly, modern-looking people began to behave in a modern way, in producing art and jewelry and doing a whole variety of other things that they hadn't done before."

Klein believes that there is a set of human genes – numbering someplace between 10 and 10,000 – that affect cognition and communication. This could be significant since, although nobody really knows how many genes we have, the *Human Genome Project* has estimated 25,000 on 3 billion 'base pairs'. Most anthropologists accept the *cultural take off* as a result of population increases, climate changes, increased life spans, and other environmental changes, but Dr. Klein stands firm in his belief that it was a genetically driven event. Which was it? Take a class in anthropology near the close of the 21st century, and the instructor will likely be able to tell you. At this point – early in the 21st century – no honest professor can answer that without some level of doubt.

Sociobiology

Sociobiology, although discussed in academic circles for decades, finally came into its own with the work of Dr. Edward Osborne Wilson. E. O. Wilson, as he is usually credited, is an ecologist, entomologist, and long term science faculty member at Har-

---

[*] Henderson, Mark <u>The Times</u>, London. February 17, 2003.

vard University. In 1975, he published <u>Sociobiology: The New Synthesis</u>, and followed that in 1978 with <u>On Human Nature</u> (for which he won the Pulitzer Prize). With those books, the battle was joined, and leading anthropologists, psychologists, theologians, biologists, and others chose sides. Outspoken supporters of Wilson include scientists, writers, philosophers, and ecological activists (*e.g.* Jared Diamond, Richard Dawkins, Ian McEwan, Michael Eisner, and Harrison Ford), while opponents accusing him of promoting thinly-veiled racist, sexist, and atheist pseudo-science have included Marxists, scientists, philosophers, and theologians (*e.g.* Stephen Jay Gould, Richard Lewontin, Steven Rose, Patrick Bateson, Phillip Johnson, Walter Ong, Pope John Paul, and others).

Why so much controversy? One of the major problems in the field of sociobiology is the fact that, for every sociobiological explanation for something, we can also identify a learned cultural explanation. This devolves into competing ways of explaining how a group passes on critical survival skills and knowledge: genetically or environmentally. Scientist George C. Boeree wrote that:

> if a society is to survive ... it must take care of the very same issues that genetics must take care of.

But, do humans work by instinct? Boeree stated that, although we may not have irrepressible instinct, when we "define instincts as 'strong innate tendencies toward certain behaviors in certain situations' ... [then] we probably do [have them]". So, do we have these *genetic tendencies*?

The most widely accepted test for genetic influence is called *twin research*, or *twin studies*, where factors are evaluated across several groups:
- o identical twins raised separately (100% genetic match; 0% environmental match);
- o identical twins raised together (both a 100% match);
- o siblings raised apart (25–50% genetic; 0% environmental);
- o siblings raised together (25–50% genetic match; but, 100% environmental match);
- o adopted children (0% genetic; 100% environmental); and,
- o complete strangers (both a 0% match).

The results of these studies are then mathematically correlated to determine the influence level that results from the genetic link, that which results from a shared environment, and that which may come from a universal 'cultural background' that influences all humans. That which doesn't correlate at all is, by default, the result of free, independent action. To date, results that have been generated clearly indicate that there is, in fact, a significant genetic influence on items that are usually considered "learned" or "chosen".

Consider some of the data involved in this controversial area:

o   correlation studies show approximately a 40% genetic component in:

   −   homosexuality; and,

   −   juvenile disorders.

o   correlation studies reveal that genetics contributes ~50% to:

   −   religiosity;

   −   political intensity;

   −   personality dynamics;

   −   general intelligence level (IQ);

   −   optimism; and,

   −   likelihood of divorce.

o   correlation studies indicate 60–70% genetic influence (*i.e.* nearly determinate) in:

   −   alcoholism;

   −   narcotics abuse;

   −   ADD (attention deficit disorder); and,

   −   Schizophrenia.

Does this prove sociobiology is 'the answer'? Absolutely not; but, it does make it a respectable subject for consideration and investigation. So, let's consider it.

Just what is *sociobiology*? Well, to begin, understand that it is not the same thing as *Social Darwinism*. That is the idea that unilineal evolutionary theory can be applied to social constructs such as culture. Under that theme, cultural traits would be determined by a "survival of the fittest" approach; and, sociobiologists simply don't go that far. What they do propose is somewhat more refined than that. It goes something like this:

- ♦ Humans are an animal species – granted, a very intelligent, self-conscious, evolved species; but, animal nonetheless.

- ♦ Humans are, in fact, a *social animal* – much like sheep, ants, bees, and wolves. In other words, we function both as individuals and as key members of an hierarchal group.

- ♦ Certain traits, behaviors, and reactions contribute positively to the survival and growth of the human community; other traits, behaviors and reactions appear to be either neutral or detrimental to human survival.

- ♦ Over millennia, physical attributes that contribute positively have been encoded genetically in the human gene pool. Bigger, stronger, faster, smarter humans naturally tend to pass on their genes disproportionately when compared to the smaller, weaker, slower, and dumber of the species – because the first group tends to live longer, eat better, more readily survive challenges, and reproduce more abundantly.

- ♦ Non-physical attributes which contribute positively have also been passed on to future generations. Hunting skills, agricultural knowledge, tool design, weapon construction, and so forth have all been passed from parent to child – making humans the most efficient and productive agriculturalists and hunters on the planet.

- ♦ Unquestionably, many of these skills and behaviors have been learned by children being taught by their elders, or by having participated in communal activities as they matured.

- ♦ If this communal exposure were the only source of these attributes, we should expect that they would quickly be discarded once they were no longer required – since, if not required, they would not be used, taught, or learned.

- ♦ For example, children raised today in the USA would have no practical reason for knowing how to hunt and kill an elephant or hippopotamus; and, typically, they don't.

◆ Six of the more commonplace phobias, however, would all have been valuable survival skills during most of our history. Human beings (*homo sapiens sapiens*) have been around for roughly  200,000 years. Most of that time (probably about 150,000 years) was spent on the African savanna (grasslands). The open spaces (above), multitude of predators, and inherent dangers in this environment were (according to sociobiologists) "imprinted" on human DNA.

◆ When we consider some of the attributes that would have been key survival instincts 20,000 (or more) years ago, they appear to be of no practical value today. However, there are indications that some of these attributes still remain within the human community. For example:

■ Arachnophobia	A fear of spiders, *arachnophobia* reduces the likelihood of a barefoot, mostly naked human being bitten by a spider – most of which are harmless, but many of which produce potentially lethal or damaging venom.
■ Agoraphobia	A fear of open spaces, any early human fearing open spaces would tend to avoid highly exposed regions of the savanna – regions where lions, tigers, hyenas, and other human predators have a serious advantage.
■ Ophidiophobia	A fear of snakes; although bunny rabbits have traditionally been a source of food, snakes have not. Bites from a venomous snake could easily result in death or, at a minimum, a physically debilitating reaction that could leave a human vulnerable to the larger predators.

- ■ Claustraphobia   A fear of small places would prevent a human from entering caves, burrows, or other enclosures where they could be easily trapped by carnivorous hunters.

- ■ Acrophobia   A fear of heights keeps people from venturing too close to cliffs, ravines and other sources of dangerous falls. In fact, chasing prey over these high places was a common strategy for humans hunting large mammals such as mammoths and elephants.

- ■ Brontophobia   A fear of thunderstorms was helpful in exposed areas such as the savanna, where lightning was a very real survival concern.

♦ The frequency of phobias among children and adolescents ranges from 3.3% to 9.2%, depending on age and gender. The perfectly logical reasons why humans might have had these fears in the past are typically no longer present. The reason why studies focus on children and adolescents is that they have not had as much opportunity to develop that fear through experience. But, they have them anyway; and, a nearly 10% frequency rate is <u>far</u> too often to attribute to a purely chance occurrence.

♦ Sociobiologists therefore think that what are phobias today might not actually be remnant genetic imprinting from key survival skills thousands of years ago.

♦ That is not to say that <u>all</u> such phobias are genetic imprints; but, only that it is distinctly possible that many of them are.

So goes the argument from the sociobiologists. Regardless of the source, however – environmental, biological, genetic, or metempsychotic – there are numerous areas where we find what can only be described as *cultural traits*. The purpose of this text is to provide a survey, or general overview, of some of these traits, and how they differ around the world.

Statistically, at least 3 students in a typical class should feel a distinct level of discomfort viewing one or more of these 3 photos. Why? Sociobiologists think they know; but, do they?

Section II
Socio-cultural Markers

Socio-cultural Markers

What do we mean by *socio-cultural markers*? Generally, we mean any cultural or social feature that serves to indicate or specifically identify someone as a member of any particular social community or grouping. Although there are many, most are either very subjective, or are far too subtle to use as examples here in this course. For example, the author has experienced situations in India where his host would observe others at a distance and announce "American", or "English", or "Australian", or "French" – which, after checking, were seemingly almost always correct. To the author, any of them could have been from any of these social communities. Clearly, my Indian host was observing identifiers or markers that were very subtle – too subtle for me.

Some markers, however, are quite obvious. In this section, we'll take a look at some of those that are readily observable:

- What language do they speak?
- How do they dress?
- What religion do they practice?
- How do they represent things artistically?
- What is their general philosophy of life (their *world view*)?
- What do they find funny or humorous?
- What foods do they consider a normal part of their diet?

We're going to try not to put too much importance on any of these, but they do provide a good introductory point to understanding that what you might consider normal may be totally repulsive or illogical to someone from a different cultural background.

Chapter 5
Linguistics (Formal)

Natural Languages

Natural languages are those languages that have developed among human groups over thousands and thousands of years. This differentiates them from languages that have been deliberately created to commune with machines (such as computer languages, machine programs, apps, and so forth) as well as those languages that have been deliberately created for the purpose of hopefully providing a *universal medium* through which humans would be able to communicate (*e.g.* Esperanto, Basic English, Volapük, Occidental, and Interlingua).

Varied Language Greetings

Hello	Hallo	Bonjour	Hola
Dydh da	Goeie	Mirëdita	Alo
Olá	Bok	Selam	Gamarjobat
Ahalan	Dobrý den	Guten Tag	Parev
Fo be song	Goddag	Aloha	Γειά σου
Салам	Goede dag	Shalom	Kaixo
Dis dhuit	Namaste	Ei Je	Saluton
Pêng-an	Zdravo	Salve	Jó napot
Demat	Tere	Góðan daginn	Sa'lam
Эдравей	Bona jorno	Nei ho	Hei
Halo	Salute	Ciao	Kon-nichi-wa
Salvëte	Sveicina-ts	Sveiki	An-nyong Ha-se-yo
Ki Kati	Helo	Ni hao	Iakwe
Adieu	Dzien' dobry	Allillanchu	Bunã ziua
Эдравствуйте	Helele	Nazdar	Zxivjo
Jambo	Hej	Kumusta	Sa-wat-dee
Dumela	Merhaba	Вітаю	Xin chào
Sut mae	Molo	Sawubona	Sholem aleychem

As you can see from the block above, there are a lot of ways that you can greet somebody when you meet them – all of which mean pretty nearly the same thing. This is the result of the fact that there are hundreds ... thousands ... actually, according to most experts, in excess of 5,000 natural languages still being used in the world today. That is a little sobering for the person who thinks that the whole world is "coming around" to English. We tend to be somewhat anglo-centric in the US – expecting that, as nations become "educated and developed", they will at least have a working knowledge of English. But, based on history, that is not really a reasonable expectation. That is the primary reason that several serious attempts have been made to develop an artificial, universal language; but, that too has turned out to be an unrealistic exercise (although Esperanto appears to have made better progress than any of the others).

If you have an American passport, (left) you will notice that the inside front cover has your photo along with some personal information (*e.g.* name, date of birth, issue date, expiration date, *etc.*). Across from that, on what is actually the first paper page of the passport, there is a 'message' to any foreign authority. It states:

> *The Secretary of State*
> *of the United States of America*
> *hereby requests all whom it may concern to permit the citizen /*
> *national of the United States named herein to pass*
> *without delay or hindrance and in case of need to*
> *give all lawful aid and protection.*

Although that seems pretty straight forward, it is then immediately followed by:

> *Le Secretaire d'État*
> *des États-Unis d'Amérique*
> *prie par les présentes toutes autorités compétentes de laisser passer*
> *le citoyen ou ressortissant des États-Unis titulaire du présent passeport,*
> *sans delai ni difficulté et, en cas de besoin, de lui accorder*
> *toute aide et protection légitimes.*

This appears to be – and, in fact, is – a repeat of the same message; this time, though, in French! At one time, a very large percentage of the American populace considered German to be their "mother tongue"; and, today, a significant percentage of our citizens consider that to be Spanish; but, at no time has more than a small fraction of our population considered French to be such. So, why would the United States government repeat the message in French in every passport?

The answer is based on the realization that the government isn't writing this message to you; it's writing the message to some unknown foreign authority. And, it was not so long ago that French was considered the 'language of diplomacy'. In other words, all educated representatives of the nations of the world were expected to be able to meet, discuss, and negotiate – in French. Consider the following example.

> When the *HMS Titanic* collided with an iceberg in April of 1912, the radio was still a new invention; but, the ship (being 'state of the art') was equipped with one of these new 'wireless' contraptions. So, the wireless operator sent a distress signal, calling "mayday, mayday" – the international signal for distress. Well, not really. What he actually called out was "*m'aidez, m'aidez*". Phonetically, this is very close; but, it is actually the French imperative "help me, help me". Why would a British ship – headed for the United States – in northern Atlantic waters – call out in French? Because that was the language that was most likely to have been understood by any other ships in the area at the time. Although few other ships had radios in 1912 (so only limited assistance arrived), it is unlikely that even those few would have responded if the ship had called out "ahyut, ahyut" (a rough pronunciation of "*Ajjut, ajjut*"). Why? Because probably nobody in the North Atlantic would have understood the message in Maltese! French was, in fact, the closest thing the world had in 1912 to a universal language. Today, that is English; but, in another hundred years, it may be Chinese or Arabic. There is nothing innately logical that would make the choice of English more likely.

The link between language and culture is best illustrated in a quote by Winona LaDuke (right). LaDuke, a Native American activist, environmentalist, writer, economist, and speaker, is a member of the Mississippi Band of the Anishinaabeg (Ojibway). She is also the

Founding Director of the *White Earth Land Recovery Project*, a former Board Member of *Greenpeace*, and the recipient of numerous prestigious awards. A graduate of Harvard and Antioch, she was the 2000 Vice-Presidential candidate for the Green Party (garnering 2,882,955 votes with activist Ralph Nader).

> The teachings of our people concerning our relationships to land are deeply embedded in our language. For instance, in Ojibway, *"nishnabe akin"* means "the land to which the people belong." This implies an entirely separate paradigm about property rights from that in the U.S. courts today. *"Nishnabe akin"* doesn't mean "the land that belongs to the people." It means that we belong to the land.

This quote clearly shows how language and one's view of the world can be linked at a very foundational level. The Ojibway see a relationship with the land that few Americans see; and, this is encoded directly into their language. But, do they say this because they all see it this way? Or, do they see it this way because they mature in a culture whose language frames it this way? In other words, does a language reflect the culture, or does culture get framed by the language?

Language Diversity

It is difficult to actually establish how many languages there are in the world, as agreement is often difficult to reach on whether certain members of the list are actually independent languages or dialects of the same language. The final total can run anywhere from 3,000 to 8,000. There is a formal listing of languages provided by SIL International (formerly known as the Summer Institute of Linguistics) – a Christian linguistic service organization which is primarily concerned about the availability of the Christian Bible in these languages. Their 15th edition (released in 2005) lists 6,912 distinct languages. Others, however, would dispute some of their language-dialect decisions. Regardless, about half the world speaks one of the "top ten". These are (along with their primary area of usage and an approximate number of native speakers):

1	Mandarin	(China)	885,000,000
2	Hindi	(India)	366,000,000
3	English	(US, UK, other)	342,000,000

4	Spanish	(Spain, S America)	332,000,000
5	Bengali	(India, Bangladesh)	210,000,000
6	Portuguese	(Portugal, Brazil)	180,000,000
7	Russian	(Russia)	170,000,000
8	Japanese	(Japan)	125,000,000
9	German	(Germany, Austria)	100,000,000
10	Korean	(N Korea, S Korea)	80,000,000
10	Wu	(China)	80,000,000
10	French	(France, other)	80,000,000

Arabic is not on this "top ten" list despite having about 175,000,000 native speakers (which would place it seventh) because it is usually seen as comprising 6 highly distinct language variants (the largest of which, Egyptian Arabic, only has about 43,000,000 speakers). The broad language diversity that we see around the world results from several factors: natural evolution, immigration, conquest, colonialism, and so forth. All but the first of these is more appropriately studied in classes on World History, Political Science, Western Civilization, or Civics.   The first, however (natural evolution), is most properly a field of study for linguists.

Language Structure

Languages can be studied structurally by identifying some of the factors that go in to making a language what it is. These include the following.

- *Phonology* is the study of which *phonemes*, or sounds, a language uses. There are a huge number of discreet sounds that humans can make; and, each language uses only a small percentage of them. Different sounds are included in different languages, in the phonology of their language – which accounts for the guttural sound used in German, the 'click' in the language of the !Kung, the 'rolled r' in Spanish and Scottish Gaelic, the *shch* (Щ) of Russian, and the lack of clear distinction between 'r' and 'l' in Mandarin.

These are all areas where the choice of which phonemes to include differs from that of English.

- *Morphology* is the study of "morphemes" – phoneme combinations that result in the collective sound having meaning. Although this could be a word, it need not be. For example, *bāk* (spelled 'bake' in English) is a morpheme that means "to cook at high temperature"; and, *mō* (spelled 'mow' in English) means "to cut down". You could argue that these are simply words; and, you'd be right. But, although *er* is not a word, it is also a morpheme. In English it means "one who ..." or "that which ...". So, when added to bake, we get *baker* (one who bakes); and, when added to 'mow', we get *mower* (that which mows).

- *Grammar* results when people combine sounds to form *phonemes*, combine phonemes to form *morphemes*, combine morphemes to create *words*, and then use the rules of *syntax* to string words together to form complete thoughts. The rules that govern these steps can be extremely complex, and differ widely from language to language. This 'set of rules' is known as the *grammar* of a language.

Language Change

Languages are not static constructs – in other words, they don't stand still. Academics can analyze a language, but only at a particular point in time. This is what is known as *synchronic analysis*. If they take two of more points of time, and compare the changes that have occurred in a language, they are analyzing linguistic change – by what is known as *diachronic analysis*. This can be illustrated by using something that is generally familiar to most Americans – the Christian "Lord's Prayer" (*aka* the "Our Father"). This prayer, which occurs in the Christian New Testament, has remained unchanged in meaning over the past millennia; but, the language in which it is reported may have changed dramatically during that time. So, by looking at something such as this (whose meaning has remained essentially constant), linguists can determine how the language has evolved over time. Consider this prayer (Matthew 6:9-13) at roughly even time intervals:

Anglo-Saxon   *(ca.* 1020; Bath, England translation)
Fæder ure þu þe eart on heofonum; Si þin nama gehalgod to
become þin rice gewurþe ðin willa on eorðan swa swa on
heofonum. urne gedæghwamlican hlaf syle us todæg and
forgyf us ure gyltas swa swa we forgyfað urum gyltendum and
ne gelæd þu us on costnunge ac alys us of yfele soþlice.

Middle English   *(ca.* 1380; Wycliffe Bible)
Oure fadir that art in heuenes, halewid be thi name;   thi
kyngdoom come to; be thi wille don `in erthe as in heuene;
yyue to vs this dai oure `breed ouer othir substaunce;   and
foryyue to vs oure dettis, as we foryyuen to oure dettouris; and
lede vs not in to temptacioun, but delyuere vs fro yuel.

Elizabethan English   *(ca.* 1611; King James Version)
Our father which art in heaven, hallowed be thy Name. Thy
kingdome come. Thy will be done, in earth, as it is in heaven.
Giue vs this day our dayly bread. And forgiue us our debts, as
we forgiue our debters. And leade us not into temptation, but
deliuer vs from euill.

Contemporary English   *(ca.* 2005; New English Trans.)
Our Father in heaven, may your name be honored, may your
kingdom come, may your will be done on earth as it is in
heaven. Give us today our daily bread, and forgive us our
debts, as we ourselves have forgiven our debtors. And do not
lead us into temptation, but deliver us from the evil one.

Virtually anyone who can speak English can read the contemporary version. And, nearly all can understand the minor spelling
changes and slightly "old fashioned" sound of the Elizabethan version. The Middle English version begins to be somewhat problematic in its spelling, punctuation and grammar. But, very few modern Americans could read the Anglo-Saxon version and be able to
say exactly what it means. This gradual change in spelling, punctuation, word order, phrase structure, *et cetera* are the result of 'language change' over a period of almost exactly one thousand years.

But, how could this gradual rate of change create nearly 7,000
languages in the world today? The most obvious answer is "tens
of thousands of years"; but, that still does not answer the question
as to how it all got started. There are several theories as to the start
of human language. The principle approaches are: biological mutation, cultural necessity, and an originary event. We'll consider
each of these three approaches in turn.

Biological mutation   We've seen that the closest living non-human relative of ours is the bonobo (pygmy chimpanzee), who shares a nearly identical DNA structure. In fact, of the tens of thousands of genes that humans and chimps are thought to have, it is likely that no more than a few hundred are different between the two species. These changes, which typically occurred as a result of gene mutation, result in the different facial structure, body characteristics, and so forth. It is probable that there are no more than perhaps 50 genes that account for cognitive differences. One such difference, however, is in the vocal system — the system including the nasal cavity, palate, lips, pharynx, velum, tongue, teeth, epiglottis, and larynx.

In adult humans, the epiglottis and larynx are much lower than in the bonobos (or infant humans). It is the larynx that uses air from the lungs to cause vibrations in the audible range; and, it is the epiglottis that alternately closes off our "wind pipe" and our esophagus (the "food pipe"). Having them higher makes it less likely that bonobos and children will choke; but, having it lower makes the entire system a far more efficient sound production system. So, speech comes at a price: a much greater chance of choking. This change, or mutation, is a biological difference. When coupled with related changes in the brain (such as the development of *Broca's area*), this results in humans possessing an advanced speech and language capability that the bonobos simply do not have.

Cultural necessity   According to this approach, humans have possessed the physical capacity for speech for a very long time; but, this does not necessarily mean that they also created language. After all, humans (and our ancestors) have also had the ability to sweat (which is severely restricted in bonobos) for at least 2 million years, but that does not lead to our having created deodorant millions of years ago. Well, if simply having the ability to speak didn't result in language, what did? The answer from this approach is *cultural necessity*. As agriculture was developed, and climatic changes occurred following the last ice age, the ability of humans to feed and support larger numbers grew. This all happened roughly 8,000 to 10,000 years ago. It is no coincidence that Çatalhöyük in Turkey (the first known human city) has been radiocarbon dated prior to 6,500 BCE (8,500+ years ago). Of similar age, but still inhabited, is the city of Jericho, Israel. It is postulated by those who adhere to 'language as a cultural necessity' that the stone-age humans who first inhabited these cities (and others like them) were forced to make use of their speech capability to communicate in order to organize these large urban settings.

Originary event　　　　　　　Finally, there is the *originary event* postulated by generative anthropology. The leading proponent of this field is Dr. Eric Gans, a UCLA French professor. Gans has published several books in which he has presented new ideas, as well as expanded on ideas developed by René Girard and others. Key to this view of anthropology is what he refers to as the *originary* event. This is described on the jacket of his The Origin of Language (1981; Berkeley: University of California Press), where it reads:

> Eric Gans, like his teacher, the French critic René Girard, posits an event, a primal scene, at the origin of language. According to Girard, it was ritual sacrifice that constituted the fusion of the latent human abilities to mean and to murder, to create, symbolically, and to destroy. At some particular point in human pre-history, man achieved through ritual a deferral of intraspecific violence, which in turn gave rise to other such deferrals and ultimately to all human institutions, including language. Though, like Girard, Gans postulates a collective event at the origin of culture, in his version of the originary scene linguistic consciousness itself, rather than ritual, plays the key role.

> Gans' theory of representation is at once richly generative and concrete. He derives from it an integrated model of linguistic evolution – a genetic theory of speech acts – progressing from the simplest "ostensive" utterances to the declarative sentence. He provides an anthropological foundation for the use of language ...

According to Gans (pp. 11-12), in explaining Girard's hypothesis, "all higher animals have a tendency to imitate the gestures of their own (and sometimes other) species. Early man, as a result of various factors, acquired greater gifts for and inclination toward such imitation than any other species." However, this imitation "leads to potential rivalry among members of the same group, which among animals is controlled by the mechanism of stable dominance relationships" (*i.e.* the "alpha animal"). He then goes on to point out that "the crisis produced by mimetic rivalry will tend to polarize the violence of the group as a whole against an individual arbitrarily designated as the cause of the crisis." The sacrifice of this victim resolves the crisis "because the victim appears to the group as both the cause of the crisis and the source of its resolution". This sacrifice not only brings about a resolution of the specific crisis, it also produces "a communal peace not otherwise accessible". Gans, unlike Girard, considers language to be the key outcome of this originary event. To him, it is the representation of the event (the use of signs or symbols to re-present it; *i.e.* language) that is of greatest import, and not the sacrifice itself. Although this shares some of the views of 'cultural necessity', it is far from a restatement of the same approach.

Regardless of whether language arose as a result of genetic mutation, cultural necessity, or some originary event, one question still remains: <u>where</u> did it originate? In answer to this question, there are 2 common answers: *monogenesis*, and *polygenesis*.

Monogenesis claims that language arose in one location, and then spread. This parallels one theory of the biological evolution of human beings. Most human paleontologists today accept the so-called *Out of Africa* theory – that all modern humans are descended from a small group of hominid ancestors who lived someplace in east central Africa. Linguistic monogenesis accepts that language first developed with this group, and spread around the world as they moved around the globe. This first language is often labeled as *proto-human*.

Polygenesis maintains that language arose in several locations around the globe, and then spread from each of them. There are some (currently a small minority) human paleontologists who believe that modern humans arose from similar ancestors in several locations at about the same time in history. Language would thus have also begun in several different locations at about the same time (resulting in the recognized "language families: Uralic, Indo-European, Sino-Tibetan, *et cetera*).

Historical Linguistics focuses on where language came from, and how it has evolved over thousands of years. Typically, the first question to be resolved is whether to rely on a *monogenesis* or *polygenesis* origin.

Typically, monogenesis schemes assume (as do geneticists) an "origination point" somewhere in East Africa (the light square on the map in Figure 5.1 on the next page). By contrast, polygenesis schemes have multiple origination points. One such scheme (the most popular) is shown on the map in Figure 5.2 (next page). Note, however, that adherents to the polygenesis theory often can not agree on where these starting points are to be found.

Once one accepts a theory as to how it all began, the next step is to decide how languages came to be "related". It is obvious to any unbiased observer that some languages are very closely related (*e.g.* French and Spanish), others are more distantly related (*e.g.* Norwegian and Hindi), and still others don't appear to be related to any other languages at all (*e.g.* Etruscan, Basque and Burushaski).

The two most popular explanations for this are the *genetic theory* and the *wave theory*. The *wave theory* suggests that, when people speaking two different languages live in close proximity to each other, they often borrow vocabulary, syntax and even structure from each other. This would account for why French and Spanish (which are geographically adjacent) have so much in common, while French and Japanese (which have no common geographic boundaries) share virtually nothing. Although intellectually intriguing, this theory has largely been abandoned since the days of its greatest popularity in the 1950s. Nearly all historical linguists today accept the *genetic theory* – regardless of whether they adhere to the monogenesis or polygenesis idea of 'how it all began'.

Historical Linguistics

Origins

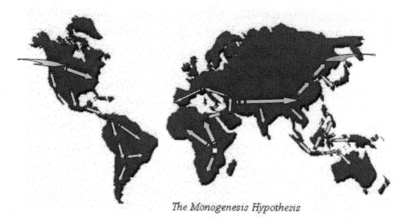

The Monogenesis Hypothesis

Figure 5.1   The Monogenesis Linguistic Hypothesis

Historical Linguistics

Origins

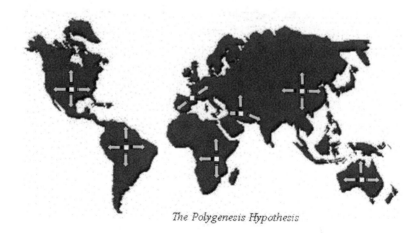

The Polygenesis Hypothesis

Figure 5.2   The Polygenesis Linguistic Hypothesis

One of the most renowned, although often highly controversial, historical linguists is Dr. Merrit Ruhlen. Dr. Ruhlen has proposed several controversial explanations regarding language relationships. The controversy arises from the fact that, not surprisingly, the further back one goes in time, the less historical evidence exists and the less general agreement there is on relationships, connections, *et cetera*. Dr. Ruhlen's more recent theories involve the Native American languages of the western hemisphere. Although his theory is highly controversial, and admittedly rather speculative, he carries a great deal of influence in this field. Earlier proposed theories of his were often similarly rejected and ridiculed by the academic establishment, only to be broadly accepted at a later date.

Typically, *Historical Linguistics* is only of minimal interest to the cultural anthropologist. Of greater interest is *how the language is used*. What does it <u>mean</u> when someone does such and such? How does your religious background change how you use the language? Can you tell the speaker's socio-economic class from their choice of words, phrases or grammar? *et cetera*. These issues do not fall within *formal linguistics*, but are <u>essential</u> to *sociolinguistics*.

Chapter 6
Linguistics (Sociolinguistics)

To the cultural anthropologist, languages themselves (and *historical linguistics*) are actually less interesting than what is commonly called *sociolinguistics*. This is the study of the social aspects of a language; and, there are many.

When two people are talking, there is always more going on than just the "content". The language they use is affected by social factors which define, or are determined by, their relationship. The tone, the sentence structure, and perhaps even the language selected (in some parts of the world) would be different for a man talking to his boss at work and the same man talking to his wife.

Factors that are considered – nearly always subconsciously – include:
   a) how well they know each other;
   b) the social setting;
   c) the social status and "role" of each;
   d) the cultural setting of the language;
   e) the purpose of the conversation; and,
   f) the topic.

Have you ever noticed that there is a difference in the way you speak to your friends, the way you speak to relatives, and the way you would speak to your professor at her office? This is often known as *code selection*; and, in some countries, this even stretches to selecting which language to use. In the United States (with the general exception of isolated non-English speaking enclaves), you can usually tell both the region and the socio-economic status of the speaker by their accent, dialect and language style.

Diglossia

Diglossia (Greek: "two tongues") is a term that sociolinguists use to describe a bilingual community where two languages or dialects are used differently for different social situations. Although less pronounced, the same effect also occurs in monolingual communities. Typically,

1) there are 2 distinct varieties — a high (H) and low (L) language;
2) each is used for distinct functions and in distinct situations; and,
3) nobody uses the high (H) speech in everyday conversation.

Examples (and the language most likely used) might include:

a) telling a joke (L);
b) interviewing for a job (H);
c) giving a speech for a charity event (H);
d) giving a speech for a friend on their birthday (L);
e) conversation in church (H); and,
f) talking in the school cafeteria (L).

In the US, this might consist of someone using Spanish, German or Chinese (the family's native language) as the "low" language, and English as the "high" language. You might also see this in Sicily, where natives use Sicilian (L) and Italian (H); or, in Minsk, where natives often speak both Ukrainian (L) and Russian (H) – or in Brooklyn (where Spanish is often the low, and English the high), northwestern Maine (French–low, English–high), or the Watts section of LA (Korean– or Ebonics–low, English–high).

One of the more common forms of diglossia results from the genders of the participants: men and women often do not use the same language. The crudest example of this might be an increased use of vulgarity between men; usually, this is significantly curtailed when a woman is present (Figure 6.1, next page; however, the use of vulgarity by women actually increases when men are present). But, it goes much further than that. In fact, men and women are very different in their entire use of a language.

Although men often think "women talk too much", Dr. Marjorie Swacker proved otherwise. Both sexes were asked to describe 3 paintings by Flemish artis Albrecht Durer. On average, the men took 13 minutes, while the women only took 3 minutes 10 seconds to communicate what they saw to another member of the same gender (Figure 6.2).

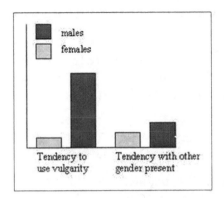

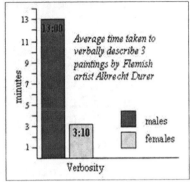

Figure 6.1 Vulgarity   **Figure 6.2 Verbosity**

This is definitely cultural. Most societies have given men a much greater opportunity to take a dominant role, be more talkative, discuss weighty matters, give long speeches, *etc*. Women, while suppressed in these areas, have been encouraged culturally to express their emotions, while men have been taught to "keep their cool", "remain calm", and "stay in control". As a result, one of the only areas where women typically talk more than men (regardless of where they're from) is in areas that revolve around emotion.

There are also many instances where different words are used by men and women – for the same thing! In Japanese, the terms for water, stomach, delicious and eat (respectively) are *ohiya*, *onaka*, *oisii*, and *taberu* <u>for</u> <u>women</u>; but, they are *mizu*, *hara*, *umai* and *kuu* <u>for</u> <u>men</u>. A similar process also occurs in English. There are no hard and fast rules about the words in English as there are in Japanese; but, word selection is frequently indicative of the gender of the speaker.

Politeness

Usually, there are many ways of getting what we want. What these methods are often depends upon the social situation. When with friends, we might say "Give me that plate", or "Shut-up"; however, at a formal function with relatives or a boss, "Could you please pass me that plate?", or "I'm sorry, I don't mean to interrupt, but I can't hear the movie." would be more acceptable (and likely). Different social situations require a change in language to fit the occasion. It would be socially unacceptable to reverse these two phrases.

Anthropologists Brown and Levinson identified four types of *politeness strategies* that essentially sum up human "politeness": *Bald On Record*, *Negative Politeness*, *Positive Politeness*, and the *Off-Record* indirect strategy.

Bald on Record refers to an "in your face", call-it-as-it-is approach. There is no attempt to help the listener "save face".

Positive Politeness recognizes that the listener has a desire to be respected, and offers a level of that respect. It also indicates that there is a friendly relationship being put forth, and implies group reciprocity.

Negative Politeness is similar, but usually either self-deprecates or acknowledges that the speaker is imposing himself on them. For example, a sentence might begin with "I was wondering if …" or "I'm sorry to bother you, but …".

Off Record is a mechanism for "side stepping" any possibility of confrontation. The desire is made known without directly imposing by asking (*e.g.* "I'm going to have to call some friends; my car will be in the shop 'til Monday"); or, the speaker begs off from a confrontation by offering a cliché avoidance (*e.g.* "I must have called you back a dozen times, but you were never there; boy, do they keep you busy.")

One indicator of politeness is the use of *honorifics*. These are *speech markers* used to show respect for the listener. Referring to someone as Mister, Miss, Doctor, Sir, Ma'am, *et cetera* is an indication of respect. These markers, however, are often linked to region and social status. For example, Southerners are much more likely to use Sir and Ma'am than New Englanders. When relocating to the South, New Englanders are constantly reminded of this when service personnel (*e.g.* waiters and clerks) call them Sir or Ma'am. To the speaker, it is a sign of respect (or pandering for a better tip); but, to the New Englander, it instinctively sounds sarcastic and disrespectful.

Gender is also a factor in the use of honorifics, but is most likely the result of cultural bias toward the relative social status of the sexes. Women have historically needed to "act like a lady", "know their place", and take a secondary role in society. One might expect that they would therefore adopt the subservient habit of using honorifics to show respect and to acknowledge their lack of social standing; and, they do. Women are much more likely to use honorifics than men. For example: female students are roughly twice as likely as male students to address their professor as "Doctor So-and-so".

The final form of politeness to be considered is the use of *hedges*. These are phrases that are added to blunt the edge of something. Examples might include beginning with "I was told that …". "A lot of people claim that …", "Mary told me that …", or "I heard that …". It is thought that, by identifying some third party as the potential source, or denying direct ownership of the idea, hedges tend to soften or deflect any offense that might be taken by the listener.

Pidgins and Creoles

A simplified language derived from two or more languages is called a *pidgin*. It is a *contact language* developed and used by people who do not share a common language. It is used in limited ways, and the structure is very simplistic. In Chinese ports at the start of Far East trading, the Chinese and American/British traders adopted a streamlined "business English"; this was corrupted by the Chinese speakers of this new 'language' as "pidgin":

Business English →
　　　→ BIZ-ness EN-glish →
　　　　　→ BIZH-ness EHN-glish →
　　　　　　　→ PIZH-neh IHN-glis →
　　　　　　　　　→ PIDG-neh IHN-glih →
　　　　　　　　　　　→ PIDG^n IHN^{glih} →
　　　　　　　　　　　　　→ PIDGIN

Ever since, all such contact languages have been known as *pidgins*.

Since they only serve a single, simplistic purpose, pidgins usually die out once the need disappears. However, when the pidgin is used long enough, it begins to evolve into a richer language with a more complex structure and a much richer vocabulary. Once this pidgin has evolved and has acquired native speakers (with children often learning the pidgin as their 'first language'), it is known as a *Creole*. An example of this is the Creole of Papua New Guinea, *Tok Pisin*, which has become the official national language.

Tok Pisin: *Yu pren tru bilong mi. Inap yu ken helpim mi nau?*
English: *You are a true friend of mine. Can you help me now?*

When slaves from Africa were brought over to North America to work on plantations in the 19th century, they were systematically separated from their community and mixed with people from other communities. They were unable to communicate with each other. The owners' strategy behind this was so that they couldn't come up with a plot to escape. In order to finally converse with their peers on the plantations, they needed to develop a common language by which they could communicate– a pidgin. For the slaves who fled to the sea islands off the coast of Georgia and South Carolina (*e.g.* Hilton Head or St. Helena), this pidgin (later, creole) is known as *Gullah* It is closely related to Jamaican Creole and a Bahamian dialect, and is closest in many ways to the Krio language of Sierra Leone in West Africa. Gullah has contributed numerous cultural customs to the United States as well as several fairly common words: *e.g.* goober (*Gullah:* guber, meaning "peanut"), and gumbo (*Gullah:* gumbo, meaning "okra"). The spiritual *Michael Row the Boat Ashore* is originally a Gullah spiritual.

Others also arose from colonization; languages such as French, Spanish, Portuguese, English, and Dutch were the languages of the colonizers as they set up ports and towns to oversee shipping and trading routes. Pidgins developed as a mix of the colonizers' language, the native language, and perhaps an African language (if slaves were involved). For example, *Papiamento* began as the pidgin used in the Dutch ports in the southern Caribbean (Aruba, Bonaire and Curaçao); it was a mixture of Dutch, English, Spanish, Portuguese, various West African languages, and Carib. Today, Papiamento has evolved into a formal Creole used extensively throughout the area.

Papiamento: *Mi no ta huma hopi. No mas cu un paki pa dia.*
English: *I don't smoke much. No more than a pack a day.*

In every pidgin or creole, there is a dominant language which contributes most of the vocabulary (called the *superstrate*), and one or more minority languages that also contribute (called *substrates*). In the examples above, the superstrates are English (Tok Pisin) and Spanish (Papiamento), with several languages serving as substrates (native Papua New Guinea languages for Tok Pisin; Yoruban, Carib, English, Portuguese, and Dutch for Papiamento).

Louisiana Creole is probably the best known American creole. It is derived from French (the superstrate) and several West African languages (the substrates). You have probably heard of *Cajun* – a well developed dialect of this Creole (the name coming from a vocal corruption of *Arcadian* – the former Canadian home of the displaced French speakers). In 1755, the French in Acadia (northern Nova Scotia) were forced to leave. They left for the nearest French-friendly port: New Orleans. A pidgin developed enabling the new immigrants to communicate with the Africans and Spanish that already lived there. That evolved into the creole.

Language Variation

This is the variation that occurs <u>within</u> a language depending on the *context* in which it is being used. In this sense, *context* refers to things such as ethnicity, social class, gender, age, geography, and numerous other factors. There are several "types" of language variation, and these are often indicative of social factors such as those just listed. The 3 primary types of variation are:

Internal Variation   different ways within a language of expressing a meaning. These are often considered ungrammatical, incorrect or mispronounced. One example of internal variation in English is "ask" *versus* "axe".

Language variety   broad term used at a number of levels. We can use it to distinguish between English and French, or to distinguish between two varieties of a language – such as Boston English *versus* Appalachian English.

Dialect   a complex, often misunderstood, concept. Dialect is actually a collection of attributes (phonetic, phonological, syntactic, semantic, and morphological) that make one group of speakers noticeably different from others speaking the same language.

People should be careful when they use the word *dialect*, for it is a commonly misused term. Dialect is <u>not</u> a negative term for linguists. Although you may hear people refer to non-standard varieties of English as "dialects" (usually implying something bad about the non-standard variety – and the people who speak it), a *dialect* really refers to <u>any</u> variety of a language. So, technically, <u>everyone</u> speaks <u>some</u> dialect of their native language.

Dialect is also not synonymous with accent. Accent is but one part of dialectal variation. Non-linguists often think that accents <u>define</u> a dialect (or, that accent alone can identify someone as non-native or foreign). Also, non-linguists usually think it's the other people that have an accent – not them.

So, what is accent? *Accent* refers specifically to phonological variation, *i.e.* variation in pronunciation   So, if we talk about a "southern accent", we're talking about the pronunciation of English common to the southern part of the US. But, a southern <u>dialect</u> has more than just particular phonological properties. *Accent* is about pronunciation, but *dialect* is broader, and also includes syntactic, morphological, and semantic properties.

A final note on accent: *everybody has one!!!* There is <u>no such thing</u> as a person who speaks without an accent. This is not just political correctness, by the way – it's a fact. So:

- a *dialect* is a particular variety of a language (and, everyone speaks in some dialect); and,
- *accent* refers to the phonology of a given dialect.   Since everybody has a dialect, everyone therefore has an accent.

Two final terms that should be understood are *idiolect* and *speech community*. An idiolect is simply the technical term used to refer to the language variety spoken by an individual speaker of the language. Just as variation occurs among groups of speakers, there is also variation from speaker to speaker. No two speakers of any language speak identically. Each person speaks their own particular variety of their language – their own *idiolect*. And, a *speech community* is any group of people who all speak a common dialect.

Standard English

One of the biggest misunderstandings regarding dialect re-volves around the problem of standard *versus* nonstandard varieties of a language. Non-linguists often simply get the wrong idea of what these are. Let's compare.

Wrong Ideas
- A language is composed of a standard dialect from which all of the non-standard dialects emerge.
- The standard dialect is the correct way to speak the language.
- Other dialects represent inferior ways of speaking it.
- The standard is more complex, logical, and expressive than the non-standard.
- Non-standard dialects are a product of lazy speech.

Right Ideas
- Languages have various dialects.
- There are a range of varieties that are considered standard. So, John Kerry, Barack Obama, and George Bush may all speak standard English, but their dialects are clearly not the same.
- What is considered standard is predominantly associated with prestige, a non-linguistic factor.
- From a linguistic standpoint, what is considered standard has nothing to do with either correctness or superiority.
- From a linguistic standpoint, all dialects are equally correct, expressive, complex, logical and so forth. That is, the term non-standard dialect only means *not the standard dialect* – it does not mean inferior or sub-standard.
- Non-standard dialects are not simply offshoots from the standard. Don't think of non-standard dialects as branches of some standard variety. People often think that the properties of a non-standard have evolved out of the standard; but, this is not true. Non-standard and standard dialects make up a range of dialects that comprise the language.

Prestige

There are many factors involved in determining the *standard* form of a language; but, they typically do not include linguistic factors. One factor that is very important is *prestige*. Basically, the standard dialect is that dialect most associated with prestige in a society. Does this mean that all prestigious people in the society must speak the standard? No. But, most do. Sicilian, Napolitano, Venetan and several other languages have gradually become secondary to standard Italian. What became the *standard* was the Romance language of the area around Florence, the area of the political leadership of Garibaldi's revolution (that led to modern Italy), literary heritage (*e.g.* Dante), and the heart of the Renaissance (*i.e.* the artistic center of Italy, with DaVinci, Michelangelo, *etc.*).

But, if the standard confers prestige on its speakers, why doesn't everyone speak the standard? That would require that everyone was welcome to speak the standard. Think about how you feel about your own dialect. Even if you speak a non-standard variety of English, do you want to be told by someone else that the way you speak is wrong or inadequate, and that you should change? When someone relocates from one region to another, it is common for people to constantly mimic or point out their accent. In practice, this usually doesn't discourage its use and get them to adopt the 'standard regional dialect' of their new area; actually, it often has the opposite effect – encouraging them to continually reinforce their accent, and thus distinguish themselves from the plebeians amongst whom they now consider themselves to be living. Dialects are intimately bound up both with identity and a sense of community. It would be naïve to think that this is not the case, and that people can simply shrug off one dialect and adopt another with no cost. In fact, once you are an adult, learning the speech patterns of another dialect may require a lot of training. It is important to recognize the prestige factors involved in a non-standard dialect. Even though a speaker may speak a non-standard variety of a language, they may gain prestige within the community by using that non-standard variety – either in the eyes of their peers or their own.

So, prestige can actually take two different forms:

Overt Prestige refers to speakers of non-standard varieties who adopt (to some degree) the standard variety – to leverage the generally prestigious perception of thosewho use this dialect.

Covert Prestige refers to speakers who choose not to adopt a standard dialect, but try to leverage prestige associated with the distinctiveness of their non-standard dialect – usually, by appearing to relate more closely with a specific group (*e.g.* a British dialect in government circles, a French dialect in culinary circles, an Italian dialect in fashion circles, *et cetera*).

In simple terms, *overt prestige* seeks prestige by assimilating to the standard, while *covert prestige* chooses not to assimilate to the standard. Clearly, both choices have distinct costs and benefits.

Classifying Dialects

When attempting to classify dialects, linguists work along a number of lines. The three primary sources of language variation are geography, ethnicity, and social class.

Geography

A major factor in dialect diversity is geography. The study of regional dialects is usually called *dialectology*. Although the lines are rarely very clear, it may provide a sense of how dialect varies with geography to view an example. In the United States, linguists usually divide the country into either 6 or 9 distinct dialect regions [Figures 6.3 and 6.4].

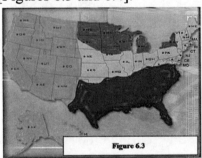 

Figure 6.3   Figure 6.4

Figure 6.3 (above, left) divides the US into 6 dialect regions: North, South, West, Upper Midland, Lower Midland, and Northeast. Many linguists, however, do not believe that this captures the unique dialect often called a 'Boston accent'. So, they further divide the country into 9 dialect regions (Figure 6.4; above, right): Eastern New England, Upper North, Lower North, Upper South, Lower South, Upper Midwest, Upper West, Northwest, and Southwest. Several groups have done extensive research to define the different accents, vocabulary, grammar, *etc.* of these regions.

Ethnicity

Another factor in language variation is ethnicity. Often, ethnicity is closely tied to a particular geographical area; but, not always. Sometimes, ethnicity is a factor <u>despite</u> broad dispersion (*e.g.* African-American *Ebonics* – linguists have always recognized the characteristics shared across the African-American English speech communities regardless of geographical region).

Class

A third major factor in language variation is social class; and, it is important to remember that class often plays a role in dialects. Class often includes economic and educational criteria. To a native Floridian, all Bostonians sound alike – because they are only hearing the major dialect distinctions. To the Bostonian, however, there are many sub-sets of the dialect. For instance, most Bostonians don't think they sound <u>anything</u> like the Kennedys. They hear wealthy, Irish Catholic, private-school, closed-society influences that put this family in a totally different sub-set from them.

Typically, these factors are all there. So, when we look at variation, we must constantly bear all of them in mind as potential *extra-linguistic* factors. In fact, we also need to factor in such things as age and sex – each of which also plays an important role in understanding language variation.

Slang

Finally, there is the fact that some words are considered *slang*. Slang is actually a tricky thing to define; but, that doesn't stop us from having a clear sense that there are words that are clearly slang words. In this sense, it is the linguistic equivalent of pornography — in 1964, Supreme Court Justice Potter Stewart wrote that "I shall not today attempt further to define the kinds of material I understand to be embraced, ... [b]ut I know it when I see it." He meant pornography; but, he could just as easily have meant slang.

So, if someone comes up to you and says, "yo, dude, that is one tight car", the meaning is not clear. Because several of the words are slang, their meaning varies across the community. An older American may think they're talking about a car with poor leg room, while a younger American may think the speaker is showing admiration for the way the car looks. In this quote, "tight", "yo", and "dude" are all examples of slang.

From a linguistic point of view, there is nothing unique about slang. They are still words, and are formed by the same processes as other words – subject to the same constraints of the language as are non-slang terms. What is special is their *sociopsychological* or *sociolinguistic* role – *i.e.* how and when we use them, and how we feel about them as words. In this context, they often share several common properties.

Informality   Slang words are almost always used in very informal contexts. Think about when someone might use *clueless* as opposed to *unaware*.

Group identification   Many slang words are markers of group membership outside mainstream society. Someone who says "dude" is probably younger (even though "dude" has been around for a long time). Similarly, the slang use of "tight" (above) would not typically be used by an older speaker. Ethnic groups also often have specific slang terms that identify people who use them as members. In fact, membership works both ways. If you <u>don't</u> know the slang, you are also clearly identifying yourself as a non-member of the group.

Short life span   Although not necessarily, slang often has a short life span. There are examples like *cram* – meaning "to study intensely over a short period of time" – that have been around for a long time. Other slang terms appear and then disappear pretty quickly. *Groovy* is an example. It never really had much staying power, and its productive use really didn't extend beyond the sixties.

Slang is scalar   Slang seems to fall on a *slanginess* continuum. Think about the following three terms: unaware, dense, clueless. Most people wouldn't see *unaware* as slang at all; *dense*, however, feels "marginally slangy"; and finally, *clueless* feels the "slangiest" of the three.

Often, if a slang term hangs around long enough, it loses its 'slanginess' and becomes acceptable as part of the standard use of the language. In most cases, it still feels informal to a degree, but it doesn't feel like slang anymore. Examples include *rip off* (*i.e.* to steal) and *ain't* (am not). Basically, the idea is that if slanginess is a continuum, there must be a middle where terms don't feel like slang, but don't feel formal either. This is what linguists call *colloquial*. It's clearly informal, but not slang.

Sapir–Whorf Hypothesis

All of these descriptions of linguistics have focused on how the language reflects, and perhaps indicates, the way that the speaker relates to the world about them. But, not all linguists have considered language to be the servant of reality; some, in fact, have proposed that it is the other way around – that reality is perhaps the servant of language. Two of the most notable holding this view were Edward Sapir [1884–1939] and his student, Benjamin Lee Whorf [1897–1941]. Collectively, their view is known as the *Sapir–Whorf Hypothesis*.

Whereas most linguists look for universal structures and processes in language, the Sapir-Whorf Hypothesis postulates that different languages actually produce different ways of thinking. They posited that the different grammatical approaches of different languages educate their speakers to view the world from a different perspective – *i.e.* to think differently. Numerous anecdotal examples have been put forward by supporters of this view.

♦ The third person singular pronouns in English (he, she) distinguish gender. The less used *it* is used almost exclusively for inanimate objects. By contrast, the Palaung (a small, Burmese tribe) have only a single, gender-neutral pronoun. The Romance languages (*e.g.* French, Italian, Spanish, *etc.*) not only distinguish the pronouns, but also assign gender to every noun – requiring that adjectives and modifiers have 'gender agreement' with the noun. The SWH (Sapir-Whorf Hypothesis) would theorize that this means that English speakers would likely be more conscious of, and pay more attention to, issues of gender than the Palaung, but perhaps less than speakers of the Romance languages.

♦ English divides time into the past, present, and future. The Hopi (a native tribe of southwestern US) do not. Instead, the Hopi distinguish between that which exists (or has existed) and that which does not (or has not yet). This combines the English perception of the present and past into 'that which is', and the future and imaginary (or hypothetical) into 'that which is not'. The SWH maintains that the Hopi thus experience time in a different manner than English speakers – because their temporal perception is fundamentally different.

♦ English routinely uses the future tense to distinguish that which <u>will</u> happen. In Portuguese, there is a *future subjunctive* verb form. This adds a sense of uncertainty to every future event described by this form. Americans assume that there are certain future events that simply <u>will</u> happen; the Portuguese qualify this by using the future subjunctive. "The stars will shine tonight <u>if</u> they didn't all go supernova during the daylight hours."; and, "I'll see you tomorrow <u>if</u> I don't get run over by a truck tonight." The English way of speaking about the future is so certain we don't even think about the possible problems; the Portuguese, however, are recognizing life is not that certain.

♦ People talk and write about what is important to them. As a result, their vocabulary often reflects their focus of interest. This is known as a *focal vocabulary*. For example, the Inuit (Eskimo) people have 4 terms for what most Americans call "snow"; the Saami (Lapps) have at least twice that. The Nuer in Africa have several dozen terms for what most Americans would call a "cow"; and, there are numerous other examples that could be cited. The key question is whether this reflects a world view, or helps create one.

There is no question that reality and language are inter-related. However, whether it is our worldview that structures our language, or our language that structures our perception of reality is not so clear. There appears to be ample anecdotal evidence for both positions. And, although the SWH fell into some academic disfavor in the sixties, it has revived with a vengeance since then under the heading of *Linguistic Relativity*.

Technically, Sapir and Whorf never co-authored anything, neither of them ever presented an hypothesis, and they never distinguished between *strong* and *weak* forms of their views. This is relatively recent: *strong linguistic relativity* is linguistic determinism (*i.e.* language dictates the range of possible cognitive processes); and, *weak linguistic relativity* is a recognition of a linguistic-cognitive correlation, but not determinant (*i.e.* language influences cognitive processes). This division into weak and strong was not original with Whorf, but was espoused by Stuart Chase (an MIT-trained American economist and engineer) – who Whorf actually described as being "utterly incompetent". Modern research into so-called *weak linguistic relativity* has been promoted by such academics as Stanford Professor Dr. Lera Boroditsky.

"Language ... powerfully conditions all our thinking about social problems and processes. ... The fact of the matter is that the 'real world' is to a large extent unconsciously built up on the language habits of the group. No two languages are ever sufficiently similar to be considered as representing the same social reality."

— Edward Sapir

"Language is not merely a reproducing instrument for voicing ideas but rather is itself the shaper of ideas, the program and guide for the individual's mental activity, for his analysis of impressions, for his synthesis of his mental stock in trade.."
— Benjamin Lee Whorf

"Each language comes with its own cognitive tool kit, almost as if each has its own parallel universe that sees the world a little bit differently. [...] How tragic then that we are losing a language every two weeks ... tremendous cultural loss ... incredible cultural treasure."

— Lera Boroditsky

Chapter 7
Food and Clothing

Food and clothing are fairly obvious social markers. Walk down a street in nearly any American city, and you will notice that different age-based social groups adhere to different standards regarding what is considered appropriate attire. It quickly becomes clear that certain clothing styles are more acceptable within some social groups than they are within others.

So-called short-shorts are not appropriate for all locations or functions, but they are certainly more generally accepted when worn by women than men, and also more so when worn by a younger rather than older individual. Similarly, so-called hip-hop shorts are typically more acceptable within a younger group, while wearing socks with sandals is probably more readily tolerated within an older group.

Similarly, food is often a cultural marker. Americans would be shocked, and possibly outraged, if they walked past a butcher shop window and saw dogs skinned and waiting to be butchered (right; Guangxi, China). However, sale of what they call "fragrant meat" (*i.e.* dog) is commonplace in China, Korea, Viet Nam, and several other countries where it is often  considered medicinal (relieves impotence, cures disease, and expels evil spirits). Of course, Indians may be offended by similar US displays of cuts of beef.

Food

Every time an American family tries to decide on a restaurant for dinner, they are reminded of the cultural differences in food.

- ◆ Enchiladas? Mexican restaurant.
- ◆ Egg Foo Yong? Chinese restaurant.
- ◆ Paella? Spanish restaurant.
- ◆ Spanikopita? Greek restaurant.
- ◆ Sauerbraten? German restaurant.

- ♦ Lasagna? Italian restaurant.
- ♦ Palak Paneer? Indian restaurant.
- ♦ Phở saté? Vietnamese restaurant.
- ♦ …

Not only are there ethnic & national differentiations, but there are regional variations, as well.

- ♦ Boiled dinner, lobster roll, or apple crisp? New England.
- ♦ Hoppin' John, sweet potato pie, or grits? The Deep South.
- ♦ Jambalaya, dirty rice, or beignets? Louisiana.
- ♦ Fried Spam & rice, poi, or manapua? Hawai'i.
- ♦ Smoked salmon, moose steak, or fiddleheads? Northwest.
- ♦ …

But, there are many other ethnic or national delicacies that may not be quite as familiar to the average American.

- ♦ Witchetty grub   (large moth larvæ eaten raw or crisped in Australia)
- ♦ Shitto   (a red pepper & fermented fish sauce popular in Ghana)
- ♦ Fried Crickets (considered a treat in the Philippines)
- ♦ Deep fried Monkey toes   (an Indonesian equivalent to chicken wings)
- ♦ Haggis   (steamed sheep stomach stuffed with oatmeal in Scotland)
- ♦ …

If you have not lost your appetite yet, then we should explore the obvious question: why do some groups consider something a delicacy or treat, when others consider it to be repulsive? The answer is culture. Let's tale a look at just one aspect of this dietary variation: meat.

In the United States, the most commonly eaten meats (excluding birds and fish) are beef and pork. Both meats are derived from animals that are primarily bred, kept, and used for food; and, you would be hard pressed to find an American household with a "pet bull". This allows the person eating the meat to disassociate the foodstuff from the living animal from which it came. Even the names are indicative of this disassociation.

For several centuries following the conquest of England by William the Conqueror in 1066 CE, the language of the English royalty was Norman (William and his troops had come from Normandy); Norman is a Romance language (related to French, but infused with Norse terms by Viking settlers). The language of the peasants was late Anglo-Saxon – early Middle English. It was the peasants who bred, raised and slaughtered the animals; and, names for them generally referred to the living animal: *e.g.* *cú* (cow), *pecg* (pig), *sceáp* (sheep), and *deór* (deer). By contrast, royalty had no direct contact with the living animal, and often only saw it once it had been killed, butchered, and prepared for the table. As a result, they most often used the Norman terms for these foods: *e.g.* *bœuf* (beef), *porc* (pork), *mouton* (mutton), and *veneisun* (venison).

The lack of direct involvement in the slaughter and preparation of meat led to the ability to divorce the actual killing and slaughter from the final food product. This separation, or disassociation, even resorted to using words from different languages when referring to the food and the animal from which it came. When no such separation is possible, a sense of revulsion often arises when the animal product is served. This lack of separation most often occurs when the situation meets the following criteria:

a)   the animal is often a household pet;

b)   the animal is often used as a draft animal;

c)   the animal has been named by younger family members;

d)   no crisis ever dictated either eating it or dying of starvation;

e)   a religious injunction precluded ancestors from eating it;

f)   it is considered dirty or diseased (whether true or not); or,

g)   the physical resemblance between the animal and the food is overpowering.

Think about which meat foods are most often rejected by Americans, and you'll soon see that at least one of these criteria is virtually always present — most likely serving as the cause of the revulsion. Consider some examples.

♦   dog or cat (a);

♦   horse (b);

♦   goat, pig, *et cetera* (c) ;

♦   moth larvæ (d) ;

◆   cows (Hindu) and pigs (Jews & Muslims) (e);
◆   fried cockroaches or rats (f); and,
◆   boiled lobster (g).

In contrast to what people <u>don't</u> eat is a long list of ethnic specialties that people <u>do</u> eat. Typically, these are foods that have a strong historical or gastronomic heritage. The Swiss are world known for their cheeses (*e.g.* Gruyère, Emmentaler, and Raclette) and chocolate (*e.g.* Cailler and Lindt). Russia and some other countries are known for their caviar (black, or sturgeon, and red, or salmon). The French are known for their wines. Germany features sausages. Japan produces sashimi.   *et cetera.*

The bottom line when it comes to cultural dietary variation is to remember that the two primary factors in food selection are *avoidance* (*e.g.* list a through g, above, for meat) and *preference* (*e.g.* the ethnic 'specialties' listed in the preceding paragraph). In the final analysis, human beings are omnivores – their teeth, stomach, intestines, and supporting systems are designed to consume and process nearly anything, either plant or animal. There are obviously exceptions (*e.g.* poisonous items such as the *puffer fish*), but these are rare compared to the variety of items that humans can eat. This means that the choices are usually based on cultural criteria, not nutrition or biology. And, without having experienced similar cultural and geographical restrictions and opportunities, it is impossible to understand why someone from another culture eats (or refuses to eat) the things that they do.

Clothing

Why don't female American students come to class topless? Seriously. Why not? It would certainly increase the attendance level amongst male students. Or would it? Clothing is every bit as culturally dictated as food preferences. Consider the clothing items in the list on the next page (left) and the ethnic groups listed (right). Can you match which ethnic group would most likely consider which clothing item 'normal'? The answers are at the bottom of the page; but, see how well you do before you check results.

1)	burqa	a)	Japan
2)	dashiki	b)	Saudi Arabia
3)	dishdasha	c)	Hawai'i
4)	kimono	d)	Scotland
5)	sari	e)	Bermuda
6)	abaya	f)	Indonesia
7)	salwar kameez	g)	Morocco
8)	kilt	h)	West Africa
9)	lederhosen	i)	Afghanistan
10)	muumuu	j)	Eskimo (Inupiat, Inuit)
11)	hooded caribou jacket	k)	United Arab Emirates
12)	sarong	l)	Punjab (northern India)
13)	walking shorts	m)	India (especially central & southern)
14)	kaftan	n)	Germany

So, if food preferences often follow from historical crises, historical usage, religious injunction, fear of disease, *et cetera*, what are the typical reasons for clothing variation? Most often, weather, environment, and tradition. Although there may be societies where the female students could come to class topless (with no physical or sexual implications whatsoever), that is certainly not true in the US. And, once American students adjusted to the change, it is actually unlikely that it would have any effect on male attendance at all; but, that might take a while.

Consider a few facts about some of the clothing items listed above.

Dishdasha The dishdasha (right) is the traditional men's clothing in Saudi Arabia as well as in most of the other Arab nations. It is essentially a long-sleeve, loose fitting tunic that hangs to just above the ankle. Many of what are now considered Arab nations were once nomadic or semi-nomadic tribes living in desert regions.  Their livelihood rarely came from agriculture (it's a desert), and was frequently based on running trade or caravan routes across the broad expanses of desert. Spending large amounts of time on camels or horses under a relentless sun, in blinding sand storms, and in torrid heat made the loose fitting dishdasha a logical choice: the free form encourages air flow, reflects much of the sun, provides

Answers to clothing–ethnic match: 1i, 2h, 3b, 4a, 5m, 6k, 7l, 8d, 9n, 10c, 11j, 12f, 13e, and 14g a ready barrier for swirling sand, and generally keeps the body several degrees cooler than it would be with other styles of clothing. Also, due to the complete coverage of the dishdasha, the use of restrictive or heat trapping undergarments is entirely optional.

Lederhosen   Lederhosen (German for "leather trousers") are actually leather shorts worn today mostly for folk events (*e.g.* Oktoberfest) or regional pride. They first appeared – primarily in rural

areas of Bavaria (southern Germany) and Austria – in the 1830s. Initially, they were worn by woodsmen, farmers, and other village people. They offered several advantages over earlier, fabric trousers: being leather, they were warmer in the cool mountain environment; they were extremely durable and long-lasting; they provided much greater protection from thorns, brambles, sharp rocks, and other objects often encountered by those working in the woods; and, properly cared for, leather pants can literally last a lifetime (making them very economical in the long run). Traditionally, they are held up by suspenders which are often heavily embroidered with village, family, or regional symbols.

Aymara bowler   The Aymara are an indigenous people of western Bolivia, southern Peru, and northern Chile. They have

lived in this area for perhaps 2,000 years, having been politically dominated by the Inca, the Spanish, and now the local, native governments. Today, they number about 2 million. The highly distinctive dress of the women includes the traditional Chola dress (often made of *aguayo*, a multi-colored, woven wool) topped by a felt bowler hat. The neighboring ethnic grouping of the *Quechua* also wear this hat. Where did it come from? And, why do they wear it? Pride.

During the 1920s, a shipment of bowler hats from Europe was destined for Spaniards working on building new railroads in Peru. The shipment (Europe to Bolivia to Peru) arrived, but the hats were too small for the rail workers; so, they were distributed free to the native Quechua and Aymara people. They fit the women. The warm and soft felt hats were considered a luxury and a symbol of status by the Aymara women, and were soon adopted as formal wear (for shopping, church, public gatherings, *et cetera*). Today, the Aymara and Quechua women still consider them a status symbol, and the bowler hat business is thriving. A woman without one is often looked down upon as an "unfortunate".

Pareo   The *pareo* is the Tahitian version of a sarong; other terms for it include *lavalava* (in Samoa), *kaily* (Kerala, India), *sulu* (Fiji), and *lap-lap* (Papua New Guinea). It can be worn by both men and women. Modern styles for women are longer than those for men, and serve effectively as dresses. Men wear shorter versions, and women in the Polynesian islands of the South Pacific also wore these shorter versions (topless) until early in the 20th century. Today, this shorter version is often worn by women as a "beach coverup", a sort of wrap-around skirt used to cover a bikini bottom when leaving the beach area.

Often all grouped under the heading *sarong*, it is essentially just a rectangular piece of cloth that is wrapped around the body and tied. Some, such as the Papua New Guinea *lap-lap*, are rather skimpy by western standards – comprising just a small rectangular cloth in the front and another in the back, tied together at the sides with a single thread. In this form, they are little more than a loincloth.

The use of these garments today is widespread (in common use from Africa and Arabia across the Indian Ocean to India and Sri Lanka to Southeast Asia, Australia, New Zealand, and the islands of the South Pacific). Originally, the garment began on the Malaysian peninsula (*sarong* is actually the Malay word for "sheath"). In its earliest form, it is a piece of cloth about 3' by 7' that is sewn into a tube shape. It is stepped into, and then pulled up to the navel. It is tightened and held in place by folding the excess fabric over onto itself and tucking it in at the waist. Other societies have enlarged it (to cover the breasts), reduced it (to immodest, almost obscene, sizes), and adapted it in many ways (such as belt loops, and worn with a dress shirt, tie, and jacket as formal business wear).

The advantages of the sarong were early recognized by people all across the warmer climates of southern Asia, northern Africa, and the South Pacific: it is loose enough to allow a great deal of freedom of movement; it allows for air flow to reduce the buildup of body heat;　it is readily adjustable in size and comfort;　it provides a modicum of modesty (unless cut way down in size);　and, it enables the wearer to wear that and little else.

Numerous western actors and actresses have worn sarongs in Hollywood movies: Dorothy Lamour, Tyrone Power, and – more recently – Pierce Brosnan (in *The Thomas Crown Affair*).

Ethnic Clothing

Unlike food choices, clothing almost always began as a functional decision.　Extremes of climate, environment, *etc.* are nearly always the driving force behind the style and design;　and, local availability of materials and skills usually drive the decoration.

 For example, the *dashiki* of western Africa is a loose, flowing, V-neck, pullover shirt.　The color and patterns (if any) are dictated by the occasion (*e.g.* a "dashiki suit" – a dashiki with matching *kufi* [cap] and dress pants – is the African equivalent of a tuxedo, and may be worn to formal events)..　The nature of the event often dictates the colors.　For example, at weddings, it will likely be white (although sometimes purple or light blue are worn). Neither red nor black would ever be worn at a wedding, as black is the color of death in West Africa, and red honors the blood shed by slaves.

Chapter 8
Religion and Art

Religion — Cults

Anthropologists often use the term *cult* in describing religion, and this can cause some misunderstandings with students. The English word cult is derived from the Latin *cultus*, which meant "culture". As such, it has evolved in common English usage with several different meanings. *Cultus* has become the Latin root for such English terms as:

- cultivate
- cultivation
- colony
- cult
- culture
- cultured
- colonial
- colonist
- colonize

The word cult is actually defined as "a system of worship of a deity." In this sense, it thus refers to almost every religion (only 'almost' because there are a very small number of religions that neither believe in nor worship a deity; they are, in practice, either agnostic or atheist). This, however, is not how most students of anthropology understand the word; and, this is almost certainly the fault of their religious leaders. Religious leaders of several faiths often use the term derisively or pejoratively – to refer to any religious group which they consider to be inferior or misguided. Although technically not an accurate definition, it has become so commonly used in this way that it has taken on this connotation.

If *cult* is to be used with this narrow, disparaging meaning, then a generally accepted set of criteria must be established to determine which groups are cults – and, which groups are not (it is simply unacceptable to consider any group with whom you disagree to be a cult). The criteria most often used by anthropologists are the following five:

- the group has, or had, a charismatic, powerful leader(s);
- it displays a group mentality that tends to restrict or deny the individuality and individual worth of the members;
- there is a definite alienation of friends or relatives that effectively "drives them away";

- it may financially abuse the individual for the perceived greater welfare of the group as a whole; and,
- it exhibits physical isolation from the surrounding community, avoiding that which might form a bond with the outside world.

Although there are some groups that do earn the title *cult* on this basis (typically satisfying four or five of these criteria), they are (fortunately) few and far between.

The way that most general anthropologists (those who do not specialize in any one of the sub-fields), and virtually all cultural anthropologists use the word is simply to refer to "a system of worship". This is very close to Webster's definition (given above), and only lacks the necessity of acknowledging a deity. This omission is not without some justification, as not dropping that requirement would make it impossible to list Buddhism as a cult (along with Christianity, Islam, and Hinduism) – even though Buddhism has the 4th largest following in the world *because so many Buddhists are atheists!*

Dr. Anthony F. C. Wallace [1923–] remains one of the most respected Psychological Anthropologists – *i.e.* specializing in the area of personality and interpersonal cultural transmission. Having earned his PhD from the University of Pennsylvania, he served as an anthropology professor there for nearly 40 years (1951–1988).

 The author and winner of the Bancroft Prize for numerous books, his work centered on Native American cultures, and the cultural aspects of the cognitive process. When his focus turned to religion, Dr. Wallace (left) identified what he considered to be four distinct religious *cults* – *i.e.* four distinct "systems of worship":

- ◆ individualist;
- ◆ shamanist;
- ◆ communal rites (or *communism*); and,
- ◆ ecclesiastic.

You can think of these as 4 different general forms (or structures) of religious practice.

It can not be emphasized strongly enough that Dr. Wallace was not being critical in his use of the term *cult* to describe the different general forms that religious practice can take. It is actually our expectations that we must watch carefully in this section. Unlike courses in *World Religions* or *Comparative Religion*, this section is not intended to introduce you to any specific religious belief systems. In practice, nearly all of the religions to which you would be exposed in one of those classes would belong to the 4th of Dr. Wallace's cults – the *ecclesiastical cult*. This section is part of an anthropology course, and is designed to initiate you to the general categories that anthropologists assign to systems of worship. Some of these (probably most) may seem strange to you; but, that is because most of that to which you have previously been exposed is really quite similar in structure. Although you may not realize it, you are almost certainly suffering from some degree of religious tunnel vision.

So, what are these "four cults" of which Dr Wallace speaks?

Individualism

In Dr. Wallace's *individualistic cult* category, individuals are understood to be their own specialists. This makes it the most difficult of the four cults to study, for there is neither an organization nor an organized body of literature to which we can turn for answers. In addition, individualistic cults occur most often in egalitarian band and village societies. The reason this makes it more difficult to study is simple: how many friends or relatives do you have that are part of a band or village society?

There are, however, some individuals even within modern, state societies (such as the United States) that follow an essentially *individualist cult* approach to religion. Perhaps one of the best recent examples is Jiddu Krishnamurti. Krishnamurti [1895–1986] was a world-known lecturer throughout most of the 20th century; and, although he had (and still has) a very large following, he adamantly refused to establish any formal organization around his beliefs. In fact, in a speech he gave (August 3, 1929) disbanding a group that had grown up around him, he said the following:

"I maintain that truth is a pathless land, and you cannot approach it by any path whatsoever, by any religion, by any sect.

> That is my point of view, and I adhere to it absolutely and un-
> conditionally.   Truth, being limitless, unconditioned, unap-
> proachable by any path whatsoever, can not be organized; nor
> should any organization be formed to lead or to coerce people
> along any particular path. If you first understand that, then
> you will see how impossible it is to organize a belief. A belief
> is purely an individual matter, and you cannot and must not
> organize it. If you do, it becomes dead, crystallized; it be-
> comes a creed, a sect, a religion, to be imposed on others. ...
> The moment you follow someone, you cease to follow Truth."

Krishnamurti was an exception in the modern world of political states and stratified societies. He was, as they say, "marching to his own drummer". He was, in fact, an excellent example of a religious individualist. Although research indicates that most individualistic cults are *animistic*, this is certainly not true in the case of Krishnamurti. His belief system is usually understood as based on Hindu beliefs with some traces of Buddhism and Taoism mixed in – never espousing any of these, but frequently sharing specific perspectives with them.

In the modern world of political state societies such as the US and the European countries, the most common occurrence of religious individualists would likely be the increasing number of people who decline to identify to which *religion* they adhere, and prefer to speak of their *spirituality*. Organized religions often disparagingly cluster all of these individualists together under the rubric of *New Age*; but, that is a gross over-simplification. First, there is no established set of beliefs to which so-called New Age followers adhere. Second, there is usually no organized religious structure to which they belong. Finally, the very term New Age is misleading, since many of the beliefs that these individuals do happen to share in common are frequently the same as those that have been espoused by Hindus, Pagans, and Buddhists for thousands of years.

Animism

Before moving on to the remaining three of Dr. Wallace's religious cults, it would help to understand what is meant by the term *animism*. It was stated above that, traditionally, most individualistic cults are animistic; but, no explanation was given as to what this implies. During the earliest days of anthropology (the early to mid years of the 19th century), it was commonly accepted that religion had developed along a progressive evolution from animism through polytheism to monotheism – with the 'highest', most logical form of religion being monotheistic belief (which, "coincidentally", just happened to be what those early anthropologists believed). Not only is this offensive to people who believe and practice systems which are not monotheistic (essentially accusing them of practicing inferior, less viable religious beliefs), sufficient historical and archæological information has been discovered to show that this was simply inaccurate. But, just what is *animism* that put it 'at the bottom' for these early anthropologists?

Animism is "the belief that all objects possess a natural life or vitality and are endowed with indwelling souls ... the belief ascribing conscious life to all natural objects, or to nature in general. Belief that men, animals, plants, stones, etc., are inhabited by souls which may exist in a separate state." Most students of anthropology, adhering to one of the largest religions of the 21st century (Christianity, Islam, Hinduism) find the idea that there are people who believe that rocks have souls to be "quaint" – often regarding them in the same manner as members of the *Flat Earth Society*.

But, it is not really absurd at all. In modern ecclesiasticism (*i.e.* all of the world's major religions of today), adherents make a clear distinction between the sacred and the profane. However, many of the indigenous populations of the world believe that everything in the material world is a direct creation or manifestation of Divine Power. As such, they consider everything to be sacred; thus, there is no sacred–profane distinction. In their world view, everything is alive (with the power of the Divine). They accept that all of reality is "saturated" with spirituality. Today, anthropologists and sociologists who study these beliefs label this view as *animism* (from the Latin *anima*, meaning "breath, wind, spirit, or life").

Shamanism

Today, there are a number of words used to describe the role of a particular person within a certain type of religious cult. These words, some of which are considered derogatory by adherents of these systems, include: sorcerer, witch doctor, medicine (wo)man, magician, thaumaturge, wizard, and shaman.

As terms such as *witch doctor* and *medicine woman* have fallen into disfavor as derogatory, the more common term for these religious practitioners has become *shaman*. This term, which comes from the Tungus language of Siberia, has none of these negative stereotypes associated with it. The late University of Florida anthropologist, Dr. Marvin Harris, defined shamans as being "women or men who are socially recognized as having special abilities for entering into contact with spirit beings and for controlling supernatural forces."[*] Similarly, but in more specific detail, Dr. William A. Young, of Westminster College (Fulton, Missouri), described the role of the shaman as follows:[#]

> "The term [shaman] comes from Siberian indigenous religion, but is now widely used for a 'sacred person' who has entered fully into the spirit world, and who thereafter is gifted with the ability to make journeys there for the sake of the well-being of his/her people. Through these ecstatic journeys, the shaman acquires a knowledge used to heal sicknesses, instruct a person or group on proper courses of action, and even cause good things to happen. A shaman, typically, not only has had a spontaneous, powerful spiritual experience that has empowered the specialist, but also has studied sacred lore with another shaman. Someone who has been called to be a shaman, and has accepted the status by passing through the process of apprenticeship, is particularly venerated and retains the position throughout his/her life."

Again, these are most often found in egalitarian band and village societies. An excellent example of a tribal society which relies on shamanism in their religious views is that of the Oglala Lakota (part of the Sioux Nation). One of the better known rituals practiced by the Oglala is the *Vision Quest* (adopted and popularized as a Klingon tradition by the *Star Trek: Next Generation* television series). This is a ritual which a tribal member undertakes to receive spiritual guidance for his (or her) life. After fasting for 3 or 4 days, the seeker is taken out to a sacred hill where they remain – without food or water – crying out to the spirits for a vision.

---

[*] Harris, Marvin and Johnson, Orna (2003). Cultural Anthropology: Sixth Edition (Boston: Allyn and Bacon)

[#] Young, William A. (2005). The World's Religions: Worldviews and Contemporary Issues (Upper Saddle River, New Jersey: Pearson Education, Inc.)

Typically, after several more days, they experience such a vision. They may be visited by animals or the *wakinyan* (thunder beings), and the vision is usually a very powerful experience. They return to the village, where the local shaman aids them in interpreting the vision, and what it means for their future life. This is typical of the type of role the shaman plays in village life – helping villagers bridge the gap between the mundane and spirit worlds.

Often, the shaman is crucial to the health of the tribe as the one who channels healing from the spirit world to individuals in need (such as with the !Kung, *aka* Bushmen), the channeler of dreams which provide critical information to the tribe (*e.g.* the Tapirapé), or the one who acts as a conduit for the spirit of a totem to pass its hunting and survival skills on to the tribe with whom it has a perceived special relationship (*e.g.* the wolf for the Tlingit).

Communal

Communal cults are those which tend to reinforce communal bonds within the society. They often make extensive use of rituals to solidify the group by transferring cultural meaning and significance to the group. In other words, the communal cult uses religious rituals to "keep it all together".

Both Native American tribes and African tribes are often primarily communal cults (all groups can only be described as "primarily" of one type, since it is rare not to find at least 2 or 3 of the different approaches represented to some degree in different activities or practices). Native Polynesians developed special dance rituals that were performed to meet specific communal needs. These dances are performed today largely for tourists; but, the traditional society saw them as a means of binding the tribe together to face an impending challenge – whether it was human, animal or environmental. Examples include the Kaibola Dancers of the Trobriand Islands, the native female dancers found among the paleolithic tribes of Papua New Guinea, the male fire dancers of Samoa, or the better known hula dancers of the Hawai'ian Islands (photo*).

---

* The hula was traditionally conducted topless, as in this late 19th century photo, but has been 'sanitized' (covered up) for today's 'tourist variations'.

Each of these dance rituals serves multiple purposes for the tribe:

♦ they strengthen the bond of communal kinship;

♦ they provide a mechanism to focus spiritual energy for the benefit of the tribe;

♦ they visually remind members of key mythical or historical events from the tribe's shared experiences; and,

♦ they serve as a means of bringing the spirit world into direct contact with the profane world in which they live.

Ecclesiasticism

Ecclesiastical cults – those religious groups with which we are all familiar – are those which have a professional clergy (*i.e.* priest-hood) organized into a formal bur-eaucracy. In fact, the term *ecclesiastical* comes from a Greek root that meant "an assembly". This gradually came to refer to "anyone who addressed an assembly" – *i.e.* a priest, rabbi, pastor, cleric, *et cetera*. This is, in practice, the religious structure with which students are undoubtedly  most familiar. No criticism is intended by referring to it as a cult, as it only defines the structure of the religious belief system.

The photograph above is one that the author took at the Roman Catholic church in Pisa, Italy (the Bell Tower is the famous *Leaning Tower* – I was not holding the camera cock-eyed).

Typically, ecclesiastical groupings are found in highly structured, centralized political states. The leaders of these groups are for-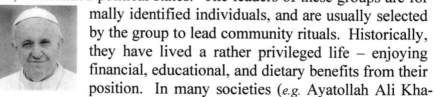mally identified individuals, and are usually selected by the group to lead community rituals. Historically, they have lived a rather privileged life – enjoying financial, educational, and dietary benefits from their position. In many societies (*e.g.* Ayatollah Ali Khamenei of Iran, His Holiness the Dalai Lama of Tibet, and Pope Francis I [left] of Vatican City), these ecclesiastical leaders also either lead, or hold, considerable secular, political power.

Something which appears quite commonly in ecclesiastical cults, but is extremely rare in shamanistic and communal cults, is the concept of the temple. Although the word used here is temple, this applies to any impressive, monumental structure intended for ecclesiastical religious purposes. A few examples follow.

First Church of Christ, Scientist
Boston, Massachusetts, USA
(Christian Science)

Peterhof Chapel
St Petersburg, Russia
(Czarist Russian Orthodox Chapel)

Tuomiokirkko
Helsinki, Finland
(Lutheran))

Grand Choral Synagogue
St. Petersburg, Russia
(Jewish)

St Peter's Basilica
Vatican City
(Roman Catholic)

Uspenski Cathedral
Helsinki, Finland
(Russian Orthodox)

Art

The What *versus* The How

If culture is the transmission of shared societal beliefs, practices and wisdom, then religion is one of the primary conveyances for the transmission of culture. Religion, in fact, quite often serves as the medium for what gets transmitted. By comparison to this, art becomes one of the answers as to what is transmitted. Occasionally (as in religious iconography), religion and art almost meld into a common medium that is 'self-transmitting'.

What does this mean? In essence, culture is often thought of as the sum total of the practices, beliefs, knowledge, experience, history, wisdom, and characteristics of a society. Religion reflects this culture, and thus becomes one of the mechanisms for perpetuating it – through ritual, theology and dogma – to the members of the group. The young frequently learn what the meaning of an event is through their religion.

By contrast, art is an expressive medium. It virtually never tells us what we <u>should</u> know or believe; but, it provides a medium through which our culture can convey how our culture interprets life (*i.e.* what we <u>do</u> know or believe; *i.e.* our *world view*).

Most people don't think of art when they think about cultural concepts; but, they should. Whereas religion is often the medium our culture is "conveyed" through, art has a somewhat different role. It isn't usually the concept that is being conveyed, as much as it is the medium through which other cultural concepts are illustrated. In simple terms, religion often is the conveyance medium, the *how*; and, art reveals the content to us, the *what*.

If that sounds a little strange, consider an example: the European Renaissance was, in many ways, intricately tied to the religious views of the day. The French Christian leader Martel had earlier defeated the Moorish Muslim leader Tarik; and, it was at this time of the early Renaissance (1492) that Ferdinand of Spain managed to claim Islam's final toehold in Europe at Granada. The Islamic Moors had been defeated, and Christianity was back in full flower in Europe. The art of the day – *i.e.* that produced as part of the Renaissance – reflected this religious shift. Paintings, sculptures, and so forth all focused on religious themes – specifically, Christian themes. By comparison, other societies and other times have often stressed alternative concepts. Art became a reflection of the dominant culture – it became the medium through which the cultural changes that had taken place were illustrated.

What is Art ?

Webster's Collegiate Dictionary Fifth Edition (1948) provides no less than 10 different meanings for the term *art*. Although all related, the breadth of the term shows some of the difficulty in trying to answer the question "what is art?" Interestingly, only one of these definitions ever mentions painting, sculpture, or music. In general, the various definitions are more closely related to "human contrivance or ingenuity". This is essentially what art is all about – the application of human ingenuity and skill to otherwise utilitarian efforts. As such, it would be extremely unlikely for it to be the same for every culture; and, as expected, it isn't. Not only does it differ; but, the fine line between art and utility is completely blurred in most non-European cultures.

If you do any research on archæology, you will discover that there are 2 things archæologists often investigate: tools and pottery. They look at tools because they tell them a great deal about the skill and technology of the society that produced them. They look at pottery for a totally different reason: they learn a great deal about the *world view* of the society that created it. They are looking at the size, shape, and – of particular interest – the decoration of the pottery.

Archæologists know that there was contact between the Indus River Valley civilization centered around Harappa (in present day Pakistan) and the eastern Mediterranean civilizations of Jerusalem and Phoenicia. They know this because they have found coins from each place in the other. But, some societies didn't use such an easily traceable item as currency (for instance, the civilization at Teotihuacán in México). We know most of what we know about the extent of their influence not from relics such as currency, but from pottery pieces. Archæologists have compared potsherds (literally, broken pieces, or shards, of pots) found at Teotihuacán to those found at Mayan sites along the Yucatan coast, with pieces from the Pueblo societies of the American southwest, and several other early civilizations. These pieces of pottery are artistically distinct to each culture, and are thus readily identifiable.

As a society changes its perception of the world, or *world view*, their artistry also changes; and, this can also be seen in the pottery produced. Consider the example of the Shipibo-Conibo tribe of eastern Peru. Today, this is an isolated tribe of about 35,000 people scattered across villages that typically count someplace in the vicinity of 100 members each. They are found in eastern Peru in the jungle at the headwaters of the Amazon River. Although now maintaining regular contact with the rest of the world, this has not always been the case. Today, the women of the Shipibo-Conibo produce pots and vases identical to patterns from their history. Although new, they give us a window through which we can view how their world view has changed over the last 1200 years.

Originally, their pottery reflected a world view that saw animistic forces all around them in the physical world. Pottery used in ceremonial rituals was usually decorated with stylized plants, spiders, birds, and lizards. This style of pottery predominated in the Shipibo area in the 9th century (left).

After the conquest by the Spanish, and an introduction to their world view at the time, the imagery of the Shipibo-Conibo pottery became more obscure (suppressing religious images offensive to the Catholic Spanish). By the late 17th century, it was usually decorated with geometric designs (with hidden ancient symbols) which often incorporated human-like spirit representations (left).

Finally, as the Shipibo-Conibo came into regular, frequent contact with modern European and South American peoples (often adopting their religion and their world view), even the human-like figure became less obvious. Most pottery from the 20th century, in fact, is decorated almost exclusively in geometric patterns; and, although ancient symbols may sometimes be found, the symbol of the cross is far more common. The cross can be seen in the example shown here (right), in which no discernible human face is visible.

What we see from this highly abbreviated look at the Shipibo-Conibo pottery is a gradual change in their perception of the world and their place in it – over a period of more than twelve hundred years. This shifting *world view* has been reflected in their hand-made, hand-decorated pottery. This type of shift may be either more or less noticeable in other societies; but, art is clearly a medium through which a culture expresses its cultural views – perhaps not vocally, but "loud and clear" just the same.

Chapter 9
Music and Humor

Humor

Humor has got to be one of the most difficult subjects for a cultural anthropologist to analyze. The problem begins by trying to define what it is that is being analyzed: *i.e.* what is humor? Anthropologists, sociologists, psychologists have all attempted to answer that; and, they have come up with scores of different results. Once a definition is settled, however, it doesn't get any easier. How do we measure it? What are the *fixed points* that we can use to compare different cultural adaptations of it? Doctoral dissertations have been written by those attempting to provide a comprehensive analysis of humor.

We'll begin here by exploring three points:
a)   a "dictionary" <u>definition</u> of humor;
b)   an hypothesis for the <u>purpose</u> of humor; and,
c)   an overview of the different <u>forms</u> of humor.

We'll begin with a definition. Webster defines humor as "discovering, expressing, or appreciating ludicrous or absurdly incongruous elements."* That is fine for our purposes so long as we all understand what Webster means by ludicrous. Today, many take it to mean outrageous, ridiculous; but, it has a more subtle meaning. That same dictionary says that ludicrous is something that has been "adapted to excite laughter, especially from incongruity or exaggeration". We'll come back to this.

Many have tried to explain *why* we have humor. What is the purpose behind it? Freud thought that humor always fell into one of two overarching categories: tendentious (promoting a cause), or non-tendentious (not promoting any specific cause). He added that

---

* Webster's Collegiate Dictionary (5th Edition) (1948; Springfield, Massachusetts: G & C Merriam Co.)
* ----- (1978) <u>American Heritage Dictionary of the English Language</u>. (Boston: Houghton Mifflin Co.

tendentious humor was generally either aggressive or sexual, while non-tendentious humor was nearly always nonsense.

Finally, our 3rd point: what forms does humor take? This could be a very long list. An admittedly abbreviated list might include:

Puns	Wisecracks	Practical jokes
Banter	Burlesque	Situational humor
Repartee	Conundrums	Freudian slips
Parodies	Hyperbole	Anecdotes
Jokes	Irony	Satire
Dark (Morbid)	Farce	Blue (off-color)
Droll	Slapstick	Epigrammatic

By and large, each of these forms most often (or always) takes a verbal form. However, this is certainly not always the case, as people may find things humorous that don't fit any of the forms on the list; and, there are always new ways in which incongruity can be expressed (not just in words). For example, a caricature is a  drawing or painting that grossly exaggerates certain prominent features of the subject to the point of incongruity (that meets our earlier definition of humor). In the caricature of President Obama (left), the artist has focused on his angular face, big smile, and prominent ears. This is an example of non-verbal humor, which does not require text to elicit a humorous reaction. Typically, it falls under Freud's non-tendentious category, since it doesn't appear to be done to promote a particular cause. That is not necessarily true, however, of all caricatures. For example, this caricature  of Adolph Hitler (left)* appeared in a 1942 drive for War Bonds. This caricature of the German Chancellor was clearly tendentious (as it had a political motivation, or cause, behind it). In the drawing, Hitler is portrayed as a threat, with the message to "insure your home against Hitler!" and a plea to "buy war savings bonds and stamps". It was clearly critical, and was drawn by an American Jew who despised Hitler.

---

* Published in *PM Magazine* (July 28, 1942); drawn by Theodor Seuss Geisel (Dr. Seuss)

Humor has been described as the tendency of particular cognitive experiences to provoke laughter and provide amusement; and, there are a number of theories about what social function it serves. People of all ages and cultures respond to humor. When people are amused, and laugh or smile at something funny, they are thus considered to have a "sense of humor".

A sense of humor is thus the ability to experience humor, although the extent to which an individual will find something humorous depends on a number of variables, including geographical location, culture, maturity, level of education, intelligence, and context. For example, children often prefer slapstick, such as *Tom*  *and Jerry*, the *Road Runner*, or the *Three Stooges* (left). A preference or appreciation for slapstick comedy appears to be related not just to age, but also to culture and gender. For example, numerous studies have shown that males are more likely than females to find the Three Stooges "funny". It is a very simple, straight-forward, visual, almost "in your face" form of humor. As a result, it is readily understood by children, and easily crosses cultural and language barriers; and, men tend to relate to the physical nature of it. By contrast, satire is far more subtle, and requires understanding the target of the humor. As a result, satire tends to appeal to more mature audiences, has difficulty crossing cultural barriers, and is usually more intellectual than physical.

Most humor relies on cultural association, and often does not translate to other languages and cultures with the same perspective; and, people from different cultures often consider different things funny. Sometimes, a culture is perceived as being without a sense of humor. This isn't true; they just find different things amusing. There is, in fact, no form of humor that is universally appreciated. A few come close, but none is truly universal.

Jerry Lewis (right) was a comedic icon in the American theater. His humor was broad, slapstick, immature, and often absurd. Although he was very popular in the United States, his appeal in Europe (during the 1950s and 60s) – particularly France – was legendary. Many maintain that this was overstated, and that the

French never did really like him any better than other cultures; but, the record speaks for itself.

- ♦ Although he won the prestigious Governor's Award of the *Academy of Television Arts and Sciences* (the highest Emmy award conferred), that did not happen until 2005 (and was in large part a result of his tireless work for charity – specifically, Muscular Dystrophy).

- ♦ On three different occasions, he was awarded *Director of the Year* by the French film industry, and was similarly honored in Germany, the Netherlands, Spain, Belgium, and Italy (but not the United States).

- ♦ In 1984, the French government made him a Commander in the *Order of Arts and Letters* (France's highest cultural award).

- ♦ And, just 2 months later, they awarded him the *Legion of Honor* (France's highest honor – period).

Clearly, appreciation for any particular form of humor is largely cultural.

Another common form of verbal humor is the so-called *ethnic riddle*. Usually, this is a two part riddle that consists of a question and an answer. Often, these address somewhat delicate areas, and the subject of the riddle is frequently a person or group that is on the outside, or periphery, of the general society. Poking fun at specific groups and stereotypes can create tension and build walls of misunderstanding; however, it can also be used either to reinforce the *status quo* by acknowledging societal boundaries (so-called *mirroring society*), or to defuse social tensions by allowing a non-confrontational outlet for aggression or resentment. It is possible to learn who is in power and who is on the periphery of a culture simply by looking at who is the subject of these ethnic jokes and who is telling them. Obviously, this varies from culture to culture.

- The English often tell ethnic riddles about the Scots and Irish.

    What's a half mile long and has an IQ of 40? The Saint Patrick's Day parade.

- Both the Dutch and the French make jokes about the Belgians.

    What's the latest Belgian invention? An airport with a roof to keep rain from delaying flights.

- Traditionally, Norwegians generally tell Swedish jokes.

    What do you get if you cross a Swede with a Gypsy? A car thief who can't drive.

■ The Germans often tell them about the Italians.

> *What is the gearing configuration of an Italian tank?*
> *Four reverses and one forward, in case they are outflanked and attacked from the rear.*

■ The Danish often tell them about the Germans, their neighbors (and World War II enemies) just to the south.

> *How do you sink a German submarine? Send down a diver to knock on the door.*

■ The US is the most culturally pluralistic country on earth, and this tends to make American humor more diverse. Nevertheless, the group that is perhaps most often the target of intellectually degrading ethnic riddles are the Polish.

> *Did you hear about the new Polish parachute? It opens on impact.*

■ Just to prove that no form of humor is truly universal, the Japanese rarely tell ethnic jokes; but uniquely, when they do, the target is almost always *the Japanese!*

> *After the baby was born, the panicked Japanese father went to see the obstetrician. "Doctor," he said, "I don't mind telling you, I'm a little upset because my daughter has red hair. She can't possibly be mine."*
>
> *"Nonsense," the doctor said. "Even though you and your wife both have black hair, one of your ancestors may have contributed red hair to the gene pool."*
>
> *"It isn't possible," the man insisted. "We're pure Asian." "Well," said the doctor, "let me ask you this. How often do you have sex?"*
>
> *The man seemed ashamed. "I've been working very hard for the past year. We only made love once or twice a month."*
>
> *"There you have it!" the doctor said confidently. "It's just rust."*

Often, cultures are either large or diverse enough to result in regional examples of this same phenomenon. For example, this applies to the US (which is both large and diverse) and Belgium (small, but with 2 predominant social groupings)

■ The heavily Cuban-American population of Miami-Dade County, Florida often tells politically motivated ethnic jokes regarding their ancestral homeland.

> *A dog swims from Cuba to Miami. When he drags himself onto the beach, a number of American dogs gather around him. The American*

dogs began to question him. "Did you not get enough food?" they asked. "No," he said, "There was plenty of food." "Did you not get medical attention when you needed it?" they continued. "No," he replied, "There were many excellent veterinarians to take care of me when I was ill." "Well, then," they asked, "Why did you leave?" "Because," he replied, "every once in a while I like to bark."

■ The more powerful Belgians (mostly Flemish) tell them about the less powerful (generally the Walloons).

> *A Flemish politician is addressing an audience of Walloon workers: "With our economic plan, you can enjoy looking forward to a 4-day work week." Enthusiastic applause.*
> *"And soon after that, we'll be offering a 3-day work week." More enthusiastic applause.*
> *"Later, you'll be able to live comfortably working just 2 days per week." Wild cheering.*
> *"Ultimately, you'll work just one day a week and still live very well." At that point, a man at the back of the hall shouts out, "That's great; but, please don't make it Monday!"*

Even non-ethnic jokes differ significantly from culture to culture. *Reader's Digest* publishes their monthly magazine in several countries around the world. In 2009, they asked readers in each of these locales to select their 'best joke'. A few examples should show how "sense of humor" varies by culture.

■ Australia

> *A polar bear walks into a bar and says, "Give me a scotch and .... Coke."*
> *"Why the long pause?" asks the bartender. "I don't know," says the bear. "I've always had them."*

■ China

> *My cousin always "borrows" money from her older brother's piggy bank, which drives him crazy. One day, she found the piggy in, of all places, the refrigerator. Inside was this note: "Dear sister, I hope you'll understand, but my capital has been frozen."*

■ Hungary

> *Doctor: Have you taken my advice and slept with the window open?*
> *Patient: Yes.*
> *Doctor: So your asthma disappeared completely?*
> *Patient: No, but my watch, TV, iPod, and laptop have.*

■ Portugal

> *A man is visiting an old friend when a little girl races through the room.*

"Diploma," the friend calls after her, "bring us two cups of coffee." "Diploma? What an odd name," says the visitor. "How did she get it?" The friend sighs. "I sent my daughter to university in Lisbon, and that's what she came back with."

■ Switzerland

Wife: Honey, did you notice? I bought a new toilet brush.
Husband: Yes, I did. But I still prefer the paper.

■ United States

A priest, a minister, and a rabbi want to see who's best at his job. So they each go into the woods, find a bear, and attempt to convert it.
Later they get together. The priest begins: "When I found the bear, I read to him from the Catechism and sprinkled him with holy water. Next week is his First Communion."
"I found a bear by the stream," says the minister, "and preached God's Holy Word. The bear was so mesmerized that he let me baptize him."
They both look down at the rabbi, who is lying on a gurney in a body cast. "Looking back," he says, "maybe I shouldn't have started with the circumcision."

■ France

President Sarkozy visits a steel factory. To the boss's surprise, the president greets an employee, Morton, with a warm hug. The same thing happens when Barack Obama visits, and again during Vladimir Putin's tour.
Unimpressed, the boss says to Morton, "I bet you don't know the pope." Morton shrugs. "We play golf together."
The gauntlet has been tossed, and the boss pays their way to the Vatican. During the Benediction, Morton slips away. Sure enough, he soon reappears – side by side with the pope on the balcony.
Two Chinese tourists tap the boss on the shoulder and ask, "Who's the guy in white standing with Morton?"

Preferred Comedic Formats

Virtually all cultures have one or more preferred comedic formats. It may be slapstick, satire, nonsense, ethnic humor, *et cetera*. Frequently, the source of this preference can be identified. For example:

Slapstick   Defined as "comedy characterized by loud and boisterous farce", slapstick humor is usually very physical, and often borders on the abusive. As stated earlier, it appeals more to children and to men. Many seem to empathize with the victim of the physical humor; while some relate to the perpetrator, as it allows them to harmlessly vent what they perceive has been abuse direct-

ed at them. As such, we might suspect it to be more valued by societies that have just undergone a punishing, humiliating event. If
so, then the European countries might be expected to have appreciated slapstick in the years just after World Was II; and, they did
(the height of Jerry Lewis' success in Europe).

Satire   This is a "work in which irony, derision, or wit in
any form is used to expose folly or wickedness." In studies, it has
been shown this usually requires an educated, informed audience
knowledgeable of the situation being satirized. (*e.g.* studies show
that the TV audience for Jon Stewart's *Daily Show* is, on average,
older and better educated than that for *Two and a Half Men*).

Ethnic Humor   This, as just seen, tends to reaffirm the speaker
as *endocultural* (within the acceptable core of society) while making the subject *exocultural* (outside, or on the fringes of society).
This can reassure the speaker of their acceptance, and can also
offer the subject a nonviolent means of "venting" frustration over
their marginalization.

Nonsense   Described as "behavior or language that is meaning-
less or absurd", this is often used to ridicule or mock established
norms. This often occurs in cultures where the norms are stable,
well established, and capable of being mocked without fear of reta-
liation. *Monty Python* made a success of ridiculing British norms
through nonsense; *Mel Brooks* has often done the same thing in
America (today, that's Brad Cooper, Ed Helms, and Zach Galifian-
akis). This requires a stable, secure, comfortable, and somewhat
sophisticated audience fundamentally able to 'laugh at itself'.

Humor exists in every culture, in every ethnic group. If you
ever encounter a society that appears to have no 'sense of humor',
it is almost certainly because humor is highly driven by culture,
and you "just don't get it". And, be vary cautious about using any
humor in contact with someone from a different cultural background. It may not be understood, and could easily backfire.

Music

Do you thoroughly enjoy the music your parents put on the car
radio? Do they enjoy the music that you like? What about grandparents? Chances are, the answer to each of these is "no, not real-

ly". Why not? Because music is another cultural feature that is subject to geographic, ethnic, age, education, social class, and other determining factors. In the case of the questions just asked, the most likely culprit is age.

♪ What were the 2 most popular new songs in 1938?
> *Begin the Beguine (Artie Shaw)*
> *Thanks for the Memory (Bob Hope, Shirley Ross)*

♪ What were the 2 most popular new songs in 1964?
> *I Want to Hold Your Hand (The Beatles)*
> *The House of the Rising Sun (The Animals)*

♪ What were the 2 most popular new songs in 2012?
> *I Gotta Feeling (The Black Eyed Peas)*
> *Rolling in the Deep (Adele)*

Not only is it hard to imagine someone who thoroughly enjoys all six of these songs, it is almost as difficult to find someone who has even heard all six. Why? What is there about the primary age demographic of music buyers that rejects the music of the prior generation (often even rejecting that of older siblings)? Preferred musical style is based on many, many factors. Among these are:

♪ Geography	♪ Education	♪ Wealth
♪ Ethnicity/Culture	♪ Social class	♪ Gender
♪ Age	♪ Psychology	♪ Personality

The six songs listed above all attained their "best selling" status in the US – an area comprising multiple ethnicities, education levels, social classes, personalities, genders, wealth levels, geographical regions and psychological attributes. What differs is age! Not the age of buyers at the time of sale (about 14 to 28), but the age demographic at the current point in time (as of 2014, about 94, 65 and 20, respectively).

But, what about these other factors? For this course, the one that is of most interest to us is ethnicity/culture. Consider some of the different traditional cultural musical styles.

♪ Bluegrass	♪ Salsa	♪ Dixieland
♪ Calypso	♪ Zydeco	♪ Steel drum
♪ Reggae	♪ Dundun	♪ Gagaku
♪ Bomba	♪ Jibaro	♪ Celtic

This categorization system based on instruments was expanded over the years by a number of different people, such as the mediæval German composer Martin Agricola and Belgian musical instrument museum conservator Victor-Charles Mahillon. Cultural anthropologists specializing in the field of music (usually called *ethnomusicologists*) more often use a system which grew out of these earlier efforts known by the names of the primary system developers (*i.e.* the Sachs–Hornbostel system). Ignoring finer distinctions and the sub-categories that often accompany this system, it essentially divides musical instruments into the following categories:

a)   ***idiophones***, which produce sound through their self vibration (examples would include the xylophone and the glockenspiel);

b)   ***membranophones***, which produce sound through the vibration of some vibrating membrane (examples here would include the drum and the kazoo);

c)   ***chordophones***, which make music by vibrating strings (*e.g.* a violin, guitar, or piano – where the strings are internal and struck by a hammer);

d)   ***aerophones***, in which a column of vibrating air creates the tone (examples would include pipe organs, flutes, clarinets, *et cetera*); and,

e)   ***electrophones***, which make sound by electronic means (*e.g.* theremins and synthesizers).

There are problems with this system, however. What if a drum is a hollowed log with no animal skin membrane; is it still a membranophone or an idiophone? Shouldn't aerophones be divided into those using a vibrating reed (woodwinds, such as a clarinet) and those with just air (such as flutes)? What if the musician must vibrate his lips to create the sound in an aerophone (such as a trumpet)? Despite the many problems, this is the system (with many subcategories added to address these, and other, questions) that is most often employed by ethnomusicologists today.

Cultural Music Determinants

Certain cultural features tend to be reflected in the musical style that is most common to a particular society. This is often dictated in large part by the choice of instruments, and this may have been driven by immigration patterns. For example, bluegrass music is primarily an Appalachian folk form featuring guitars, fiddles (violins), drums, and occasionally mouth organs (harmonicas) – almost all of which came with them, their parents, or grandparents from Germany (the predominant source of Appalachian immigrants). Those instruments that were not brought with them were generally either very inexpensive or were capable of being made at home. This was a very poor community that simply could not afford to purchase expensive instruments. Interestingly, the music itself tends to most often be very lively, upbeat, and positive-mood evoking. These were people who were poor, but were getting a new opportunity, a new chance; life was hard, but it was good.

By contrast, the traditional Celtic music of Ireland ranges from the hauntingly melancholic to the raucous celebratory. It is hard to imagine the same culture producing both *Irish Step Dancing* (*e.g.* Riverdance) and *Danny Boy* (3rd verse lyrics below)[*]. The Irish people had periods of great celebration often mixed with times of intense suffering, and their folk music reflects both.

> And if you come, when all the flowers are dying
> And I am dead, as dead I well may be
> You'll come and find the place where I am lying
> And kneel and say an "Ave" there for me.

Another example of a traditional culture developing a musical style on the basis of the natural functions of society is that of Bavaria (southern Germany), Austria and Switzerland. One of the common folk music styles of this region is known as *yodeling*, which began as an effective communication method between shepherds on mountain fields high in the Alps.

All human voices have at least two distinct vocal registers, called *head* and *chest* voices, which come from different ways of producing a tone. Most people can sing tones within a range of lower pitch in their chest voices, and then a different range of higher pitch in their head voices (also called *falsetto*). There is often a noticeable gap between these two ranges, although experienced singers can often control their voices to the point where the two

---

* Although *Danny Boy* was written in 1910 by an Englishman (Frederic Weatherly), it was quickly adopted by the ethnic Irish in both the US and Canada.

ranges overlap. This allows them to easily switch between the ranges to produce high-quality tones in either. Yodeling is an application of this technique, where a singer might switch between these registers several times in just a few seconds (usually at high volume). Repeatedly going back and forth over this *voice break* produces a very distinctive type of sound.

Audiologically, the best places for Alpine-style yodeling are those with an echo. These include lakes, rocky gorges (or anywhere with a distant rock face), outdoor canyon-like areas between buildings, down a long hallway, and (best of all) a mountain range. Shepherds watching their animals (sheep, goats, cows) used this ideal setting and the unique acoustic features of yodeling to communicate with other shepherds, often over distances of many miles; and, this evolved into the yodeling folk music of the area.

Don't like steel drum music from the Caribbean?

Don't appreciate Indian ragas?

Find Scottish bag pipes irritating?

Think the didgeridoo sounds like a flatulent bull?

No problem – they weren't developed with you in mind!

Section III
Ethnic & Cultural Systems

Systems

What do we mean by *system*? And, how do these differ from the *Cultural Markers* just reviewed? Here, we are referring to the procedural methods that are typically employed by a cultural group to accomplish one of the essential functions of group governance: economy, home life, reproduction, family, legality, politics, *etc.* Each of these presents a variety of optional methods to accomplish what is ultimately the real goal: social stability and survival.

The *Cultural Markers* just reviewed were cultural phenomena that tend to be "the norm" for a given society. They could, in fact, be called *stereotypes*; however, that term often carries negative connotations. Defining them as cultural markers enables us to see them as norms without engaging those connotations. Systems, however, are more than just the norms of a society; they are actually the methods a society uses to regulate and control social processes.

Chapter 10
Economic Systems

Production

One of the most basic concepts in understanding a communal organization and structure is their *energy capturing technology*. This is the idea – because there are limits to what the environment can provide – that the challenge for human civilizations is to become as efficient as possible in this effort. If all a society gets for energy is what nature has provided through wild plants and animals, then that society will be limited severely by their location, climate conditions, *et cetera*. But, if a society were to develop interplanetary agriculture, fossil fuels, nuclear fuels, and even fission technology, the amount of energy to which they would have access would become virtually infinite; and, there would be effectively no limits to the growth of that society. Unfortunately (or, perhaps fortunately), humans do not have this infinite energy capturing technology. Therefore, all societies face some limitation.

This may occur with raising food, transport energy (*e.g.* gasoline), warmth (*e.g.* firewood), *et cetera*. The level of this limitation is known as the *carrying capacity* of a particular environment. This is the point where the available resources and the available technology have reached their limits. If a society attempts to go beyond this carrying capacity limit, an inevitable crash occurs. It is generally believed that this is what happened to the ancient mesoAmerican civilization at Teotihuacán.

Teotihuacán (Nahuatl: "city of the gods") is in the Valley of México, roughly 30 miles northeast of México City. Today, it is an area of impressive archæological finds – including the *Pyramid of the Sun*, the third largest pyramid in the world (right). At its height around 500 CE, Teotihuacan was a city of 125,000 to 200,000 people, making it one of the 6 largest cities in the world at that time [along  with Rome; Luoyang, China; Seleucia, Babylon; Alexandria, Egypt; and, Antioch, Turkey]. Although there is a great deal that we just don't know, there are some things that are generally agreed upon.

Located roughly in the center of mesoAmerica, it was ideally situated as a trade center for the extended region (as Jerusalem was for the Middle East about the same time, and Singapore is for Asia today). Traders from the Mayan communities in the Yucatan to the southeast, the Andean communities to the southwest in South America, the Nahuatl areas in modern México and the US to the northwest, and even as far as the 'mound builder' cities of the Mississippi valley to the distant northeast all filtered goods through this central Teotihuacán conduit. The city flourished as a center of trade, art, religion and culture. Planned development expanded the city to more than 2,000 mason homes and countless wooden farm houses on the outskirts. The city, founded around 200 BCE, grew by 500 CE to over ten square miles and an amazing population density a little higher than that of Boston today (but without any high rise apartment buildings).

To feed this huge city, and to provide the necessary resources, the residents had to keep expanding their lumber, mineral and agricultural base. In other words, they had to keep increasing the size of the area that was supplying the core city. Eventually, the distances involved made this a virtual impossibility (they had no domesticated beasts of burden, and had yet to invent the wheel). The city's economy simply imploded (collapsed in upon itself). In Cultural Anthropology terminology, Teotihuacán had exceeded its *carrying capacity*. Around 675 CE, the population began to disperse; and, by the early 700s CE, the city was essentially gone. In one final act to protect their economic, religious and cultural secrets, the last departing citizens burned the entire city to the ground (sort of a "last one to leave turn out the lights" approach).

There are other theories as to what happened to Teotihuacán (invasion, plague, natural disaster, *et cetera*); but, the 'carrying capacity argument' appears the most likely given all of the archæological evidence currently available.

There are a number of ways in which humans can meet their energy requirements (predominantly, with food). Different anthropologists count these methods differently, but typically come to between 4 and 8 different systems. The differences result from the fact the 4 basic approaches can be sub-divided into narrower, more specific approaches. The four 'basic methods' are:

- **Foraging** – gathering energy as food provided by nature

- **Agriculture** – production of energy by planting, feeding and harvesting plants

- **Pastoralism** – production of food through the exploitation of animals

- **Industrialism** – generation of energy through mechanized processes

How each of these categories can be subdivided is easier to see when we look at exactly what is meant by each term.

- *Foraging* refers to those societies that rely on what they can <u>find</u> as food (both plant and animal). Also known as **Hunter-Gatherers**, there are 3 forms this may take:
  - ➢ *pedestrian foraging* (essentially, walking around looking for food);
  - ➢ *equestrian foraging* (riding around on horses hunting food); and,
  - ➢ *aquatic foraging* (fishing for food).

In all cases, however, population densities for foraging societies tend to be low simply because nature doesn't reliably provide enough food to support a larger population.

- o !Kung – the pedestrian foragers of Angola, Botswana and Namibia (Kalahari Desert area of southern Africa) who live in groups of 10-30 adults and eat whatever roots, berries, fruit and nuts they can find, and any  small game they can kill. They speak an ancient *click* language.

o   Métis – equestrian foragers, the Métis Nation resulted from a mix of male French and Scottish fur traders with Cree, Ojibwa, Saulteaux, and Assiniboine women. Different from (and often rejected by) both European and Native communities, they became a distinct people in northwest Canada during the 18th and 19th centuries – highly skilled buffalo hunters with a national income, at that time, greater than that of either Canada or the US.

o   Kwwakiutl – the Native American aquatic foragers around Vancouver Island, Canada who speak the Kwakwala language. They became extremely efficient harvesting salmon, candlefish, shrimp, crabs and other marine life. Today, there are still Kwakiutl villages making their living from the sea.

◆   *Agriculture* provides increased food (over foraging) as a result of an increased reliance on technology. This also may take several forms.

➤   *Swidden agriculture* (*a.k.a.* "slash and burn") opens up arable land by burning off whatever was previously on the land. This generates a nutrient-rich ash covering, but the soil reclaimed in this manner is quickly depleted of nutrients, and the farmers generally move on to burn new virgin fields within just a few years;

> *communal agriculture* (sometimes referred to as *horti-culture* rather than agriculture – as is Swidden farming) results when small scale societies, large families, or local communities come together to enhance crop production through coöperative, additional labor; and,

> *large-scale agriculture* (the so-called "super-farms" common in the American west).

Agriculture, which was "invented" roughly 8,000 – 10,000 years ago, enables a population density of roughly 50 times what a foraging community can support. Examples of the different agricultural / horticultural techniques include the:

o Maya – the native peoples of what is today Belize, Guatemala, and southern México. They practiced several variant forms of Swidden agriculture, and founded an impressive culture on the back of this *slash and burn* approach. Mayan society in central America, however, was plagued by limited supplies of food and resources.

o Amish – the Amish are a religious community that follows a Christian Anabaptist philosophy, and takes the instruction to "come out from among them, and be ye separate" [2 Corinthians 6:17] as literally as any group on earth. Amish families tend to be large (averaging 7 – 10 children), and communities tend to be close knit, and practice communal farming.

o Archer Daniels Midland (ADM) – plants, grows, harvests, and distributes agricultural products on a vast scale. This is by use of highly mechanized and technologically advanced equipment and infrastructure.

◆ ***Pastoralism*** is for animals what agriculture is for plants – it refers to those societies that rely on domesticated animals for their energy supply. These animals, usually ungulates (*i.e.* hoofed mammals such as sheep, cattle, pigs, goats, horses, camels, *et cetera*), are used to provide food, transportation, clothing, housing, and so on. This often requires a more mobile society, or *transhumance*, as the herds must be tended to and kept in situations that are most productive for their health, growth and reproduction.

◆ ***Industrialism***. So far, this has all been about food production; but, that is only part of the story. Food is just one (albeit the most important) form of energy. As population increases, other forms of energy become more critical – light, warmth, mobility, *etc.* Societies that reach that size find that *specialization* makes energy production more efficient. In fact, technology applied to agriculture typically enables a society to produce more food (and more of these other energy resources) than it requires. Therefore, as a result of *industrialization*, a percentage of the population can be applied to areas not related to energy production: weavers, tailors, cobblers, millers, soldiers, artists, writers, …

As with food production, industrialization also has three primary forms:

○ *Cottage industry* refers to small, flexible, labor-intensive businesses. Mohandas Gandhi, as part of his vision for India, supported cottage industries. India had a huge population, and yet was still able to produce a food surplus (it still does). Gandhi realized that this enabled India to specialize; but, Gandhi feared that specialization through large scale industrialization would wreak environmental havoc on India. He thus encouraged cottage industries – specialization without large-scale industrialization: *i.e.* people working at specialized trades that tended to be very labor intensive (*e.g.* hand weaving; right).

o *Non-material Production* is the production of services or non-material products. Examples of this (and the trade that produces them) would include justice (lawyer), finance (banker), music (musician), art (artist), poetry (poet), protection (police, military), faith (clergy), fashion (designers), *et cetera.*

o *Large-scale Industrialization* is what most people think of when the term industrialization is mentioned. In this case, examples might include Honda®, Florida Power & Light®, MicroSoft®, Dell®, General Electric®, Boeing®, *et cetera.*

Economic Organization

An economy comprises the decisions people make, and the means by which they make them, when there are limited resources but greater demands or desires. In other words, "when there ain't enough for everybody to get everything they want; how do we decide who's going to get what?"

The key part of the definition just given is that phrase "and the means by which they make them", and describes the *economic system* that is employed to administer resources for the group. There are a number of different economic systems that have emerged around the world; and, they tend to have different strengths and weaknesses. But, to understand the various systems, we must also understand a variety of concepts linked to them.

■ *Personal Property Ownership*

North Americans (along with Europeans and people from several other areas) adhere to a concept of *private property rights.* In fact, these are so ingrained in American thought that it is difficult to convince the average American that they need either to be defined or explained. But, they do.

Ownership means simply that the "owner" has unrestricted, absolute, permanent, and exclusive rights to something. An owner can sell it, rent it, trade it, gift it, or simply ignore it. It doesn't matter – they have total rights to it, and they can do whatever they please with it (whatever "it" is).

Significantly, many parts of the world do not share this concept of personal property rights. This ethnocentric view of ownership has been described by some (*e.g.* Gary Ferraro, University of North Carolina) as *cultural myopia*. He uses examples from East Africa, where the "rights" to a cow may change hands within the community on a daily basis; and, the Kikuyu of Kenya, who rebelled against British colonial government in the 1950s (*ca.* 1952-1960). The revolt, known to the British as the *Mau Mau Rebellion*, arose in protest over the appropriation and redistribution of fallow native land that the British administrators thought was therefore "un-owned". It was owned – just not in the same manner as land back in England was owned (it was owned by the "tribal lineage"). Understanding how different cultures define ownership can greatly impact understanding of how goods and services are produced and distributed.

■ *Production*

To *produce* is, according to Webster, "to make, or to create so as to be available for satisfaction of human wants" In other words, production consists of the growth, manufacture, or fabrication of resources for the purpose of meeting human desires. All societies must find means to do this. Failure to meet the wants of their communal members would inevitably result in the eventual dissolution of the community. The means used to enable production, however, vary widely by society.

☐ **Household**   The household – the family – is the smallest of all possible production facilities. In the case of industrial production, it is the base for the *cottage industries*; in the case of food acquisition, it is the focal point for both *Swidden horticulture* and the small "family farm"; and, in the case of foragers, it is generally the most efficient unit size for *pedestrian foraging*.

☐ **Specialization**   As the size of the production unit increases (to extended families, kinship groups, tribes, nations, …), efficiency is gained through the specialization of certain members to tasks that they learn and perform as part of an integrated effort across the production unit.

- *Gender*   Perhaps the earliest specialization, or *division of labor*, was between genders. Even Neanderthals, as prehistoric foragers, appear to have relegated men to hunting and women to gathering. Although gender-based specialization is today termed sexist, there are some biological factors that often made this division a matter of rational efficiency, and not simply male dominance.

- *Age*   The very youngest members of a society are rarely expected to participate in the same production activities as adults – primarily due to physical size, limited strength, diminished endurance, and lack of training. The age where this is no longer considered productively inefficient varies according to need; children in subsistence situations in Asia and Africa are far more likely to be enlisted in productive activities than are their peers in Europe or North America. Similar constraints are often found among older members of the community.

- *Labor*   Henry Ford is credited with having revolutionized the manufacture of automobiles by employing *labor specialization* at his assembly plant in Dearborn, Michigan in 1913. Neither the concept nor its implementation was original with him. But, he did succeed at it in such a way as to forever change work practices. Each member of the community (in this case, his company) was trained for a certain function. This tends to make them faster and more productive than if they have to learn multiple functions, and enables the community to become more highly productive at their collective enterprise than they would ever be individually.

Distribution

Producing resources to meet human wants is only the first half of a solution to the problem (getting everyone what they need); and, it may be the easier half. Once production has occurred, the newly created products or services must still be distributed to satisfy those human needs. How it gets distributed varies as much as how it was created – perhaps, even more.

☐ **Reciprocity**   This is better known to most Americans as *bartering*. Fundamentally, this is simply an exchange of goods (or services) of roughly comparable value without the use of money.

▪ **General**   General reciprocity is essentially the act of gift giving. You don't give a gift with any consideration of whether you will get something back of comparable value; you simply give it because it's "the right thing to do". We see this all the time when parents give birthday, Christmas or Hanukkah gifts, a new bicycle, college tuition, *et cetera*.

▪ **Balanced** Helping out a friend in their time of need is an example of *balanced reciprocity*. You aren't expecting immediate payment for your generosity; but, you do expect that the 'favor would be returned' if you were ever to find yourself in a similar situation of need. It is the giving of a product or service to someone who you expect would compensate you for it; but, you don't know at the time of the gift when that will be, and you suspect that it may be in the distant future, if ever.

▪ **Negative** This is when product is received as a result of deception, falsehoods, leverage, hard bargaining, dishonesty, cheating, or even theft; *i.e.* not nice. It works as a means to distribute product; but, it almost always alienates the giving party. As a result, this is almost never employed when dealing with close friends, relatives, or others who might be able later to 'return the favor' (*e.g.* you don't steal from the local Mafia boss).

▫ **Redistribution** *Redistribution* usually involves someone in addition to the giver and receiver. Usually, this added person holds a position of authority with the responsibility to see to it exchanges are made as the parties expect.

▪ **Egalitarian** In an egalitarian redistribution scheme, everyone is treated as having equal value and worth to society. If it is a farming community, everyone contributes whatever they have produced, and everyone in the community gets to withdraw from the supply according to their needs. In an idealized setting, this is the basis of *communism*. It was also the founding principle behind *Brook Farm* (photos, right, are of the founders of Brook Farm: George Ripley [top] and Nathaniel Hawthorne [bottom]).

George Ripley, an ordained Unitarian minister, founded the Brook Farm in April 1841 in West Roxbury, Massachusetts. He wanted an egalitarian, intellectually stimulating, morally superior society. His goals for this new experiment (which attracted numerous famous American authors, thinkers and transcendentalists) were put forward in a letter Ripley wrote following his resignation as pastor of his church. It read:

> "Our objects, as you know, are to ensure a more natural union between intellectual and manual labor than now exists; to combine the thinker and the worker, as far as possible, in the same individual; to guarantee the highest mental freedom, by providing all with labor, adapted to their tastes and talents, and securing to them the fruits of their industry; to do away with the necessity of menial services, by opening the benefits of education and the profits of labor to all; and thus to prepare a society of liberal, intelligent, and cultivated persons, whose relations with each other would permit a more simple and wholesome life, than can now be led amidst the pressures of our competitive institutions."

Founding members (with Ripley) included such notables as Nathaniel Hawthorne, and encompassed regular stays by the likes of Ralph Waldo Emerson and Horace Greeley.

- **Stratified**   Not all societies have a 'share and share alike' approach to redistribution. Most, in fact, have a much more stratified approach. In this case, the redistribution is based on equity rather than equality. In other words, the recipients of the redistribution receive their produce on the basis of either their "need" or their "deservedness". The problem with this is that someone has to determine need, and who is deserving.

□ ***Tributary***   Tribute paid to a leader serves to re-affirm the power and authority of that leader; and, serves also as a means to redistribute societal products on the basis of equity. This is a fairly common method of redistribution in tribal societies with a chief. Almost without exception, the chief fares well under this type of economy, and the average tribal members don't fare anywhere nearly as well.

□ ***Reward***   In smaller groups, where they have yet to develop a tribal political system, it is usually the *big man* that is in charge. Typically, someone becomes a big man by being a highly motivational and successful producer. Drawing others to his leadership (since they want the benefits of his skill and wisdom), he ends up leading a small group. Befitting his status as the best producer, the other members of the group give their produce to him for storage and redistribution. He then often uses this supply of goods to throw a feast – as a means of demonstrating his generosity, hospitality, and leadership skills. This reinforces the allegiance of his group to him as the leader; and, the more generous he is, the more it tends to secure continued status as leader. The rest of the goods are then distributed to his group *as he sees fit*.

□ ***Bridewealth***   Both bridewealth and dowry will be discussed in greater detail in a later chapter; however, they also serve as a means of redistributing wealth within a community. When a daughter is to be married, it is expected (with bridewealth) that the groom's family will compensate the bride's family with a certain level of gifts (*e.g.* cows, goats, chickens, *et cetera*). In communities that maintain a dowry system, the same thing happens, but in the opposite direction: the bridal family gifting the groom's family. In both cases, it is a means of transitioning goods between families within the community (*i.e.* redistribution). The amount of the dowry / bride-wealth is usually a function of the relative status of the recipient family (*i.e.* it's stratified).

□ ***Potlatch***   The final method of stratified redistribution to be mentioned here is what is known as a *potlatch*. Common among certain Native Americans of the west coast (from California to Alaska), this is essentially the 'stratified reward' feast system used by big men (see above) when carried out by the head of a tribal society. Originally, *potlatch* was from a Chinook pidgin used in the fur trade, and meant "to give". This is the term usually used by anthropologists, but each Pacific tribe has its own word for the practice; some of which are far more descriptive than "to give". The word in Kwakwala (the language used by the Kwakiutl and other Vancouver Island tribes) is *pasa*, and meant "to flatten". They understood it to mean "to flatten guests under the weight of gifts". Well known examples of the potlatch exist among the Kwakiutl, the Tlingit, and the Suquamish.

The chief would attempt to validate and confirm his status in the tribe, over and above whatever hereditary claims he might have, by hosting a party where he would either give away or destroy all of his personal possessions. This would include food, fish oil, weapons, shields, clothing, blankets, boats or canoes, and anything he might have acquired from traders or Europeans. All the while doing this, he would boast about the great wealth that enables this largesse, and the comparative poverty of other area chiefs. In a state of embarrassment, the other chiefs would reciprocate and hold a potlatch of their own – each, in turn, trying to out do the other.

▫ ***Market Exchange***   This is a distribution scheme in which it is the value of the product (rather than the worthiness of the recipient or the prestige of the provider) that governs the transaction.   There are two basic forms in which this can occur: through barter, and through the use of a currency.   Value, regardless of which subsystem is used, is based on the simple rule of "supply and demand".

▪ ***Direct Barter***   In the case of a *direct barter* system, the value of two or more items are determined relative to each other, and an exchange of what is perceived as equal value occurs.   In its American form, this may involve a service as well as (or in place of) a tangible product.   Essentially, a "help me put on my new roof, and I'll help you renovate your shed".   Services aren't required; but, they are commonly involved in a barter situation in the US.

In other societies (and even occasionally in the US), tangible products are often involved.   It basically becomes a one-to-one flea market without money.   In this case, it might be an even exchange of products neither party needs to gain something they each desire.   Where it does happen in the US, it often involves agricultural products.   One farmer may devote all of his fields to the growing of tobacco.   This can later be harvested, dried, and sold so that it serves as a source of income.   But, there is a minor loss of value when it is sold to a distributor (who only does this to make a profit, so prices must be kept as low as possible).   The farmer's neighbor has used all of his land to grow corn.   It tastes great, and it is nutritional; but, it is actually a poor source of income (since most potential buyers, such as supermarkets, want a year long supply, they contract with big distributors who import from all over the hemisphere).   But, an exchange of some of one farmer's tobacco crop for some of the other's corn benefits both.   They can both eat; and, they both have a potential product to sell to the distributor the next time he visits.   No money changes hands; so, this is a *direct barter* system.

- ***Standardized Currency***   This is the system that virtually everyone in America knows and loves: *money*. Because a person willing to part with a particular item may not want anything that a potential recipient might have, a form of standardized currency is developed to act as an intermediary. It provides a means to make exchanges between providers and recipients who might not otherwise meet each other's wants; and, it allows for the indefinite storage of value while something is being sought to satisfy a particular desire. Without the existence of money, the farmer (above) who grows tobacco would need to also become an expert cigar wrapper, cigarette maker, or pipe-tobacco packager. This would be necessary in order to be able to provide a product for which there would be a potential partner in a direct barter arrangement.

But, money enables the farmer to sell what is essentially a raw material (since he can harvest and dry it without turning it into a consumer-usable item). Having currency enables the distributor to be able to buy the tobacco for future sale without having to come up with something that the farmer desires at that particular point in time.

Each product and service available within a society has a comparable amount of currency associated with it (*i.e.* a price). And, this can be set either by supply and demand (where the price is determined by how much money the recipient is willing to exchange for the item), or through the direct intervention of the societal leadership (a government, or chief). Direct intervention generates a relatively inflexible economy, but is often done to protect certain segments of the society. When this is done by government, it is called *price control*. When it is done by whoever controls the supply of an item (*e.g.* a monopoly of either one supplier, or a cartel [several suppliers collaborating]), it is illegal (under US law). The US government has rarely instituted any form of price control (usually, only in cases considered to be a national crisis); and, they are generally avoided. Examples would include gasoline during the Nixon administration, certain high-end food products during the Roosevelt administration (*i.e.* during World War II), and state-licensed property repairs following the 2004 hurricane season in Florida (to prevent what is commonly known as *price gouging*).

The only problem with currency is that there is a clear need for some type of regulation and control (it wouldn't work if everyone printed their own); and, that gives tremendous redistribution control to whomever is entrusted with responsibility for the monetary system.

Despite this problem, however, there are 5 primary advantages to a monetary/currency system. Money is:

1) Anonymous – everybody's money is the same;

2) Divisible – usable in small or large transactions;

3) Portable – easy to "take along" anywhere;

4) Legal – value is protected & regulated by government oversight and control; and,

5) Generic – nearly anything can be 'converted' into it.

Chapter 11
Domestic Systems

The Sequence

There are four distinct categories that need to be reviewed regarding domestic life; and, there is clearly a direct linkage between them. These categories are marriage, sex, reproduction, and family. One could argue that dating ought to precede marriage; but, that is an ethnocentric attitude, for dating doesn't always occur – at least not in the American sense of the word. What does seem to be universal, however, are these four areas.

Typically, one ends up with a family as a result of reproducing (*i.e.* making a "mini-me"). Similarly, one ends up reproducing by having sex with a member of the opposite gender at the right point in time – provided there was no introduction of any foreign object, substance or practice to prevent it. And, most traditions hold that the only socially acceptable member of the opposite gender with whom one has these sexual relations is the one to whom you are married. So, it goes:

Marriage → Sex   → Reproduction   → Family

It all seems so straightforward. But, unfortunately, it isn't. Every generation, the necessity of having marriage prior to sex seems to become less and less required. This is not a text on ethics, so this is not the best place to consider that; but, suffice it to say that traditional social patterns make marriage a moral prerequisite to sex – at least in most societies. Prior to a Massachusetts Supreme Court decision forbidding the Commonwealth from barring *homogamy* (*i.e.* gay marriage), scholars had no way to know that the issue would get so complicated so quickly. So, what is consistent? What is changing?

Family Structure

According to the 5th Edition of <u>Webster's Collegiate Dictionary</u> (1948), the primary (first) definition for a family is: "The body of persons who live in one house, and under one head; a household." It will likely surprise some students when they realize that Webster didn't see fit to make any reference to these people being related. In fact, though, it does; for the same source continues and, in a later definition, defines a family as "the group formed of parents and children" – but, that is not offered until the <u>fourth</u> definition!

You may think that Webster was being "politically correct" in this definition. After all, we all know what a family really is, what it has 'always been'. But, politically correct in 1948? *Politically Correct* wasn't even a phrase until roughly 20 years after this dictionary was printed; so, how could it? And, what does the word "family" actually mean? How did it get into English in the first place? Where did it come from? What do its 'roots' mean?

Another well-respected language reference specialist (Wordsworth Publishers, England, UK) has provided a derivation for the English word "family" that goes like this:

- English   *family*   comes from the
  - French   *famille*   which comes from the
    - Latin   *familia*   which is derived from the
      - Latin   *famulus*   ("slave") which comes from
        - Oscan   *famel*   which is a form of the
          - Oscan   *faama*   meaning "house".

So, not once on its tortured path from Oscan (a pre-Roman Italic civilization) to modern English has it specifically meant "parents and children". The question then becomes if "the body of persons who live in one house, and under one head; a household" is how we define the family unit, what constitutes the establishment of a household?

Defining Family Forms

Typically, a family describes a group of people affiliated by a consanguine, affinitive or residence relationship. Although consanguinity literally means "by blood", many societies understand the family through concepts other than genetic distance. One of the primary functions of the family is to produce new persons, biologically and socially. Therefore, our experience of family often shifts over time. From the perspective of children, the family is a *family of orientation*: *i.e.* family serves to locate children socially, and plays a major role in their enculturation and socialization.

From the point of view of a parent, the family is a *family of procreation*: *i.e.* the goal of the family is to produce, enculturate and socialize children. However, producing children is not the only function of a family; in societies where there is a sexual division of labor, marriage or some other stable relationship is necessary for the establishment of a functional household.

- ☐ A *conjugal family* (often called a *nuclear family*) includes only the husband, the wife, and any unmarried children who are not yet of age.

- ☐ A *consanguineal family* consists of at least one parent, his or her children, and other biologically related individuals (*e.g.* brother, sister, aunt, *et cetera*).

- ☐ An *extended family* consists of a larger group of related individuals. It commonly includes siblings as well as offspring, and frequently spans multiple generations – including children, parents, grandparents, siblings, aunts, uncles, cousins, *et cetera*.

- ☐ A *polygamous family* results when an individual has multiple spouses and may have children with one or more of them. The family includes the focal point (wife or husband), all spouses, and any resulting children. The focal point may be either male with multiple wives and children (a *polygynous family*), or female with multiple husbands and children (a *polyandrous family*).

- ☐ A *polyamorous family* consists of multiple adult males and multiple adult females (with a complex network of sexual access across all of them) and all resulting children. If this arrangement is long lasting (which it usually isn't), it is called a *polyfidelis family*.

China is currently the most populous nation in the world, and the nuclear family is considered the most common family arrangement. In India (particularly urban areas), the second most populous nation, the percentage of nuclear families is increasing, and is gradually exceeding other familial forms. In the United States, the third most populous nation, nuclear families comprise less than a quarter of the family units.

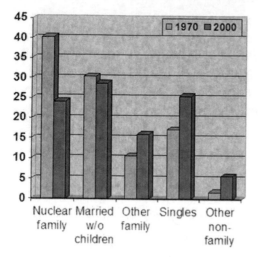

A hundred years ago, China was mostly extended families, and India was mostly *joint families* (a type of extended family identified within the Hindu religion); over that time, both are seeing more nuclear families. In the United States, the trend has been in the opposite direction. During the 30 years from 1970 to 2000 (left), the percentage of American families that were nuclear dropped from 40% to 24%. Married pairs (no children) remained roughly constant; but, people living alone and extended families both increased by about 50%.

Variety of Family Orientation

There are typically 4 possible "orientations" that a family can take with regard to day to day functions and decisions. These are:

- *Matrifocal* – a family consisting of a mother and her children, or perhaps including a father with little or no input to the decision process. The father in a matrifocal family may be deceased, divorced, separated, or marginalized; but, all key decisions are within the purview of the mother.

- *Patrifocal* – a family consisting of a father and his children, or perhaps including a mother with little or no input to the decision process. The mother in a patrifocal family may be deceased, divorced, separated, or marginalized; but, all key decisions are within the purview of the father.

- *Parentalfocal* – a name coined by Dr. Roni Berger of Adelphi University (in her 1998 book <u>Stepfamilies: A multi-dimensional perspective</u>). Both adult parents share in the key decisions, and the focus is on effective parenting, with neither parent assuming a dominating role. This is sometimes known as *maritalfocal*.

- *Democratic* – a family (of whatever form) in which all members of the family have direct input into the decision process. All key decisions are made with the approval, consent, or acquiescence of all family members.

When and where are these forms most common, or most effective?

- *Matrifocal* tends to be rather difficult to identify, since there are some roles and functions (*e.g.* warrior and hunter) nearly always held by males (called *cultural universals*). There are societies, however, where the role of females, although not totally dominating, is cetainly primary. An example might be the Nair community in Kerala, India. Individual families may adopt this form if male influence has been either eliminated or marginalized for any reason (male death, divorce, separation, prison, military duty, *etc.*).

- *Patrifocal* is by far the most common across the world's cultures. Male strength naturally tends to give men dominance in the fields of hunting, warfare, and so on; and, this often carries over into the domestic realm – giving them a primary role in familial decision making. European families are nearly always patrifocal.

- *Parentalfocal* appears to be most effective when there is not a complete biological link between children and both parents (*e.g.* in stepfamilies). Nevertheless, this is the form that most American adults would say they have, or intend to have, in their families. In practice, this is rarely the case. Usually, it devolves into a form of *power sharing*, assigning different decision arenas to specific parents. One parent may be primary in finance, employment, residence, *etc.*, while the other may take the lead in transportation, parenting, friends, and so on.

- *Democratic* nearly never works in biological families. Allowing minor children an equal say in critical family decisions is a path begging for disaster. Where this does often work is when the "family" is neither consanguineal (genetically related) nor affinitive (legally related), but is a voluntary association of individuals.

Data collected from ethnography, history, law and social statistics clearly shows that the family is a cultural institution and not a biological fact founded on biological relationship.   The different family forms occur in a wide variety of settings, and their specific functions usually depend on their relationship to other social institutions.

Chapter 12
Marital Systems

Marriage

There are a lot of relationships that are classified as marriage, and that might result in a 'household'; and, that was true even before the issue of gay marriage became a political 'hot potato' in the United States (not so much in many other countries, where it has been regionally or nationally legalized*). An etymological dictionary will show that the term "husband" comes from the Icelandic *húsbóndi*, which is actually a contraction of the earlier Icelandic term *húsbilandi*. This, in turn, is a conjunction of *hús* (meaning "house"), and *bilandi* (being "dwelling in"). So, "husband" originally meant – literally – a 'person dwelling in a house'.

Similarly, we discover that *marriage* merely refers to the act of being given to a husband. This last term comes from Latin, and does include the implication that the husband is male, although it does not necessarily infer that the one given to him is female. *To marry* (English) coming through *marītāre* (Latin: "to marry") from *marītus* (husband) from the Indo-European root *mer* (meaning "young man"). Words do alter their meaning as time progresses; and, it would be easy to carry this too far (in fact, that may already have been done – one could give a new householder a potted plant as a house-warming gift; but, would that mean he was married to it?).

So, rather than open that can of worms, let's look at some derivative terms, and terms occasionally used by anthropologists and sociologists to describe a few of the many marital forms found around the world:

---

* Countries where *gay marriages* may be performed include (as of June 1, 2013): Argentina, Belgium, Brazil, Canada, Denmark, France, Iceland, Netherlands, New Zealand, Norway, Portugal, South Africa, Spain, Sweden, and Uruguay. In addition, México, and the United States perform them on a regional basis (México: 2 districts; United States: 12 states, the District of Columbia, and 3 Native tribal jurisdictions).

- Monogamy   Gk μονο (one) + Gk γαμος (marriage) – marriage to just one person for the rest of their lives

- Serial Monogamy   Latin *serere* (to connect) + monogamy – marriage to just one person *at a time*

- Bigamy   Lat *bi* (double) + Gk γαμος (marriage) – marriage to two people at the same time

- Polygamy   Gk πολύ (much) + Gk γαμος (marriage) – marriage to multiple people at one time (includes bigamy as a sub-set)

- Polyandry   Gk πολύ (much) + Gk ανδρος (man) – a woman married to multiple men

- Polygyny   Gk πολύ (much) + Gk ηψνε (woman) – a man married to multiple women

- Homogamy   Gk θομος (one, the same) + Gk γαμος (marriage) – marriage of two people of the same gender

- Pedogamy   Gk πειδ (child) + Gk γαμος (marriage) – marriage to a child or infant

- Endogamy   Gk ενδον (within) + Gk γαμος (marriage) –marriage to someone from within the 'group'

- Exogamy   Gk εχοδυς (going out) + Gk γαμος (marriage) – marriage to someone from outside the group

- Morganatic marriage Lat *morganatica* (morning gift) – marriage of a male of high rank with a woman of low rank

- Endogenogamy   Gk ενδον *(within)* + Gk γενος (race) + Gk γαμος (marriage) – marriage to someone from the same race

- Exogenogamy   Gk εχοδυς *(going out)* + Gk γενος (race) + Gk γαμος (marriage) – marriage to someone from a different race

- Sibling marriage   Old English *sibb* (blood relative) marriage between a brother and sister (sometimes *sibogamy*)

Confused? Don't be. There is a simple description for each of these types of marital arrangement, and also a time and place when each of them seems more likely to "make sense". So, to review them in more detail:

<u>Monogamy</u>   This is what most Americans *think* they are thinking of when they use the term 'marriage'. It is derived from two Greek words that, together, mean "single marriage". Implicit in the derivation is that it is "until death do us part".

Example: Traditional Roman Catholic beliefs require monogamy unless one of the partners dies. [In practice, this appears to work best in a stable society with a relatively short life span]

<u>Serial Monogamy</u>   This is what most Americans *actually* think of when they think of marriage. Again, it means *single marriage*; but, it does not require that it be forever. It only requires that one only be married to one person – at a time.

Example: The laws of most western nations permit divorce and re-marriage to another individual. [This appears to work best in stable societies with long life spans]

<u>Bigamy</u>   This means one person who is simultaneously married to two people. We often expect that it is a man married to two women, but that is simply sexist. There is nothing in the term that would preclude it from being a woman married to two men.

Example: Societies that have had the male population decimated by war have been known to 'look the other way' when one of the remaining males takes 2 wives simultaneously. [This works best in societies with an abnormal deficiency of one gender]

<u>Polygamy</u>   Why stop at two? This is one person married to multiple people at the same time. It could be two; or, it could be three, four, or more.

Example: The Church of Jesus Christ of Latter Day Saints (the Mormons) openly engaged in polygamy <u>in the 19th century</u> – they no longer do. [See the next 2 for where this 'works the best']

<u>Polyandry</u>   Finally, a term with gender implications. This is the relatively rare form of marriage in which a woman is married to multiple men – often brothers [*fraternal polyandry*] – at the same time.

Example: Local ethnic tribes in northern India, Tibet, Nepal, and parts of Africa are officially polyandrous. [This typically works best in a society where the number of offspring must be restricted to preclude economic or environmental disaster – e.g. a subsistence economy with inadequate resources. Since multiple men are tied to a single woman, offspring are naturally limited.]

<u>Polygyny</u>   Not to be left out, this is a fairly common situation when a man is simultaneously married to multiple women – often sisters [*sororal polygyny*].

Example: Muslim society, Mormon society during the nineteenth century, and both Hebrew and Egyptian societies in Biblical times. [This works best in labor intensive societies with ample natural resources. Most societies have some women who never marry, which reduces the societal offspring; however, in a polygynous society, virtually all women are married and reproducing.]

<u>Homogamy</u>   More commonly known today, in all its political glory, as *gay marriage*. This is a marriage in which both partners are of the same gender. Technically, a homogamous marriage could also be monogamous, serial monogamous, or polygamous. And, very few (outside theological circles) consider this to be an abhorrent behavior. In fact, chimpanzees, bonobos, and other primates also engage in homosexual behavior and "pairings".

Example: Those countries listed in the footnote on page 127. Although this may relieve situations where offspring are unacceptable for any one of a number of reasons (economic, environmental, religious, etc.), it is more often simply a concession to the "sexual orientation" of the parties involved.

<u>Pedogamy</u>   Many societies have their children marry when they are very young. Although more often young girls, it could also refer to the marriage of a young boy.

Example: Mediæval societies, some Asian cultures, and early Greek society. [This works best when young people must be married to preclude falling victim to societal predatory behaviors – such as young women being raped or becoming prostitutes, or young men being sold into slavery.]

<u>Endogamy</u>   Some tribal, cultural and religious groups restrict marriage of their members to other members from the same tribe, culture or religion. Marriage within the defined 'group' (regardless of how the group is defined) is known as endogamy.

Example: Zoroastrians and Jews. [This works best when a society is trying to maintain its racial, ethnic, social, or religious 'purity']

Exogamy   This is marriage to someone from outside of the defined 'group'.

Example: Jews during the time of Solomon, numerous Polynesian and African tribal groups, and Pacific northwest totemic societies. [This works best to reduce the impact of hereditary deficiencies, and forms a natural barrier to incest]

Morganatic Marriage In this type of marriage, the young bride is – quite literally – considered a "morning gift" to the male, and is the marriage of a high ranking male (through wealth, title, privilege, *et cetera*) to a lower ranking female. Embodied in this marriage is a contract whereby the wife and any children that result from the marriage are barred from all rights of inheritance – financial, titular, *etc.*

Example: European monarchies often preserve the royal line through Morganatic Marriages.   Prince Charles and Princess Diana were both of royal blood – and William is thus a Crown Prince. Were Charles and Camilla to have children, however, the Morganatic Marriage rule would govern, and the children would not be in line for the throne.

Endogenogamy   Marriage within the same 'race'.

Example: State law in Louisiana and some other southern states until declared unconstitutional; often, the social 'norm'. [This works best in societies where fear of the 'other' is heightened, or where the 'other' is seen as inherently inferior]

Exogenogamy   Marriage outside the 'race'.

Example: modern inter-racial marriages are becoming fairly common. [This appears to work best in cases where hereditary 'flaws' can be marginalized through a more diverse gene pool]

Sibling marriage Marriage between siblings (*i.e.* brother and sister). This has been most often employed to maintain an hereditary line when the title passed to the eldest daughter, who would then be in danger from the male military leaders.

Example: the throne of the Pharaoh in ancient Egypt was inherited by his oldest daughter; so, the eldest male in the family married this daughter (his sister) to legally assume the throne.

In addition to these, there is one form that is really 'beyond the pale' with respect to marriage: *interspecies marriage.* If your reaction is "whhaaaaaatt?" then you are probably in the vast majority; however, your reaction is not universal. There are those who consider this very seriously – really! In fact, there is a web site (http://www.MarryYourPet.com) that declares on its Home Page: "So, you adore your pet, consult with him when channel switching, and give him fish every Sunday. But, if you really love him, and you're in this for life, isn't it time  you married your pet?"* There was even a Republican representative in Colorado who argued that gay marriage was just a 'slippery slope' leading eventually to interspecies marriage. That appears (at least to the author) to be more than just a little bit of a leap.

Phew!!! So, there are actually examples where virtually any of these types of marriage (excluding interspecies) might be the social norm; and, there are circumstances where any of them might be a religiously, economically, genetically or medically advantageous option for the people involved. So, how did we ever get to see just one of these as "the only acceptable form"?

The answer is *culture.* American culture (*i.e.* the blended, polyglot, 'melting pot' of predominantly European-American culture) has religiously frowned on nearly every form of marriage except forms of monogamy. Originally, when the typical life span was about 40 years, it was strict monogamy. As life spans have increased, nations who had made divorce illegal (*e.g.* Ireland and Italy) have revised their laws to permit serial monogamy. Where there was adequate protection for the young, pedogamy became undesirable. As societies saw their culture and traditions erode, they shifted from exogamy to endogamy to shore up their traditions. Modern knowledge of heredity and genetics made sibling marriage offensive; and, industrialization removed the advantages of a polyandrous society. In other words, we became predominantly a serially monogamous world because it was the logical thing to do. It wasn't decreed; nobody thought it out; it just evolved.

---

* The photo is of Koko and Kali, who were married on October 29, 2003 by the woman who manages the *MarryYourPet* web site.

Reproduction

All societies require a continual replenishment of the population for one simple reason: people die! If Americans stopped reproducing, the United States would cease to exist at some point within the next 60 years or so. The key for all societies is to reproduce at that rate which optimizes success for society as a whole. During its early years, the United States had a need to reproduce at a rapidly expanding rate (*i.e.* many more children being born than people dying). There was a whole continent to occupy, a Native population to displace, and foreign powers to be kept at bay. By comparison, modern China needs to maintain a negative population growth to ensure sufficient food and resources for its people; and, China has implemented specific government policies to establish a negative growth rate. Officially known as the *one-child policy*, surveys show it is supported by 76% of the Chinese, although is is often considered Draconian by others. It has been undeniably effective, with studies showing that it has improved their health care, increased savings rates, stimulated economic growth, reduced unemployment, relieved pressure on schools, and stabilized the world's largest national population.

Sex

A society's views on sex are usually determined by its views on reproduction. Middle Eastern society has always been in need of a high birth rate in order to maintain population in a very harsh environment, to secure disputed claims to land, to protect political boundaries, and to provide human labor for an area of the world where food production (along with most other trades) is highly labor intensive. It should come as no surprise, therefore, when religions which trace their roots to this area (Islam, Judaism, Christianity, Zoroastrianism) all document their opposition to anything that threatens society through restriction of the birth rate: homosexuality, abortion, masturbation, infanticide, sodomy, birth control (*i.e.* pregnancy prevention), recreational sex, *et cetera*. Some of these practices may be abhorrent to you on other grounds; but, they are also clearly offensive to any society that desires a high birth rate.

Cultures differ in which sexual activities they either restrict or forbid.   Sexual activity can be seen as existing on a sort of continuum. This includes, (from most to least restrictive):

- Monastic Orders (*e.g.* Roman Catholic nuns) and celibate societies (*e.g.* Shakers)
- Cultures that separate males and females unless procreation is in the interest of the tribe (*e.g.* the Marings of New Guinea)
- Cultures that value virginity to the point that violation can result in the deliberate murder of the offending girl and boy by relatives (*e.g.* rural Greeks & Pakistanis)
- Cultures that respond to violations of virginity by completely ostracizing the offender from the group – *i.e.* 'shunning' them (*e.g.* Old Order Amish & Sikhs)
- Extreme modesty as a means of keeping women from being 'soiled' by the thoughts, as well as the actions, of society (*e.g.* many Islamic countries and the Hindu culture)
- Loyalty to a single mate (for life), and sex solely for the purpose of creating life (*e.g.* Roman Catholic laity in many areas)
- Sex restricted to the confines of marriage, but allowed for pleasure as well as for procreation (*e.g.* most Protestant laity)
- Sexual encounters outside of marriage "frowned upon", but with little condemnation if they occur (*e.g.* many Americans)
- Sexual encounters outside marriage "understood" (*e.g.* many Europeans)
- Frequent, tolerated – even encouraged – sexual contact prior to marriage (*e.g.* Trobriand Islanders of Melanesia)
- Expected extra-marital relations from husbands actually loaning their wives to friends or guests (*e.g.* Chuckchee and Inuit)
- Expected sexual freedom of women with no marital restrictions (*e.g.* Toda of India)

It should be noted that individuals in every one of the societies above (given as examples in the list) also vary widely in their personal attitude toward sexual relations. One shouldn't be surprised to find either a virginal Toda or a sexually active monk any more than to discover that their next door neighbor has a different attitude toward sex than they do.

Sex, probably because it is such a universal desire, has become the center of a number of other issues – from power to economics. This is usually associated with the view that a society has of the sex act itself. Some, such as Australian Aborigines, view sex as a positive, unifying, community-supporting activity. Others may consider sex a form of spiritual pollution. And, there are also those that view sex as a negative event in the life of the community.

The United States and the countries of the Middle East are among the few remaining nations where prostitution is still illegal (although the pictures to the right show the logos of two well-known brothels in Nevada). In fact, brothels are legal in most of the counties in Nevada (as of this writing, eleven of Nevada's sixteen counties have legal prostitution). Prostitution is not just an issue for the wealthy, developed nations – it is, in fact, related to the appearance of gender inequality;  and, as such, it is often referred to as "the oldest profession". It shows up in virtually all societies where there is unequal status for the two genders.

Regarding legality, the list is impressive. Prostitution (being paid for sex) is legal (sometimes with minor restrictions) in:

- Argentina
- Australia
- Austria
- Belgium
- Bolivia
- Brazil
- Canada
- Chile
- Columbia
- Costa Rica
- Denmark
- Ecuador
- France
- Germany
- Greece
- Hungary
- Ireland
- Israel
- Italy
- México
- Netherlands
- New Zealand
- Peru
- Poland
- Portugal
- Switzerland
- United Kingdom

and more than a hundred others!

Article 11, Section 1(c) of the *United Nations Convention on the Elimination of All Forms of Discrimination Against Women* requires those countries that sign the convention to grant women a "free choice of profession and employment". Among those professions specifically identified as being part of this free choice is prostitution. Although the US has not ratified this treaty (and is highly unlikely to do so), a total of 165 countries (out of 192) have signed it to date.

It is estimated that India may have as many as 2½ million prostitutes. This results largely from poor, rural girls going to serve the wealthier urban residents. But, as in Nevada, it also attracts many middle-class women who find employment opportunities much more restricted than for their male counterparts. Dr. Michael C. Howard (of Simon Fraser University) summarized this by writing that "Sex is not simply a matter of love or recreation or producing offspring. It is an inextricable part of the totality of human society; above everything else, it is a social and cultural phenomenon."

The "Bottom Line"

If you get nothing else from this chapter, recognize that marriage, reproduction and sex are all significantly influenced by environmental, biological and cultural factors. In other words, it appears there is no universally proper form for any of them. And, as much as we might like to think that God decreed a certain mode was the only acceptable one, changes in environmental and biological factors in the US could easily result in pressure to alter our laws regarding what is acceptable (and what is not). In addition, even if one does accept that God decreed sexual practices either good or bad, and also decreed which practices were an abomination, the next question must be: "Which God do we mean?"

- Jews and Christians worship Jehovah; and, salvation tends to be an eternal residence in *heaven* – a place where sex clearly has no place.

- Muslims worship Allah; and, salvation for a Muslim male is commonly believed to be met with a host of virgins for his entertainment in *paradise*.

- Hindus worship a number of Gods (henotheistically), but generally consider the gods to have created sex to be one of the acceptable pursuits of humanity. As such, sex is seen as both noble and desirable.

- … and the list (and disagreements) go on, and on, and on.

Chapter 13
Kinship Systems

Who's your Daddy ?

Ignoring the slang meaning, this really isn't as simple a question as it might appear to be. Let's begin by using an analogy.

Suppose we take a pair of twins (Fred and Bill), and split them up at birth. Fred is adopted by the Johnsons, and Bill is adopted by the Smiths. Fred Johnson is taught that the visual sense impression he gets when looking at something that reflects energy with a wave length of approximately 0.75μ (microns) is called *red*. And, the visual sense impression he gets looking at something reflecting energy with a wave length of approximately 0.45μ is known as *blue*. Your parents most likely taught you the exact same thing, although they probably didn't explain it in precisely that way.

By contrast, Bill Smith is taught that energy with a wave length of 0.75μ is called *blue*, and that of 0.45μ is called *red*. You might think that they have this backwards; but, do they? The terms *red* and *blue* are simply symbols that English-speaking humans have mutually agreed to use when referring to the sense impressions processed by the brain when the retina of the eye is stimulated by a particular frequency. In fact, there is absolutely no reason why the terms could not be reversed; and, absolutely no way of knowing if two people have the same sensory experience when they encounter energy of identical wave lengths. In other words, what something is called (*i.e.* the verbal symbol used by consensus) may represent totally different physical realities to different individuals; or, the exact same physical experience may be represented with totally different symbols! Joe might say "it is hot" once the temperature exceeds 74°F; but, Mary might not say "it is hot" until the temperature exceeds 90°F. They are experiencing identical stimuli; but, their sensory experiences of them are very different. Similarly, this could also apply to visual stimuli such as colors.

When it comes to biological relationships, the exact same problem is encountered. In American and European culture, the term *daddy* (or *father*) is typically used to refer to the source of the male sperm that impregnated the female ovum that eventually became the child. But, it could also mean the adult male that married the mother and raised the child from infancy. One could object that that would technically be a *stepfather*, but that too (unfortunately) is simply an accepted, symbolic norm. Americans agree that that defines a stepfather; but, in reality, it has no meaning other than what is given to it – what everyone has agreed that it represents.

The difficulties arise because other cultures often do not use relationship labels in the same way Americans and Europeans do. In fact, only about 10% of the world's cultures do it the way that most Europeans and Americans do. For that reason, a foreigner's idea of *kinship* (*i.e.* who is a relative, and what is the relationship involved) may be very different from yours.

There are four terms that need to be understood to make sense of this chapter. These are listed here; and, we'll go through them in greater detail as the chapter progresses. There are also numerous other terms that may sound familiar, but still not be totally understood. These will be explained as they are introduced.

- **Kinship**   This answers the simple question "who is a relative?" As will be discussed below, relatives may be either *consanguineal* (genetically related) or *affinal* (legally related). As examples, your biological parents and siblings are consanguineally related to you – you all come from the same gene pool. An adopted sibling or your brother's wife would be affinally related (relatives because the government sanctioned that fact).

- **Lineage**   All of the descendants of a certain ancestor who is considered to be the founder (*i.e. patriarch* or *matriarch*) constitute your lineage.

- **Descent**   This refers to identifying parentage from a common ancestor. Descent is usually traced through the paternal (father's) line in the US, and is usually the basis of genealogical research – something which appears to be far more important to Europeans and North Americans than it does to many others.

- **Locality**   A declaration of where a newly married couple will "set up house", this is usually culturally constrained to favor one of several possible choices: near the bride's family, near the groom's family, near a maternal uncle, *et cetera*.

Kinship & Descent

Fundamentally, there are 2 primary means to establish kinship: *descent* and *affinity*. *Descent* is the *consanguineal* connection (literally, "with the blood"; or colloquially, a *blood relative*). While relying on both of these methods, every culture also has a preferred method of classifying relationships. For example, the Trobriand Island people do not believe that male semen has any role whatsoever in pregnancy – at least not traditionally (with so much contact with the outside world, it would be naïve to assume they are still unaware of the connection). It has been reported that the Trobrianders unabashedly practice premarital sex; but, girls are generally married by the time they are capable of becoming pregnant – hence their lack of any empirical evidence which might contradict their beliefs. Why, if frequent sex has been occurring for some time, would anyone assume it had anything to do with the sudden attival of a baby? After all, it didn't result in a baby last year!

Since most females are capable of becoming pregnant sometime between ten and twelve years of age, that means premarital sex most often occurs while the girls are younger than that. Although this may offend the sensibilities of a western student, *sexual contact* is virtually synonymous with *childhood play* amongst pre-pubescent Trobriand Island natives. That does not mean, however, that they are necessarily a sexually promiscuous society. In fact, numerous studies have shown that these sexual activities become increasingly constrained once an individual (male or female) is of marriageable age (*i.e.* at the onset of puberty).

As just mentioned, there is a wide variety in the method used to identify both who is a relative and assigning *relationship tags* to identify just how that person is related. These relationship tags comprise the field of *kinship terminology*. This only makes sense. If you consider your father's sister and your mother's sister to be comparably related to you, you might as well use the same term to designate both – and, you do: *aunt*. Anthropologists refer to this particular form of *naming convention* as either *Eskimo* or *Inuit*. Although this system might appear to you to be the only logical system, this is only because it is the one into which you were born. Actually, only about 10% of the world's societies use this system. 90% of the world uses one of the other 5 known naming conventions. A graphical representation of each will make discussion much easier; but, first we need a set of accepted "symbols" to use in diagrams. So –

These are the basic symbols (right) used in constructing *kinship diagrams*. All males and females have a symbol, and 'ego' (*i.e.* you) can be either gender. When two

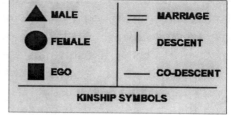

people pair off for the purpose of procreation, it is called a *marriage bond* (regardless of whether it fits your definition of marriage). The off-spring from this union are designated by the *descent bond*; and, if there are multiple off-spring from the same pairing, they are jointly shown using the *co-descent bond* symbol. These bonds (with the exception of the marriage bond) may be either consanguineal or affinal – *i.e.* by blood, or by legal acceptance). With that established, it now becomes possible for us to diagram the world's six major *kinship systems*.

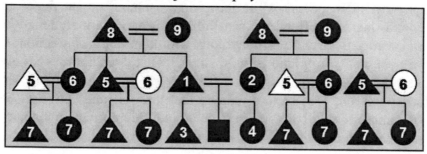

The *Inuit System* (above; *a.k.a. Eskimo System*, although "Eskimo" is pejorative for these natives) is the system commonly used in Europe and North America. The numbers that appear in the symbols on this "family tree" indicate their relationship to ego. In this case, you (*i.e.* Ego, the square) are shown as having a *father* (1) and *mother* (2). You also have siblings from the same parents: a *brother* (3) and a *sister* (4). In this system, a male sibling of either parent is called your *uncle* (5), and a female sibling of either is called your *aunt* (6). If all of your aunts and uncles were married (the block for the spouse is left unfilled to indicate an affinal relationship to you), their spouse would typically assume the same title as your parents' consanguineal siblings (5-uncle; 6-aunt). All of the children of all of the aunts and uncles are referred to as a *cousin* (7). Finally, this system extends to prior generations by simply adding 'grand' to the title: *grandfather* (8) is the father of either parent, and *grandmother* (9) is similarly the mother of either parent. Further generations are identified by repeatedly adding the prefix *great*. This system should be relatively easy to follow, since it is the naming convention that is commonly used throughout the United States.

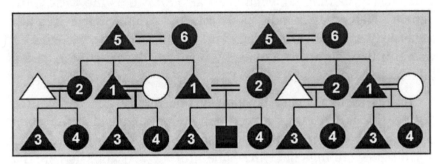

A far simpler system – and far more commonly encountered – is that known as the *Hawaiian system* (above). In this case, a common term is used for all members of the same gender and generation (sort of like the occasional use of the expression "my brother" or "my sister" to refer to a peer). Note that all male relatives of your generation (what you would probably call brothers and male cousins) have the exact same title in Hawai'ian: *hoăhānaŭ ka'nĕ* (3); similarly, all female relatives of your generation (your sisters and female cousins) have another, common title: *hoăhānaŭ wăhi'nĕ* (4). What you call your mother is the same term you would call any aunts: *makuăhi'nĕ* (2); and, what you call your father is what you would call any uncles: *makuăka'n*. This continues on with prior generations as well. Note: most Hawaiian System users include the affinal relations in this scheme; but, some do not, which is why they have been left un-coded in the diagram.

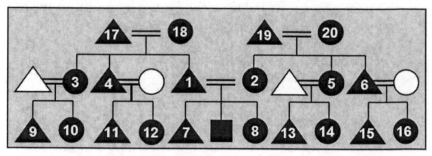

As much simpler as the Hawaiian System is than the Inuit System, the Sudanese System (above) is comparably more complex. This kinship naming convention is also known as the *Descriptive System*. Named after indigenous tribes in South Sudan, it is also used today in Arab, Bulgarian, Turkish and Chinese societies. It was also used in ancient times by many of the Anglo-Saxon and Latin cultures.

In this system, every position on the family tree has its own distinct title – reflecting gender, generation, and 'side of the family'. It isn't each person that has a unique title – each position does (*e.g.* all male siblings have the same title – 7). It appears here that each person has a unique title only because the chart only shows one sibling of each gender in each family unit. Using the Old English (Anglo-Saxon) terms for these relationships (limited to those we can determine from ancient writings), they are:

- 1–*Faeder* (Father)
- 2–*Modor* (Mother)
- 3–*Fathu* (Father's sister)
- 4–*Faedera* (Father's father)
- 5–*Modrige* (Mother's sister)
- 6–*Eam* (Mother's brother)
- 7–*Brothor* (Brother)
- 8–*Sweostor* (Sister)
- *Sunu* (Son)
- *Dohtor* (Daughter)
- *Nift* (Nephew)
- *Nefa* (Niece)

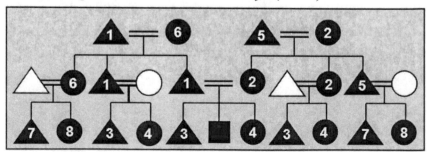

The figure at the bottom of the prior page shows the *Iroquois System*. This system is what is known as a *bifurcate merging* – it bifurcates by separating relatives as maternally or paternally related; and, it merges by combining same gender siblings as well as same gender *parallel cousins* (abbreviated PC below) and siblings.

For example, the Yanomamo tribe (native to the Amazon region) use the following terms:

- 1 – *Haya* (Father, and his father)
- 2 – *Naya* (Mother, grand-mother)
- 3 – *Elwa* (Brother, male PC)
- 4 – *Amiwa* (Sister, female PC)
- 5 – *Soaya* (Mother's brother/father)
- 6 – *Yesiya* (Father's sister/mother)
- 7 – *Soriwa* (Male cross cousin)
- 8 – *Suaboya* (Female cross cousin)

This is the first system in which we encounter what are known as *parallel cousins* and *cross cousins*; so, let's define those terms so there is no confusion.

- **Parallel cousins** are cousins by virtue of the fact that your parent and one of their parents are siblings – of the <u>same</u> gender (*i.e.* your father's brother, or your mother's sister).

- **Cross cousins** are cousins by virtue of the fact that your parent and one of their parents are siblings – of the <u>opposite</u> gender (*i.e.* your father's sister, or your mother's brother).

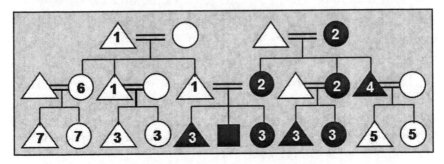

This (above) is the *Crow System*. This system follows a *matrilineal descent* pattern (see below). In this system, siblings and parallel cousins of the same gender are grouped together under the same title (3); mother, her mother, and mother's sisters are also grouped (2). Note that, since siblings are grouped with parallel cousins, parallel cousins have a fairly high status in this view of the extended family. Cross-cousins who are part of the matrilineal line are also given a special title (5). Father's relatives (other than the parallel cousins) are identified through his matrilineal line, and are all grouped together. This reflects the lower importance which paternal relations hold in a matrilineal society.

The Akan people (from Ghana and Côte d'Ivoire in west Africa) use the Crow system:

- 1 – *Agya* (Father, his father & brothers)
- 2 – *Ena* (Mother, her mother & sisters)
- 3 – *Nua* (Siblings & parallel cousins)
- 4 – *Wofa* (Mother's brother)
- 5 – *Wofaba* (Mother's brother's children)
- 6 – *Agyawa* (Father's sister)
- 7 – *Agyawaba* (Father's sister's children)

Matrilineal descent applies when you primarily follow the generational links through the female line. Both males and females are considered part of a matrilineal descent, but only until a generational change occurs; then, a male's off-spring become associated with their mother's *line*. In the above example, only those with filled symbols are strictly considered part of the "family lineage".

Patrilineal descent is the exact opposite. Descent applies when you follow the male line. Again, females are considered part of a patrilineal descent, but their children would not – being seen as part of their father's line. The diagram at the top of the next page (the Omaha system) shows a patrilineal family lineage.

Finally, the next figure (next page) shows the *Omaha System*. This is essentially a mirror image of the Crow System, except that it follows a *patrilineal descent* pattern. If we use the naming terms of the Dani (a people from the highlands of Papua, Indonesia on the island of New Guinea), we get:

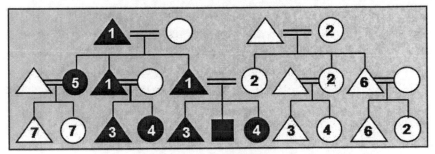

- 1 – *Opaije* (Father, his father and brothers)
- 2 – *Akoja* (Mother, her mother, her sisters, and her brother's daughters)
- 3 – *Oe* (Brother and male parallel cousins)
- 4 – *Oe-etu* (Sister and female parallel cousins)
- 5 – *He-opaije* (Father' sister)
- 6 – *Ami* (Mother's brother and his sons)
- 7 – *Ejak* (Sister's children, and father's sister's children)
- 8 – *Abut* (Brother's children and Ego's children)

Popularity

It is generally believed that about 60% of the world's social groupings use one of the two *unilineal descent* systems – either matrilineal or patrilineal. These are known as "unilineal" because they each only follow descent by a single (*i.e.* uni-) criterion. This is often the determinant in such decisions as inheritance, and so forth. To make it easier to visualize, assume that when a man and woman get married, each of them retains their family name; but, their children are given their father's family name. Determining whether someone is in their patrilineal descent is simple: do they have the same family name as their father?

To determine a matrilineal line, assume that each keeps their birth name, but any children are given the family name of their mother. Is someone in their matrilineal line? Do they have the same family name as their mother?

The remaining 40% of the world's social groupings use one of the *cognatic descent* systems. These are systems that use both male and female lines to determine such rights, duties, privileges, and responsibilities as family, class, rank, nationality, race, inheritance, ethnicity, title, *et cetera*. The most common form of cognative descent is known as *bilateral descent*, in which descent is traced through both male and female ancestors equally. This accounts for at least three-quarters of the world's cognatic descent systems. The remaining quarter consists of what is called *ambilineal descent*. In this case, each generation makes a determination as to whether to trace their descent through their male or female parent. This is usually done to ensure that the greatest benefit (with the least expense) accrues to the next generation.

With respect to frequency of use, it goes (roughly) as follows:

- ◆ Hawaiian (40%) – widespread: Hawaii, Polynesia, ...
- ◆ Iroquois (28%) – widespread: Iroquoian Native Americans, rural Chinese, ...
- ◆ Crow (15%) – common: Crow, Hopi, many Africans, Central Asians, ...
- ◆ Inuit (10%) – narrower range: Inuit, Europe, Canada, US, ...
- ◆ Omaha (5%) – narrow: certain Native Americans, Australian Aborigines, ...
- ◆ Sudanese (2%) – very restricted: So. Sudan, Turkey, ...

Lineage

Simply put, a *lineage* is a "descent in a line from a common progenitor, race, or family." This lineage is the information to which most people are referring when they say they are going to "trace their genealogy". What they are saying, in effect, is that they are going to determine their *lineage*. In order to do this, they must first decide what they are going to include in the finished product, and how they are going to determine whom to list. They can choose to merely go from their father to his father to his father, which would create a highly restrictive patrineal genealogy. If they were to include information on the brothers of each of these individuals, they would be adhering to a broader, more traditional, patrilineal genealogy. This is what is typically followed in both Jewish and Christian scriptures – women are rarely, if ever, mentioned; and, they are virtually never included in the 'begats' (*i.e.* the genealogical listings), and are generally only mentioned in stories when they are directly involved in something that involves the males. For example, the probability that Jacob (Israel) had 12 sons and no daughters would be less than 1 in 4,000. Adding a single daughter to the list would not have significantly altered this probability. There may, in fact, have been numerous daughters – the patrilineal lineage followed by these Hebrews would have simply ignored their presence, and never recorded them. The reason only one (Diana) is recorded is that she was raped (the primary reason for a war in which the males were engaged).

It is likely that the various types of kindreds and lineages will be confusing on your first pass. Don't worry; that's common. In fact, we are so conditioned to think that 'our way is the only way' that we often have a mental block to understanding or accepting other methods of determining who is related to us. For example, can you legally marry your "first cousin"? In most states, the answer is "no"; but, that assumes we know what we mean by "first cousin". In the US, we typically mean the son or daughter of any sibling of either our mother or father. But, for many cultures, it matters whether this is a *parallel cousin* or a *cross cousin*.

Locality

Once you get married, where do you live? Traditionally, there are 9 different possible patterns that answer this question. Albeit this is potentially as confusing as the kinship relationship terms, a detailed review shows both what it is, and what might cause it.

- *Patrilocality* locates with (or close by) the husband's father; in this type of living arrangement, the husband, his brothers (who have also located here), and any sons tend to form the center of the domestic unit. It most often occurs in a highly patrifocal society where sons must learn a "family trade" from their elders (*e.g.* carpentry or farming).

- *Matrilocality* locates with (or close by) the wife's mother; in this type of living arrangement, the wife, her sisters (who have also located here), and any daughters tend to form the center of the domestic unit. This often occurs in a highly matrifocal society, where daughters must learn key skills from other females (*e.g.* in cultures such as India, where food preparation is highly complex and extremely labor intensive).

■ *Ambilocality*   locates with <u>either</u> husband's kin or wife's kin; in this type of arrangement, it is the nuclear family (husband, wife and any children) who tend to form the focus for the domestic unit, although there is a marked tendency to favor either the male or female line. This is often followed in the US, and is common among bilateral societies. It allows the husband and wife to choose where future success is most likely to be.

■ *Bilocality*   locates with <u>both</u> husband's kin and wife's kin, moving back and forth. Again, this type of arrangement tends to make the nuclear family the focus of the domestic unit; but, it favors neither the male nor the female line. This occurs when both sons and daughters need the support of older same-gender relatives to ensure their growth and maturity.

■ *Neolocality*   is the most common system used among the better educated in the US. Employment or education may draw the couple to a location which is near neither the husband's family nor the wife's family; and, they "set up house" in a new, unrelated environment. This seems to work best in a culture where transmission of a trade to the next generation is something that is learned apart from their elders (such as at school – *e.g.* engineering, medicine, law, *et cetera*).

■ *Avunculocality*   locates with the husband's mother's brother. Although this may seem strange, there are many societies that do this. If the society is matrifocal, males can easily get "lost in the shuffle" when they wed and become secondary members of their wife's kin group. By locating with their uncle, they develop a male core for their domestic group that consists of a group of brothers and their sisters' sons. This supports a male learning a trade from his elders, and makes military service a more reasonable path.

■ *Amitalocality*   locates with the wife's father's sister. This is the mirror image of avuncolocality, and enables the creation of a strong female cluster within a patrifocal society. Girls have older females from whom to learn, and in whom they can confide, in the presence of a group of sisters and their brothers' daughters.

- ■ ***Virilocality*** locates with the general clan comprised of the husband's kin. A sort of catch all, several of the patrilineally focused options could be practiced under this umbrella.

- ■ ***Uxorilocality*** locates with the general clan comprised of the wife's kin. Another catch all, several of the matrilineally focused methods could be practiced under this umbrella.

Bottom Line

Dr. Marvin Harris (of the University of Florida) wrote that "kinship is one of the central organizing principles of human social life, but there is always room for negotiation of kinship status. ... The flexibility of kinship systems makes it possible to transform relationships through reclassification in order to invoke a desired role relationship."[*] Whhhaaaat? He clarifies this by defining *fictive kin ties*, and offers them as a means by which individuals manage to "transform relationships ... in order to invoke a desired role relationship". What is meant by a "fictive kin tie" can best be seen by giving a very simple example.

> If your mother and father have a couple with whom they are very close (they may have been the best man and maid of honor at their wedding; they may have become your God-parents; or, they could simply be close personal friends), you may grow up calling them 'Aunt and Uncle'. Biologically, they aren't related to you. But, they have a *fictive kinship status* which is comparable to that of a biological aunt and uncle (hence the use of those terms). This is not an affinal relationship because there is no legal recognition of their role (unlike what happens in a marriage or an adoption – either of which establishes an *affinal kinship status*).

Dr. Harris also referred to children who do not mature in the manner accepted as the societal norm as "incompletely launched young adults". Know anybody like that?

A lot of new terms have been introduced in this Chapter, so let's recap these terms in a "kinship glossary".

---

* Harris, Marvin and Johnson, Orna (2003) <u>Cultural Anthropology (Sixth Edition)</u> (Boston: Allyn and Bacon; page 150).

Glossary

Affinal, Affinity a legally recognized relationship.

Ambilineal descent each generation selects the line followed.

Ambilocality location with either husband's or wife's kin.

Amitalocality location with the wife's father's sister.

Apical the founding progenitor of a lineage.

Avunculocality location with the husband's mother's brother.

Bilateral descent cognatic descent that relies on each line equally.

Bilocality alternating location with husband's and wife's kin.

Clan a group of lineages who all claim descent from a (possibly fictitious) apical ancestor [Gaelic: *clan*, "off-spring"]

Cognatic descent follows matrilineal and patrilineal lines to some degree.

Consaguineous biologically related (literally, "with the blood")

Cross cousin someone with a parent who is the opposite-gender sibling of your parent.

Crow System matrilineal descent.

Eskimo System *a.k.a.* Inuit System

Fictive accepted relationship that is neither genetic nor legal.

Hawai'ian System the simplest descent system.

Inuit System common European and US descent system.

Iroquois System a bifurcate sys.

Kin group of persons of the same stock, race, or family.

Kindred the family to which one belongs, consisting of close bilateral relatives.

Kinship the quality or state of being kin.

Lineage lineal descent from a common progenitor, race or family.

Matrilineal descent descent that follows the female line.

Matrilocality location with the wife's mother.

Moiety a major division that divides a society into reciprocal groups for multiple functions. For example, the Seneca Iroquois moieties perform funerary services for each other.

Neolocality location separate from both sides of the family.

Omaha System a patrilineal descent system.

Parallel cousin someone with a parent who is a same-gender sibling of one of your parents.

Patrilineal descent descent that follows the male line.

Patrilocality location with the husband's father.

Phratry a descent group composed of several supposedly related clans, the actual connection often unrecognized.

Sudanese System rare, extremely complex descent system.

Tribe a social group comprising families, clans, phratries or moieties, together with slaves, adopted strangers, *etc.*

Unilineal descent a single line, either patrilineal or matrilineal

Uxorilocality location with the wife's kin group.

Virilocality location with the husband's kin group.

Chapter 14
Legal Systems & The Causes of War

Law

Most societies find it advantageous to systematize their recognized norms, and raise them to the level of *laws* – binding rules that define reasonable and expected behavior. This results largely from the fact that people often have conflicting interests, and not everybody wants the same thing at the same time – inevitably leading to conflict at some level; and, every society must have some means to determine what is "right", and to resolve these internal conflicts before they escalate to confrontation or violence.

Order

Laws are norms that have been incorporated into set rules; but, without any means of enforcement, they are little more than guidelines for acceptable behavior. Since not everyone in a society is willing to forego their personal wants and needs to maintain acceptable social behavior, there usually needs to be some societal power behind them to guarantee that they are followed. This power may be financial (*e.g.* fines), physical (*e.g.* incarceration), forfeiture (*e.g.* surrendering real property to authority), ostracization (*e.g.* expulsion or deportation), *et cetera.*

Every law rests upon some unwritten, but understood, basis tacitly acknowledged by all members of the society. The United States is a large, highly organized, state society; and, many citizens assume that the basis for law in the US is the United States Constitution. It isn't. The Constitution is simply the highest level of law; but, it isn't the basis on which all laws rest. That basis is the general, tacit agreement of all Americans that: (a) there is a need for established norms; (b) these norms should limit or restrict actions only to the degree that is required to protect the activity of others; and, (c) an over-arching framework that establishes boundaries for these actions is required so that all laws are compliant with the wishes of the people. The Constitution is simply how Americans have chosen to codify that over-arching framework.

Jurisdictional Conflict

It is actually a fairly common situation where the legal system, or set of laws, of one group are in conflict with those of another – at the same place, at the same time, with the same people. In cases such as this, it is necessary to have some form of understanding as to which system takes precedence in the case of such a conflict. Australia has a national legal system; the various aboriginal bands each have their own legal system; and, occasionally, these come into conflict with each other. Australian law dictates that aborigines are allowed to rely on their own legal system; but, if it conflicts with Australian national law, Australia wins. The aborigines may not always like this, for aboriginal law is a major ethnic identifier for them; but, only the national Australian government has the power necessary to enforce its will.

The Pokomam Maya of what is now Guatemala and the state of Quintana Roo, México are another example of this. Prior to his death in 1541, these southern Mayans were subjugated by Spain under the leadership of the cruel, but resourceful, Pedro de Alvarado. Even so, there were major insurrections by these Maya in 1847, and again in 1860. They were in formal rebellion against the Mexican leader Porfirio Diaz as late as 1910. Small scale skirmishes still arise periodically in this area. Again, the Mayan legal system is considered to be "the law of the saints", and adhering to this legal system is a mark of Mayan ethnicity. Both Guatemala and México have come to recognize the rights of the Maya to live by their own laws – so long as it doesn't interfere with, or contravene, national law.

Perhaps the best example of this type of jurisdictional overlap, however, is much closer to home. Many of the Native Americans that reside within the borders of the United States live on so-called *Indian Reservations*. Technically, according to US treaties, these are *Sovereign Domestic Nations*. Although the exact governing body and process varies from native group to native group, the Blackfeet Nation (a member of the Algonquin family) in northwestern Montana is fairly representative. They state on their web site that:

The Blackfeet Tribal Business Council is the governing body within the exterior boundaries of the Blackfeet Indian Reservation. The Blackfeet Nation, in its relationship with the federal government as a "domestic sovereign" Indian nation, is recognized as a nation within a nation through treaties, agreements, laws and executive orders. ...

The Blackfeet Tribal Business Council consists of nine Council members that are elected into office based on two and four year terms. The Blackfeet Tribal Business Council is the duly constituted governing body within the exterior boundaries of the Blackfeet Indian Reservation; and the Blackfeet Tribal Business Council has been organized to represent, develop, protect, and advance the views, interests, education, and resources of the Blackfeet Indian Reservation.

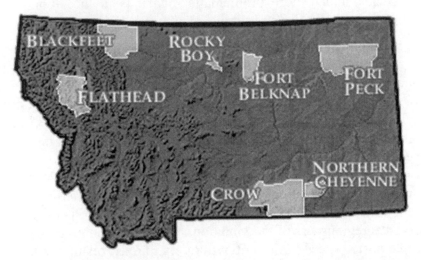

The Blackfeet Tribal Council was formed in 1934, just ten years after Native Americans were granted US citizenship (1924). This council, known today as the Blackfeet Tribal Business Council, is the legal governing body of the Blackfeet Nation. As a result, Blackfeet laws apply; however, when in conflict with US national law, it is the US law that supersedes. Although the Blackfeet do not operate casinos, many other tribes do. These are legal so long as the games offered do not directly violate either federal or state law. In other words, if a state allows a casino anywhere, operated by anyone, then they can not legally object to a Native casino run under their own jurisdiction – and, the Natives need not apply for a license. Again, Native Law applies, but US and state laws supersede only when (and if) they are in conflict.

Enforcement, Mediation, and Conflict Resolution

Laws are essentially an abstract formulation of social standards. All societies have norms by which they live; but, not all societies have reduced these norms to abstract concepts that can be written as general laws. For example, the Australian Aborigines have a very well formulated set of laws and rules by which they live; by contrast, the Comanche Nation has never been able to reduce tribal norms to the abstract principles that are required to formulate them as laws. This makes enforcement of law in Comanche society much more problematic than it is in the Aboriginal culture – for their rules and standards are not well defined.

It is not just in formulation, however, that societies vary. They also vary in the degree to which they expect (and demand) compliance. This is also true for different laws within a given society. For example, every state in the United States has a law against murder; and, there is no state that routinely fails to require citizen compliance. By the same token, every US state also has highway speed limits and laws against serving alcohol to minors. Observation, however, will show that both of these laws are "selectively enforced" – *i.e.* sometimes they are enforced, and sometimes they are not. Usually (although not always), the difference is in the perceived egregiousness of the violation. Going 63 mph on a highway with a posted speed limit of 60 will rarely, if ever, result in a traffic ticket; going 120 mph on that same road almost certainly will. A priest or minister serving eucharist/communion wine (typically about 25 proof) to a 16 year old parishioner won't raise eyebrows at the local police station; but, a local bar serving a *Harvey Wallbanger* (Vodka, Galliano and Orange Juice – a mixture that is also roughly 25 proof) to that same 16 year old most certainly will.

Foragers need very few laws regarding property – because they usually don't own any. However, they do have conflicts over food and sex. These societies can often minimize these conflicts by: (a) devising detailed, explicit rules regarding them (*e.g.* Aborigines); (b) having minimal hard rules, but extensive social norms that govern the sharing of food; (c) setting rules governing equitable, reciprocal division and distribution of food; and, (d) imposing fairly liberal rules regarding sexual access. The logic in this last one may not appear obvious; so, consider this as an analogy: *you can neither break into an open store, nor steal something from a box labeled "Free! Take as many as you please.".*

Agricultural and industrial societies have more areas of potential conflict than foragers (land and other resources being more critical to their society); but, the general approach to these added pressures remains pretty much the same: (a) rules; (b) norms; (c) reciprocity; and, (d) lack of constraints. When these fail to resolve or mediate the conflicts, then the only recourse left to society is enforcement. As listed earlier, this includes financial, physical, forfeiture, or expellant penalties. But, there are other pressures that enforce the rules of society more than just fear of punishment.

Small Scale Societies

Small scale societies (more on these in the next chapter) typically rely on a *subsistence economy*. This means that the society does not have the ability to produce a surplus; hopefully, supplies of food, housing, tools, technology, and so forth meet the basic needs of the community – but, not much else. Sometimes this occurs due to harsh environmental conditions (such as for the Inuit in the Arctic, or Aborigines in the Australian outback); sometimes it results from a marginally developed understanding of technology that precludes exploiting the natural resources that are present (such as many of the native tribal groups of New Guinea); and, sometimes it happens this way because the number of people simply exceeds what would otherwise be an adequate resource supply (such as some areas in Pakistan, India and China).

Societies that are both *small scale* and rely on a *subsistence economy* also tend to be *egalitarian societies*. These are groups which are basically structured around the principle of "all for one, and one for all" – in other words, the members of society are precluded by their cultural structure from gaining any level of control over more than their "fair share". In simple terms, these are societies in which a Bill Gates or a Warren Buffet is not possible. Frequently (but, not necessarily always), the members of these societies are closely related.

In virtually all subsistence economies (including both foragers and small horticultural societies), there are several points that seem to be commonplace:

- each domestic unit tends to be self-sufficient;
- every domestic unit tends to resemble every other unit;
- access to resources and power tend to be egalitarian, not hierarchical;
- groups are almost always small in size; and,
- domestic ties and kinship are key to societal integration.

What these all mean can be summed up fairly succinctly: "Everybody knows everybody else, and is probably related to them." This has a very positive effect on the application of laws and social norms. Basically, it's a lot harder to steal from Uncle Joe than it is from a complete stranger; and, the guilt and selective correction that can be applied by your family is far more stringent than what could be applied by an industrial state. As a result, jail time, fines, and other common enforcement penalties in an industrialized society are generally not required in a small, egalitarian society.

By contrast, a *political society* (again, more on these in the next chapter) is one which employs a *political economy* – an economy in which technology has evolved to a sufficient level to permit production of a surplus, as well as individual specialization. This requires the society to find ways to manage both the surplus and the work distribution. This permits the growth of larger societies, and individual members usually no longer know, nor are related to, the other members of the society. Kinship pressure is no longer effective as a deterrent to crime. As societies grow in size and sophistication, resolution of conflicts may still come from the presence and pressure of *kin groups* (*i.e.* relatives), but, this is generally insufficient to prevent open aggression. Sometimes it is; but, not always.

War

On occasion, conflicts arise <u>between</u> societal groups, rather than <u>within</u> them. Typically, this occurs when groups of people align themselves into distinct territorial groupings or political communities in preparation for a potentially violent resolution of some mutual grievance.

Students in the 21st century often react with surprise or bewilderment when they read in a history class about the approach of the British military during the American Revolution: marching into battle in even rows, kneeling down to fire, and then dropping back to reload while their comrades step to the front. American rebels, fighting in a manner that was unconventional at that time, hid behind trees and rocks, fired at the British soldiers while they were falling back or reloading, and then scurried off to avoid return fire. To most students, the British approach seems stilted, unrealistic, and grossly inefficient. To the British of the 18th century, the American tactics appeared uneducated and cowardly. However, this is a good illustration of warfare as it is often practiced by subsistence societies.

Typically, the enemy forces return from the battlefield to their camps at dusk, or when a few of their warriors have been injured. Casualties are not all that common because it is usually the most experienced (*i.e.* the elderly) who shoot the arrows and throw the spears. And those injured are often the old women who are slower to get out of the way of incoming projectiles than their younger peers. This is clearly not the type of war usually fought by the US or any of the other technologically advanced nations today.

Why War?

It seems that the more a society has invested in their territory, the more likely they are to defend it; and, the more likely they are to seize territory from a defeated enemy to add to their resource pool. In considering small scale societies, a total of five reasonable explanations have been offered by anthropologists for why wars actually occur . These are:

■ *War is instinctive.* This theory maintains that humans are genetically predisposed to be aggressive and violent. They also maintain that no human society has ever been found that is not inherently violent, and that violence is simply "in our blood." Examples are usually given to illustrate that only humans engage in organized warfare; and, that this is evidence that it is something that is inherently human. After all, if war was a logical result of emotions, survival, *etc*, then other animals, which share many of these same attributes, would also resort to warfare. Although this view has a large following, the fact is that there has been observational research with chimpanzees that shows that they, too, occasionally engage in organized warfare. So, humans are not unique in that after all.

- *William Tecumseh Sherman (US Civil War General):* *"War is hell, and I mean to make it so."*

■ *War is revenge.* Another theory offered to explain war is the concept of revenge. In this case, the idea is that revenge is "to inflict harm or injury in return for a perceived harm, or to vindicate by avenging." This assumes that the initiator of a war is attempting to retaliate for some prior perceived injustice committed by the enemy. There is no doubt that some wars may result from this motivation; but, it appears to be quite a stretch to maintain that all (or even most) wars are caused by revenge.

- *Paul Gauguin (French artist):* *"Life being what it is, one dreams of revenge."*

■ *War is a struggle for success.* This essentially means warriors have a particular status within society and across societies; and, to maintain the role of warrior, one must periodically have a war. This can often be substantiated in small scale societies; but, extrapolating it to large, industrial, state societies becomes much more problematic.

Simultaneously, however, this tends to secure the position of the ultimate leader. During his 1864 campaign for re-election, President Abraham Lincoln [1809-1865], in paraphrasing an unnamed "old Dutch farmer", told a delegation from the National Union League that "I do not allow myself to suppose that … the League have concluded to decide that I am either the greatest or the best man in America, but rather they have concluded it is not best to swap horses while crossing the river, and have further concluded that I am not so poor a horse that they might not make a botch of it in trying to swap." Just as warriors are maintained by war, the position of a leader is also often secured by war.

- *Paddy Chayefsky (US author):* "*In peacetime, they had all been normal decent, cowards, frightened of their wives, trembling before their bosses, terrified at the passing of the years, but war had made them gallant. They had been greedy men. Now they were self-sacrificing. They had been selfish. Now they were generous. War isn't hell at all. It's man at his best, the highest morality he is capable of.*"

■ ***War is a struggle for resources and benefits.*** In essence, this is: "You have it; I don't. I want it; you won't give it to me." Therefore, I am going to have to go to war with you to acquire it – whatever the *it* happens to be. This is the argument that most often appeals to the non-academic. The reason for this is simple: wars are inherently territorial; and, as such, territory and/or property is often secured as a consequence of victory.

There is a common logical error that is known to logicians as *Post hoc ergo propter hoc.* In essence, it means "A followed B; therefore, B caused A." Frequently, B did cause A; but, not always. Consider the old superstition: "I washed my car, and it rained." *Post hoc ergo propter hoc* would argue that it rained because I washed my car. This may be a common superstition, but it certainly can't be true – when every city in America has at least one car wash washing numerous cars every day; but, it doesn't rain in all cities, every day. So, washing a car can not be what makes it rain.

It has been a long tradition that winners get to profit from their victory; but, it was not until 1832 that Senator William Marcy (D-NY) [1786-1857] used a phrase during his speech to the Senate that has gone down in history: "They see nothing wrong in the rule that *to the victor belong the spoils* of the enemy." The problem is that it is too tempting to apply faulty logic (of *post hoc ergo propter hoc*) and conclude that it was the acquisition of the spoils that caused the war. Sometimes, it clearly is; but, certainly not always.

- *Socrates (Greek philosopher): "The fewer our wants, the nearer we resemble the gods."*

■ ***War is entertainment.*** In this view, war is little more than a big game. War gives all combatants an opportunity to test their mettle while fortuitously resolving some conflict or reducing some threat at the same time. Typically, this is the proposed cause for war that is the least acceptable to the average person. This is becase it is offensive to most people to believe that anything as serious and dangerous as going to war would ever be considered for such a "trivial" reason. But, do we?

Apparently, the answer is yes – perhaps; but, we have to be careful here. There is no question that wars do allow military and political leaders to get first-hand information on the durability, reliability, and effectiveness of new weapon systems and previously untried troops. But, is that the primary (or only) reason they went to war? The caution once again applies to the *post hoc ergo propter hoc* logical error. Just because this information was gained does not mean that was the reason for the war having been initiated; but, it might.

- *Ian Hay (British author): "War is hell and all that, but it has a good deal to recommend it. It wipes out all the small nuisances of peace-time." (Note: among the "small nuisances" to which Hay alluded, he listed suffragettes, the tango, and golf).*

- *Jonathan Swift (Irish satirist): "War! that mad game the world so loves to play."*

All five of these proposed "causes" for war have been offered by anthropologists in response to the question of why small-scale societies go to war. They were never intended to necessarily apply to the so-called *state societies*. These are societies that have developed into very large, organized structures where there is virtually no familial relationship amongst the members, and it would be extremely rare for someone to know very many of the other members of the society. Examples of such *state societies* would be France, Spain, Iraq, Russia, the United States, and so on. So, is war really all that different in a state society? Perhaps; but, probably not.

At the risk of "getting political", consider the Second Iraq War. All Americans heard the Bush Administration's explanation for why they took the US to war – the perceived threat that Iraq had, or was developing, new *weapons of mass destruction* (although this rarely was discussed later, after it was established that there weren't any).   Absolutely nobody in the world believed it was possible for the United States to lose the war – not even Saddam Hussein. Some may have thought that it would get too bloody, too expensive, or too unpopular for the US to pursue it, and that the US would just quit and go home;   but, nobody actually thought Iraq would defeat the US. So, it was an opportunity to test US mettle, field test new weapons systems, hone strategic skills, and (at the same time) resolve a potential threat. At face value, this matches most closely to the final cause listed above (*war is entertainment*) . You may not like the term entertainment;   but, that is what it is usually called in anthropological circles.

Administration critics, however, offered several other possible reasons for the war:

♦ Many of the world's modern state societies (probably a majority of them) consider the United States to be inherently violent and aggressive. Some have blamed the war on this JWS (the so-called *John Wayne Syndrome*). This comes not just from unfriendly states;   some of America's best friends also view the US in this way.

♦ Some in the press suggested that the war was about personal revenge. Hussein had put a contract on the President's father (President George H. W. Bush) following the First Gulf War;   and, these critics maintain, the war was simply revenge by President George W. Bush for Hussein's audacity against his father.

♦ Some (such as documentary film-maker Michael Moore) claimed that the war was all about oil – that it was, in the final analysis, a war over resources.

That proposes four of the five recognized causes for war as a probable cause for the Second Gulf War. The only one not generally proposed was *war is a struggle for success*. But, Americans don't have to go very far to find a case where that was offered as the justification for American involvement in a war. In fact, the administration immediately preceding Bush (Bill Clinton) was indirectly (but rather obviously) accused of exactly that for the war in Kosovo in the movie *Wag the Dog* (starring Dustin Hoffman).

This is not a text on Political Science, so this text will take no position on any of these claims. What is clear, however, is that virtually all of the explanations for the Second Gulf War (*i.e.* the *War in Iraq*) between two *state societies* are the same as those traditionally proposed by anthropologists for *non-state societies*. So, it appears that there really isn't a great deal of difference after all.

The author does not believe that any US review of war can be concluded without referencing the early 20th century American Socialist, Eugene Victor Debs [1855-1926]. His views can best be summarized by quoting from a speech he gave in Canton, Ohio on June 16th, 1918. The US had entered World War I on April 6th of the preceding year, and Debs was an outspoken pacifist. In 1918, at the time of his speech, the US was deep in the throes of the war.

Debs (above) said "[Many of us] have come to realize ... that it is extremely dangerous to exercise the constitutional right of free speech in a country fighting to make democracy safe in the world. ... I realize that, in speaking to you this afternoon, there are certain limitations placed upon the right of free speech. I must be exceedingly careful, prudent, as to what I say, and even more careful and prudent as to how I say it. ... They have always taught and trained you to believe it to be your patriotic duty to go to war and to have yourselves slaughtered at their command. But in all the history of the world you, the people, have never had a voice in declaring war, and strange as it certainly appears, no war by any nation in any age has ever been declared by the people."

The reason for quoting Debs' speech is not to share the content of his talk as much as to introduce the fallout from it: as a direct result of this speech, Debs was arrested and charged with interfering with the American war effort. This was legally classified as *sedition*, and Debs was found guilty – solely on the reading of this speech into the court records. When he was sentenced (ironically, after the war had ended), Debs was a 63 year old man, in poor health, who had run for President in 1900, 1904, 1908 and 1912 (see below). He was sentenced to 10 years in prison, disenfranchised (all of his rights were stripped away), and his citizenship was revoked. Although legally no longer a US citizen, unable to campaign from his jail cell, and not even able to vote for himself, he again ran for President – from jail – in 1920. Despite not even being a citizen, Debs finished third – with 920,000 votes (3½%). Clearly, war "cuts deep" in the human psyche – on all sides.

One More Possibility

In addition to these 5 traditional causes for war, the 21st century has provided one more: *validation*. Historically, wars occurred between two territorial powers; but, beginning late in the 20th century, and culminating in the attacks on September 11th, 2001, the nature of war changed. The terrorist group *al Qaeda* essentially declared war on the United States and its allies. The US was a territorial power; but, al Qaeda was not. So, what could be posited as the potential cause of the attack (and others in a similar vein in Israel, England, France, Spain, Russia, *etc.*)? *Validation.* It seems that many of the terrorist attacks (wars?) that have been conducted go back to some group feeling marginalized, ignored, or oppressed by the established powers. Their actions are apparently motivated by a desire to address this imbalance.

Do these groups expect to "win" the war? Almost without exception, the answer is "no", if what is meant is a military victory by the attacker. However, if the goal of the action is to address the perceived imbalance, then "winning" is a very real possibility.

Footnote: US Presidential election results of 1912:

William Taft	Theodore Roosevelt	Woodrow Wilson	Eugene Debs
3,486,000	4,119,000	6,293,000	900,000

Effectively, what the terrorist group is seeking is validation. They are seeking to get the powers in place to acknowledge their valid right to participate in the process (the extent of this desired participation can vary from advisory to outright control of their own destiny). This would apply to *al Qaeda* (Muslim), *Provisional National Liberation Army* (Ireland), *Euskadi Ta Askatasuna* (Basque) , *Hezbollah* (Middle East), *Lashkar-e-Taiba* (Pakistan), *Kach and Kahane Chai* (Israel), *et cetera.*

The greatest danger in all of this is that – if the non-territorial group succeeds – what was once a "terrorist group" is usually written into history as freedom fighters, founding fathers, and heroes. For example, the *Sons of Liberty* became America's Founding Fathers, the *African National Congress* became the post-apartheid government of South Africa, and the rebel *Transitional National Council* evolved into the official post-Qaddafi Libyan government. Yet all of these were branded "terrorist" by the sitting powers when they first formed.

Bottom Line

Although anthropologists have proposed five possible different causes to account for war (and we have just added a sixth), exactly why a war begins is often less a clear, definable impetus than a function of the political viewpoint of the person making the call. Regardless of the cause, however, there can be little doubt that war is expensive, damaging, violent, and aggressive. As several have said (quotes above), "war is hell". And, this can be seen no more clearly than when Debs said that "it is extremely dangerous to exercise the constitutional right of free speech in a country fighting to make democracy safe in the world."

Chapter 15
Political Systems

Types of Groups

There are several types of human societies. Two of these were touched upon briefly in the previous chapters in order to see how they differed in their economies and their need for laws. What wasn't discussed was how these societies are actually structured. To begin, the method used most often to categorize them is the numerical size of the population involved. Although there are those who would further subdivide one or more of the following groupings, one of the most common identification schemes identifies just three basic groups. These are:

◆ Small–scale societies

◆ Tribal groups

◆ Political states

Small Scale Societies (S³)

Sometimes referred to as either *band societies* or *village societies*, these often survive as foragers, or hunter–gatherers, although they may also be small horticultural societies. They are – of necessity, and as their name implies – small in size. Why "of necessity"? Since they function without the presence of either a formal leader or anyone who specializes in law-and-order, they need a bond that firmly ties the members to each other and to the group as a whole. When societies become very large, this inevitably results in the inclusion of members with more distant, obscure, or even nonexistent ties; and, the social pressures inherent in strong kinship ties either weaken or disappear altogether. An illustration should make this clear:

> You, your siblings, your parents, their siblings, and the children of their siblings decide to pool financial resources, purchase 50,000 acres of undeveloped land in eastern Oklahoma, and relocate there –establishing your own rural, self-sufficient community (sort of a family survivalist center). Although you will technically still be subject to the laws of Oklahoma (and of the United States federal government), you will be too far

physically removed for either of these to be very concerned about you unless: (a) you notify them; (b) somebody files a complaint; or, (c) something blatantly and unignorably illegal occurs.

In practice, your new community will likely never contact either state or federal law officials, and communal law and order will rest informally, but effectively, with your new, local, kin-based society. In all probability, this will function quite well. Everyone in the community is related to everyone else, and no relationship is further separated than first cousin. To steal, assault, murder, rape, or in any other way violate the group's accepted ethical, social behavior, you must do so to your siblings, parents, aunts & uncles, or cousins – *because there isn't anyone else!*

In seventy years, you'll have great-grandchildren in the community, as will the others of your generation that originally founded the society. These children will be no closer than fourth cousins to each other. In addition, over the years, members of the community will meet and marry outsiders (since the alternative would be incestuous) – people they meet while away at college, on vacations, *et cetera*. So, there will be some in the community who will only be related through affinal bonds, and no longer even resemble the original family – with skin color, height, facial structure, hair and eye color, *et cetera* completely different than yours and the others who first formed this community.

Assuming that every family unit in the community will have 4 children, the original social grouping of 48 closely related souls will number 3,392 mostly remotely related souls (assuming that only your parents' generation will have died). The social pressures of kinship that had prevented inappropriate actions no longer applies for the newest generation; and, formal laws will be needed to maintain a functional society.

Clearly, if a society is to avoid law-and-order specialists, and avoid establishing a formal sovereign over them, the society must remain small in size. So, it is "of necessity" that the society be small in size.

Tribal groups

As small-scale societies grow, it seems inevitable that some of the key facts of life will also change. More people means there is a need for more food, clothing, shelter, energy resources, and so on. For a foraging society, natural resource level is fairly constant per unit of area over a general region. In other words, in the wild, only so many blackberries grow per acre. So, if you need more black-berries (or apples, or firewood, or whatever), the expanding group must also expand its territorial foraging. If the group doubles, it will need to scour twice the area to supply the same amount of re-source per person. Similarly, in horticultural societies, the amount of a crop harvested must increase to meet an expanding population.

When resources (be they food, clothing, shelter, energy, *etc*) are depleted, societies typically resort to more intensive production techniques. Rather than pick only apples that are within reach of the ground, trees may be scaled or even cut down to reach the fruit at the top of the tree; clubs and axes are replaced by spears and bows-and-arrows for hunting; horticulturalists often shift to more environmentally damaging practices to produce additional food; and, so on. Ultimately, as an area becomes more crowded with the increasing population, the potential for resource shortages increas-es and, while intensification occurs, competition for resources also becomes more aggressive.

This typically leads to two simultaneous developments: better, more formal, control of resource production; and, improved de-fense of what resources one has. In other words, the growing soci-ety coördinates the gathering or production of food and other re-sources to ensure there is a sufficient quantity; and, the society develops the necessary means to defend its resources from compe-titive groups to avoid losing control of them.

Anthropologists Allen Johnson and Timothy Earle, in <u>The Evolution of Human Societies from Foraging Groups to Agrarian States</u> (Stanford University Press; 2000) identify three major pro-cesses that result from this shift: economic intensification, social stratification, and political consolidation. That is, resource pro-duction is intensified (and better coördinated); a formal leadership pattern forms to organize and defend the group and its resources; and, society as a whole becomes stratified as the society develops a need for specialists (agrarian, technical, military, management, *etc*). This is the evolution of a small scale society into a *tribal group*.

Political states

As population continues to increase, resource coördination and management results in accumulated resources (requiring long term control to level sporadic surpluses and shortfalls), and restrictions begin to be applied to the local population which limit their flexibility in either joining or separating from the community. These processes lead tribal groups to evolve into what are commonly known as *political states*. Political states are those human groupings that typically have:

- grown very large in number;

- developed their resource production and management to a fine art (producing sufficient surpluses to withstand the vagaries of nature);

- formulated well-defined rules and laws to govern internal group behavior and maintain order among competing group members (while employing means to enforce them);

- established organized defense strategies (such as a military) to defend the group and its resources from external, competing groups; and,

- evolved into a collection of specialists, where each member of the group performs that function within the group which best serves both the individual and the group – relying on others to perform functions which they do not do as well.

Political states vary considerably in both size and resources:

- some are extremely large, but are modest in terms of *per capita* resource availability (*e.g.* China, numbering 1,350 million, or India, with 1,170 million);

- some are quite large, and have also excelled as producers of resources (*e.g.* the United States, numbering 307,000,000, or Japan, with 127,000,000);

- others (also quite large), have only modest resources available for members (*e.g.* Brazil, numbering 198,000,000);

- some are large, and have provided well for their members (*e.g.* France, with 62,200,000, and Germany, 83,000,000);

- other large societies only have modest resources available *per capita* (*e.g.* México, at 112,000,000);

- some are relatively small, but have provided well (very well) for the group members (*e.g.* Singapore, with just 4,600,000);

- others may be very small, but manage to effectively leverage their natural attributes to provide abundant resources (*e.g.* Brunei, at 384,000);

- some may even be extremely small, but still manage to provide very well for their followers (*e.g.* Monaco, numbering just 33,000)

- a few (ranging from small to extremely small) may, or may not, have well developed resources, but have other features that define them as political states (*e.g.* Palau with 21,000 residents – geographically isolated but defined by virtue of being an island; Vatican City with 557 residents, and religiously defined; Andorra with 84,000 souls, or San Marino with 30,000 – both topologically isolated and defined by mountains; or Albania with 3,600,000, and Macedonia with 2,100,000 – both of which are ethnically defined).

Regardless of the classification of a society (small-scale, tribal, political), or the relative size of the state (from tiny to enormous), the type of leadership that is employed is crucial to the success and continued existence of the group.

Types of Leaders

As was discussed [above], small scale societies are typically *acephalous* (literally, "headless"). The cohesion of the group usually relies on either the biological relationship of the members, or on a strong emotional bond shared by the group (*e.g.* the Old Order Amish, Hutterite, and Shaker communities – each bound by a shared theological, ecclesiastical vision). Tribal groups and political states are defined by their larger size and more organized infrastructure; they, therefore, all have some form of recognized leadership. But, the form that leadership takes (in any of these societies) may vary widely.

Elders

It is common in small scale societies for age and experience to be equated with wisdom. As a result, the *elders* of a community often exercise considerable influence over the group. It is not ac-tually a form of control;   but, it nevertheless has many of the earmarks of leadership. Although the Yakima were a tribal society, several of the smaller villages along the Columbia River (in Washington state) were virtually acephalous – relying on elders such as this [left] to guide their small scale community of foragers (fishing for salmon, and gathering roots, berries and nuts).

Shamans

Shamanism refers to the religious and magical practices of a group which accepts a particular individual (or group of individuals) as having a recognized ability to make contact with the spirit world. Through this contact, they are believed to be able to influence, or even control, certain supernatural forces. Particularly in small scale societies, this can be crucial to the welfare and survival of the group: essentially enlisting the spirits to aid in war, hunting, horticulture, health, *et cetera.* Shaman is from *šaman* in Tungusic (a language from Eastern Siberia), and has generally replaced the somewhat more derogatory term *medicine man.* This photo [above] is of a male Navajo shaman (shamans may be either male or female).

Big Man

As small scale societies begin to grow and expand, the changes listed above begin to occur. A need soon develops for leadership that can organize the group to intensify, and make more productive, their resource production. The individual who assumes this role is commonly known as a *big man.* Success is determined in large part by an ability to entice good workers to align with their group; and, this often depends on the apparent success and wealth of the group (nobody wants to join a starving group; but, everyone wants to join a winner).

In order to demonstrate this wealth and success, the big man holds what today would be called a party, or festival. He assembles all of the people in his group for a massive feast – inviting key members of competing groups in the area (those he would like to enlist), and proceeds to give them gifts of great recognized value. The hope is that the members of these other groups, seeing the material success of his group, will want to align themselves with his group. The problem is that competing groups, to keep their members firmly in line, respond with feasts of their own.

In the Pacific northwest, this annual feast became known as a *potlatch* (a Chinook word from the Nootka *patshatl*, that means "gift"). Rivalry being what it is, each big man had to outdo his rivals; so, the extravagance of the potlatch steadily escalated. The gifts became larger, more valuable, and more impressive. When they reached a point where there were no greater gifts to give, they began to destroy large quantities of valuable resources just to demonstrate that they had more than would ever be needed by their group. Many anthropologists believe that this blatant and frivolous generosity was one of the primary causes of their eventual communal implosion and societal collapse.

An important point to remember is that the big man actually had no more wealth than any other member of the group. He was essentially a highly respected entrepreneur – one who showed a talent for attracting good workers away from other groups, and had demonstrated success in organizing either their horticultural or foraging resource efforts. He was more akin to a *city manager* than a *mayor*. In other words, he had no real authority, but was effectively in the employ of the group to make the group more effective and successful. In the photo [right], a big man of the Kwakiutl (Hamasaka) is holding a *speaker's staff* (also called a *talking stick*). Pacific northwest natives always had a speaker's staff that was passed around during gatherings – the person holding the staff had the floor, and was the one to whom everyone else was supposed to be listening. He is also wearing what is known as a *button blanket* – a blanket with numerous decorative buttons (made from shells, bones, rare minerals, *et cetera*) sewn on. This was simply a highly visible sign of wealth – the group's wealth, not his personal wealth.

The presence of a big man could be considered the final stage of an acephalous small scale society, or the first stage of an emerging tribal society. Although he had no direct authority (indicative of a small scale society), he did wield tremendous influence over the success or failure of the group (indicative of a tribal society). The big man might be thought of as sort of a Small Scale – Tribal *leadership bridge*.

Chiefs

Tribal societies require a leader who maintains a level of actual control over the group. In addition to serving as the resource manager for the group, he also serves as the primary coördinator for their defense. Typically, the chief leads a tribal society comprised of multiple villages or bands. In return for management of both production and dispersal of resources, he receives direct payment (*i.e.* taxes). And, the chief uses the value of these payments to solidify his rank within the group. Contrary to popular American media myth, native American tribal chiefs (*i.e.* "Indian Chiefs") were neither vicious nor blood-thirsty. Some, such as Chief Joseph of the Nez Perce [left] only went to war when forced to do so; others, such as Chief Seathl (Seattle) of the Suquamish & Duwamish nations, avoided war at all costs.

Just as the Big Man can be seen as a bridge between the small scale and tribal societies, chiefdoms can exist in tribes of widely varying size. Small chiefdoms are sometimes difficult to distinguish from big man societies – the Kwakiutl, Tlingit, Duwamish and Suquamish groups of the Pacific northwest fall into this no-man's land between big men and well-established tribes. The most apparent feature that separates chiefdoms from big men societies is the social stratification that occurs in chiefdoms.

Social stratification is the process whereby an inherently elite layer of society forms, and from which its leaders are drawn. Other status levels or subgroups also form, and are indicative of a well defined cultural recognition of fundamentally unequal social rankings – from inferior to superior. We'll come back to this later in the chapter when the concept of *class* is reviewed.

Political states generally evolve one of five distinct forms of leadership: dictatorship, democracy, republicanism, monarchy, or committee rule. Although distinct (in the sense that they are readily, individually distinguishable), these are not necessarily discrete (in the sense of being separate, discontinuous forms).

Dictators

The definition of a dictator is "one who dictates; specifically, one who exercises, or in whom is vested, supreme authority in a state". The sense of a dictatorship being illegitimate or unwanted (by society) is entirely a connotation – a meaning attached to the word by common usage, but not actually part of the definition. Although holding the title "President", Fidel Castro [right] was the dictator of Cuba; *i.e.* he held "supreme authority". It is often assumed that the citizens of a political state are opposed to a dictatorship; but, there are many examples where they clearly are not. Although Pope Francis I holds supreme authority in the Vatican state (*i.e.* a dictator), Vatican residents clearly show no inclination or desire to remove him – *they chose him!*

Committees

In some states, authority resides with a committee that 'runs things'. Typically, the committee elects a chairman to serve as the front man for the committee with the society. This chairman may be little more than a spokesman for the committee; or, this chairman may assume extensive authority to the point where the committee becomes virtually powerless. Usually there is a balance some place in the middle. Xi Jinping [right] is the current General

Secretary of the Chinese Communist Party. Although he exercises great authority, he has nowhere near the level of authority that was exercised by Chairman Mao Tse-tung [left].

Republicanism

The third form that political state authority may take is what is known as *republicanism*, and this has nothing to do with the US political party of that name (the GOP; the Republican Party). The concept of republicanism is that supreme authority rests with the members of the society – the citizens; but, they maintain it would be impractical in a large group to ascertain the will of the citizens on every issue that arises. It would be too complex and time consuming for the more mundane issues, and would be grossly unresponsive in emergency situations (such as the bombing of Pearl Harbor, or the New York World Trade Towers terrorist attack).

Consequently, the members of the society select a few of their members to represent their wishes, and to act on their behalf. Occasionally, there is widespread agreement on who it will be that will represent the state to other political states in the world (*e.g.*

 President Reagan [left], who was re-elected with the support of 54,281,858 voters in 1984 – the largest plurality in American history). Reagan's impressive vote total accounted for 59.2% of those who expressed an opinion between him and former Vice President Walter Mondale; but, the greatest percentage approval of any candidate in history was the election of Warren G. Harding (over opponent James Cox) in 1920 – with 63.8% of the vote. Occasionally, the system used by a particular political state (*e.g.* the electoral college in the US) can result in someone winning the post with a minority of the citizens in support. Most Americans think this is extremely rare; but, it has actually occurred 11 times – John Q Adams, Zachary Taylor, James Buchanan, Abraham Lincoln, Rutherford B. Hayes, Grover Cleveland, Woodrow Wilson, Harry Truman, Richard Nixon, Bill Clinton, and George W Bush. On three occasions, the winner not only didn't have a majority, they didn't even have the most votes: JQ Adams, RB Hayes, and GW Bush.

Note: the lowest support level of any US President ever elected was John Quincy Adams (with just 29.9% of the vote). The next lowest, with only 39.9%, was Abraham Lincoln.

Hereditary Monarchs

At one point, most of the major societies in the world were led by hereditary monarchs (*i.e.* a King, Queen, Prince, *et cetera*). Gradually, this became less common; but, it still exists in a number of political states (more than most Americans suspect). The 37 modern states that maintain an hereditary monarchy include:

- Andorra (principality)
- Bahrain (kingdom)
- Belgium (kingdom)
- Bhutan (kingdom)
- Brunei (sultanate)
- Cambodia (kingdom)
- Denmark (kingdom)
- Japan (empire)
- Jordan (kingdom)
- Kuwait (emirate)
- Lesotho (kingdom)
- Liechtenstein (principality)
- Luxembourg (duchy)
- Malaysia (kingdom)
- Monaco (principality)
- Morocco (kingdom)
- Nepal (kingdom)
- Netherlands (kingdom)
- Norway (kingdom)
- Oman (sultanate)
- Qatar (emirate)
- Saint Kitts & Nevis (kingdom)
- St Vincent & the Grenadines (kingdom)
- Saudi Arabia (kingdom)
- Spain (kingdom)
- Swaziland (kingdom)
- Sweden (kingdom)
- Thailand (kingdom)
- Tonga (kingdom)
- United Arab Emirates (7 autonomous emirates)
- UK (kingdom)

In addition to these, there are other political states where the status of the monarchy is more symbolic than anything else; so, unless a state indicates that it is a monarchy, they have not been included here (examples of others would include Australia, Canada, New Zealand, and other member states of the British Commonwealth). The photo [above] is of the reigning British monarch, Queen Elizabeth II.

The authority level of a monarch can vary dramatically. In most of the states listed above, the monarch is limited in power by an elected parliament (*e.g.* UK, Norway, *etc.*); but, in some cases, the authority of the monarch is virtually absolute and unrestricted (*e.g.* Oman, Brunei, Qatar, *et cetera*).

Democracy

Most Americans believe (incorrectly) that the United States is a democracy; but, a democracy leaves all decisions to the citizens of the political state. In a country the size of the United States, this would require a massive interactive communication system. In fact, this was proposed by Independent Presidential candidate H. Ross Perot in 1992; but, it does not currently exist. What most Americans think is democracy is really republicanism (page 174). One of the very few places where true democracy (often, "pure

democracy") is the governing system for a political entity is in the New England Town Meeting*, where every citizen is invited to participate in, and help formulate, all governmental decisions.

Communism – in its theoretical form – is virtually identical to pure democracy. An example of this was given in the reference to *Brook Farm* [page 115].

Stratified Society & Class Divisions

Social stratification was mentioned (and defined) on page 172. At that point, it was stated that we would "come back to this later in this chapter when the concept of *class* is reviewed." Well, we're here. So, what do we mean by social stratification?

Stratification is a process whereby we form, or arrange, in strata, or layers. In the case of social stratification, this consists of dividing a society into layers – with each layer having particular functions, responsibilities, privileges, prestige, and status.

The average layman recognizes only 2 or 3 social strata, or class distinctions. But, there are several other recognized systems related to class categorization. Typically, societies identify class distinctions with levels of power, wealth, education, or birth. In some societies (*e.g.* the United States), the idea of social classes is considered offensive, as many associate the founding of the society with a presumption of equality, *i.e.* the elimination of class distinctions. Communist states typically reject it outright. RH Tawney, in his book Equality (1931), wrote that "The word 'class' is fraught with unpleasing associations, so that to linger upon it is apt to be

---

* Photo is public domain photo of a Town Meeting gathering in Plymouth, Massachusetts. All resident adults are invited to participate.

interpreted as the symptom of a perverted mind and a jaundiced spirit."* Sociologist Paul Blumberg referred to class as "America's forbidden thought."# So, let's tread forbidden ground and exercise our perverted minds – in other words, let's take a look at *class*.

Traditional Class Structure

Traditionally, there were just two social classes: *upper class* and *lower class*. This was exemplified in the British BBC situation comedy *Keeping Up Appearances*, starring Patricia Routledge as "Hyacinth Bucket" (pronounced *bouquet*). In the show (frequently shown in reruns on American PBS stations), Hyacinth is clearly a member of the British *lower class* who has an indomitable drive to stake her claim to recognition as a member of the British *upper class* – to no avail. Examples of terms that would generally fall into one of the two classes in this scheme include:

Upper Class	Lower Class
Rich	Poor
Employer	Worker
Landlord	Tenant
Bourgeois	Proletariat
Polished	Boorish
Couth	Uncouth
Aristocratic	Common
Educated	Uneducated
Skilled	Unskilled

The list could go on and on; but, these 9 pairings should suffice to illustrate the point. Note that, although Americans prefer to consider the United States a class free society (classless is something altogether different), the US clearly has a tacit class system. It may not be as well entrenched or recognized as the British system; but, it's there.

Popular Class Structure

Nobody likes to be considered *lower class*; but, few can lay legitimate claim to being *upper class* (as Hyacinth always discovers). What to do? In popular terminology, a third class is inserted

---

* Quoted in Fussell, Paul (1983) Class: A Guide through the American Status System (New York: Simon & Schuster).
# *ibid.*

between the two traditional classes: the *middle class* (essentially an American invention that has spread globally). It provides a class label, or distinction, that carries none of the pejorative associations tied to the term "lower class", while not claiming the elite status of being the "upper class". In fact, Americans appear to accept the idea that 'lower class' refers only to the dregs of society, and that 'upper class' is elitist and snobbish. This makes recognition of oneself as middle class to be the optimal distinction in the United States. It connotes the idea of having earned one's status, rather than having either failed miserably or having had it handed to them. Examples of where terms would generally fall in a three class scheme include:

Upper Class	Middle Class	Lower Class
Rich	Comfortable	Poor
Employer	Management	Worker
Landlord	Superintendent	Tenant
Royalty	Bourgeois	Proletariat
'Cultured'	Polite	Crude
Aristocratic	Privileged	Common
Prestigious Education	Functional Education	Uneducated
Professional	Skilled	Unskilled

Theoretically, if there are two classes, one might expect that the size of each class would be comparable. Similarly, with three classes, one might also expect that their populations would be either comparable or "bell shaped". In other words, as a percentage of the population, one might expect either an even distribution (*e.g.* 33–34–33), or some sort of a *normal distribution* (*e.g.* 20–60–20). Studies have repeatedly shown, however, that this is not the case.

Consider the United States, for example. If we were to use family income as the criterion on which to base class distinction (although not exclusively so, it is arguably a dominant criterion in American society), the "break points" for 2007 that would have divided the three classes at 20 – 60 – 20 would have been $19,178 and $91,705. By comparison, if the distribution were to be 33 – 34 – 33, these break points would have been about $30,000 and $65,000.

To put that into simpler terms: if we were to use an "even" three class scheme (based on family income in 2007), the three classes would consist of:

- **Lower Class**   families with an income below $30,000/yr;
- **Middle Class**   families earning more than $30,000/yr, but less than $65,000/yr; and,
- **Upper Class**   families earning more than $65,000/yr.

By comparison, if we use a *normal distribution* of 20–60–20, the three classes shift to:

- **Lower Class**   families with an income below $19,178/yr;
- **Middle Class**   families earning more than $19,178/yr, but less than $91,705/yr; and,
- **Upper Class**   families earning more than $91,705/yr.

Interestingly, however, Americans with an annual family income of a hundred thousand dollars per year (or more) usually consider themselves to be middle class. The reason is quite simple: to identify yourself as upper class carries the connotation of elitism, snobbishness and self-aggrandizement; by comparison, self identification as lower class carries a connotation of shiftlessness, failure and worthlessness. Polls have repeatedly shown that nearly 90% of Americans self-identify as being *middle class*, while less than 10% self-identify as "lower class". An amazingly paltry 1–2% self identify as "upper class". If this were graphed based on income (2007), it would be:

- **Lower Class**   families with an income below $12,000/yr;
- **Middle Class**   families earning between $12,000/yr and $250,000/yr;
- **Upper Class**   families earning more than $250,000/yr.

Common Sociological Class Structure

Sociologists and anthropologists recognize the difficulty in trying to force an entire society into just 2 or 3 strata – recognizing the negative attachments that are often associated with the top and bottom classes (and the resultant "rush to the middle", as was seen in the American polling results). As a consequence, the most common class structure scheme utilized by academics is a five tiered system. In this system, descriptors that would normally be applied would include:

Designation	Financial	Power	Social	Education
Lower Class	Poor	Powerless	Excluded	None
Lower Middle	Struggling	Blue collar	Awkward	Little formal
Middle Class	Comfortable	White collar	Uncomfortable	HS – AA
Upper Middle	Well off	Managerial	Comfortable	College
Upper Class	Rich	Powerful	Enviable	Top College

The obvious advantage to this class structure scheme is that, by dividing society into five strata, it allows for a level of differentiation that the more common "three level scheme" doesn't provide. In addition, the terms upper and middle don't seem to have the same sting when followed by "middle". If we look at 2007 American society (as we did above), we find that these five classes will divide, on an even basis, as follows:

- *Lower Class*   none   to $19,178
- *Lower Middle Class* $19,178   to $34,920
- *Middle Class* $34,920   to $56,984
- *Upper Middle Class* $56,984   to $91,705
- *Upper Class* $91,705   to   unlimited

Paul Fussell's Class Structure

Paul Fussell, from whose book we quoted RH Tawney [page 176], has gone one step further – dividing society into nine distinct strata, or classes. He adds these additional strata because he claims that his research indicates that there are actually some classes of which society, as a whole, is generally unaware. As a result, he ends up with these nine classes (along with his definitions):

- *Bottom Out-of-Sight* Prison inmates; mental hospital patients, *etc.*
- *Destitute*   Homeless, Bums, Bag Ladies, Town Drunks, *etc.*
- *Low Proletarian*   Longshoremen, Migrant, Labor, Undocumented, *etc.*
- *Mid Proletarian*   Secretaries, Technicians, En. Military, Factory, *etc.*
- *High Proletarian*   Teachers, Carpenters, Plumbers, Electricians, *etc.*
- *Middle Class*   Engineers, Military Officers, Managers, Clergy, Small Business Owners, *et cetera.*
- *Upper Middle*   Doctors, Lawyers, College Professors, Recognized Sports & Entertainment Stars, *etc.*
- *Upper*   Inherited or Earned Wealth – on display..
- *Top Out-of-Sight*   Inherited Wealth – not seen by the public.

Notice that in Fussell's system, it is not strictly a matter of income; it's a combination of income and occupational prestige (actually in keeping with our national recognition of individuals). In one of the best indications of how the American public identifies a "superior person", it is not through polls or questionnaires, but in national elections. Consider the following statistics:

- Since 1900: Theodore Roosevelt, Franklin Delano Roosevelt, John F Kennedy, George H W Bush, George Bush, and Barack Obama all went to Harvard; and,
- William H Taft and William J Clinton both went to Yale.
- In the 29 quadrennial presidential elections from 1900 through 2012, over 48% of the winners attended either Harvard or Yale; and,
- During the same 29 election cycles, the winner attended either an Ivy League school or a US Military Academy over 72% of the time.

The reason that these figures are indicative of the American view of superiority is that, statistically, based on the number of schools they could have come from:

- less than one-half of one-tenth of one percent should have come from either Harvard or Yale (not the 48% that did – 964 times the expected result); and,
- less than three-tenths of one percent should have come from either the Ivy League or a Military Academy (instead of the 72% who did – 260 times the expected).

Evidently, the American view of class superiority dictates that the likelihood of being elected president goes up by a factor of nearly 260 if you go to an Ivy League school or a Military Academy; and, it goes up a whopping 928 times if you graduate from either Harvard or Yale. It seems to influence even being nominated: *e.g.* John Kerry went to Yale; and, Mitt Romney, Michael Dukakis and George McGovern all went to Harvard.

Most anthropologists acknowledge that virtually all cultures have some form of class structure, but modify them to distinguish between an *open class system* and a *closed class system*. To these anthropologists, a closed system is one in which it is impossible, or at least highly improbable, that someone can rise above their class into what is perceived by society as a higher class; by contrast, an open system is one in which it is relatively easy to migrate up or down the hierarchy. Typically, these anthropologists identify the

United States as having one of the most open systems in the world. But, it appears to be far more difficult to change classes than some might have you believe.

In the example of the presidential elections, there is a tremendous correlation with the two premier northeastern colleges (Harvard and Yale); and, admission to Harvard or Yale appears often to be less a question of merit than a result of the American class system. This results from what is commonly called the *legacy system* – *i.e.* if a parent attended the college, the child is virtually guaranteed entrance. Consider the following example.

> The Bush family has had 18 family members attend Yale since 1800. President George W. Bush graduated high school near the middle of his high school class rankings, but was admitted to Yale as a legacy admission (despite having grades considered inadequate for admission) because his grandfather had been a Yale trustee. And, it reportedly continued: in 2004, it was reported Yale academically rejected a student (Jay Blount) who turned out to be the boyfriend of Barbara Bush (one of the President's twin daughters). The President wrote a letter to Yale, and within a month, Blount was not only granted admission, but was awarded a full first-year scholarship.*

The American class system is more open than most, but it does not appear to be as open as some sociologists and anthropologists claim it to be. Who says America ignores class status?

---

* Derived from the article *Admission to Yale: The Unfair Legacy Continues* by Eric Jaffa on www.moveleft.com (April 18, 2005).

Section IV
Otherness

Otherness is the anthropological analysis of a natural human function: the "other". All human groups, as well as a number of our closer animal kingdom relatives (*e.g.* gorillas, chimpanzees, bonobos, *et cetera*) and even some very, very distant relatives (*e.g.* porpoises, dogs, cats, *et cetera*), have a tendency to recognize which individuals "belong", and which do not. We instinctively label certain individuals as being peers, as viable members of the social collective to which we belong. Even animals do this: you'll notice this if you ever introduce a new cat to a household that already has 2 or more. The "new cat" likely will be repelled, threatened, or even attacked by the "old cats". The reason is quite simple: "she's not one of us!" After a period of this, they will gradually accept that the new kid isn't going anywhere, and will begin to include her in the household hierarchy. Dogs at a public dog park will often congregate and play with other dogs of the same or a similar breed even if they don't know each other (the author's Sheltie is definitely a "breedist").

Humans do essentially the same thing. The question arises, however, as to how to determine the boundaries of the social collective. How do we determine what defines whether someone new "fits in" or not? And, is the criterion chosen a social distinction, or is there some biological distinction?

There are numerous criteria that might be used. For example, a social group could be determined on the basis of:

- race
- class
- school attended
- accent
- faith/religion
- neighborhood
- sports team allegiance
- personal experiences

- ethnicity
- caste
- fraternity/sorority
- income
- political views
- marriage
- hobbies
- caste
- and many, many more

- nationality
- legal status
- state/region of birth
- language
- job
- sexual orientation
- interests
- dialect spoken

We'll take a look at the predominant sources of *otherness* encountered in the United States (and elsewhere) in Chapters 18 and 19. But, in order to determine whether those sources are inherent, biological, and genetic (rather than social and physically arbitrary), there needs to be a better understanding of the *human genome*. To do that, this course uses a video by Dr. Spencer Wells in class (this PBS documentary is also available in book form from Princeton University Press).

Chapter 16
Journey of Man (part 1)

The *human genome* is the complete set of genetic information that is stored in deoxiribonucleic acid (*i.e.* DNA) sequences in 23 chromosome pairs in the human cell nucleus and in a small molecule in the cell but outside the nucleus (known as *mitochondrial DNA*). There is an international, scientific, research project known as the *Human Genome Project* that began work in 1990. The goal was to "map" the more than 3.3 billion nucleotides that make up the entire DNA string. Initially funded by the US Federal Government (the National Institutes for Health and Department of Energy), the hope was that this information could potentially lead to new therapies for certain human diseases.

Nearly all of the research has been done in Universities and Research Centers in the US, UK, Australia, France, Japan and Spain. Although initially laid out as a 15 year effort, a rough draft of the entire human genome was jointly announced by President Bill Clinton and Prime Minister Tony Blair on June 26, 2000 – five years ahead of schedule. The speed at which this mega-project was completed resulted from financial support from several foreign sources, as well as impressive scientific collaboration from several international sources. The entire "genome map" was declared complete on April 14, 2003 (again, ahead of schedule).

Two years later (April 13, 2005), the *National Geographic Society* and *IBM* jointly launched *The Genographic Project*. The intent of this multi-year project was to collect thousands of DNA samples from populations around the world to be able to use the human genome data to map the historical spread of human populations. The Project Director (a *National Geographic Explorer-in-Residence*) since its inception has been Dr. Spencer Wells (right). Wells, a professor at Cornell University, published *The Journey of Man: A Genetic Odyssey* in 2002, and later wrote the PBS/National Geographic documentary by the same name.

Part 1 of the PBS video introduces the genetic methodology used by Dr. Wells. Once that is established, he traces human ancestry from its "beginning" in southern east central Africa. Wells maintains that the genetic evidence is conclusive that all modern human beings are descended from a single human male that lived in Africa between 60,000 and 90,000 years ago. Wells follows the male line because he analyzes the DNA on the Y-chromosome (the chromosome that makes males male). This gets passed from father to son every generation without change (although there are periodic, accidental alterations in the DNA sequence, known as *mutations*). By following these mutations, Wells can follow the flow of humanity across the globe as it migrated out from Africa, and can place approximate dates for when these migrations occurred. Genetic researchers at Oxford University in England (*e.g.* Dr. Bryan Sykes) have concentrated primarily on mitochondrial DNA, which similarly flows from mother to child without change. The results of the work by Wells and Sykes reveal nearly identical findings as to paths, processes, and dates for the global spread of humanity.

In Part 1 of the documentary, Dr. Wells begins in Africa with the !Kung people (*a.k.a.* Bushmen). He identifies this tribe as the "oldest" human population on earth, and then looks at when (and why) some of them migrated out of Africa. He then follows this first migratory wave out of Africa, across India, and into Australia (the source of the Aborigine population).

A second wave of migration followed later bringing humans through Central Asia down into India and east (both to the north and south around the mountains) into China. Another group went west across the steppes and into modern Europe.

Chapter 17
Journey of Man (part 2)

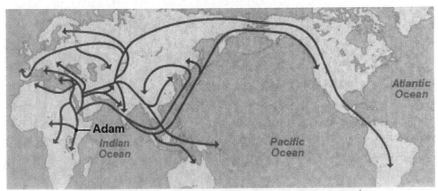

The Genographic Project **Migration Map**[*]

In Part 2 of the documentary, we join Dr. Wells as he follows the Central Asians we met in part 1 westward into Europe, and eastward into Siberia and on to the Americas.   The map (above) illustrates the various paths that appear to have been followed by early humans as they spread across the globe. If any student is really curious, this web site will sell you a DNA self-test kit[#] which they will then analyze and provide detailed information regarding either your mitochondrial DNA or Y-chromosone DNA markers (either, but not both) from which you can trace you're ancestors' journey around the world.

After exploring their journey into Europe, Dr. Wells follows the other group up into Siberia, visitng the Chukchi people north of the Arctic Circle. From here, the last ice age provided a pathway to the Americas. The lower sea levels during the ice age enabled them to cross what is now the Bering Sea into Alaska. As the ice

---

[*] Map, courtesy of *The Genographic Project*, shows the migratory paths of humanity based on more than 10,000 DNA samples from indigenous populations around the world. Map and further information are available at:
https://genographic.nationalgeographic.com.

[#] Cost of the kit, including testing, analysis and reports is $100 plus S&H.

age ended, the rising sea levels cut off retreat and opened an ice-free corridor south along the Rockies into central North America.

Dr. Wells visited with Navaho natives in the American southwest, and then followed their spread throughout North America and then down the land bridge (*i.e.* Central America) to South America (the last of the continents to be inhavited).

The purpose of Wells' documentary (and the reason it is embedded into this course) is to show that all of the "others" that we see in the world (different races, ethnicities, *et cetera*) are, in fact, all "cousins" descended from a common ancestor. The various divisions and markers humanity commonly uses to distinguish between their peer group and outsiders are, without exception, social inventions and not biological facts.

Chapter 18
The Other: Race, Ethnicity, Caste

The 'Caste System'

The caste system is: (a) nearly exclusively restricted to the Indian sub-continent; and, (b) a perfect example of a closed class system. The questions regarding caste thus become:

- What is the caste system?

- How many castes are there, and what are they?

- How did it come into existence, and what maintains it?

- Just how rigid, or closed, is it?

We begin with an introduction into how it came into existence in the first place, and what maintains it today. First, the term *caste* is the English word for this class structure; it is not the term used by Indians. In fact, the English term is the Anglicization of a Portuguese term, *casta*. This was the term Portuguese invaders used to describe the ritualistic, social and task divisions they discovered when they first encountered Indian society. Technically, in Portuguese, *casta* refers to one's "lineage or ancestry". The earliest apparent references to the system appear in the *Ṛg Veda* (the oldest Hindu scripture, generally attested to have been written down around 1500 BCE, and – based on astronomical references – originating orally perhaps as early as 4000 BCE).

The system was "clarified" in the *Manu Smriti* (*circa* 200 CE), and four *varnas* were identified: the *Brahmin, Kshatriya, Vaishya,* and *Shudra*. These varnas are to what most Westerners are referring when they use the term caste. The problem is that it gets more confusing – much more confusing. Non-Hindus also use the term *sub-caste*; and, this is not actually referring to divisions of the varnas as much as it is to the many Hindu *jati*.

A jati is essentially a community which shares something in common. This may be based on any of several attributes, such as:

- occupation (similar to the mediæval European feudal craft guilds);

- language (or dialect, since five to six thousand years ago, the predominant languages of today were still dialects of Sanskrit – just as 1600 years ago, the Romance languages of today were still dialects of Latin);

- religion (Hinduism is actually a collective term for a number of very different religions from "beyond the Indus River" – from which the term *Hindu* came);

- origin (*e.g.* a common historical or mythical ancestor); or,

- homeland (*i.e.* the specific geographical area from which they originally came).

In practice, the four varnas serve as collective groupings for dozens, if not hundreds, of different jati. So, on the surface, the jati might appear both to be true sub-sets of the varnas as well as based almost exclusively on occupation. It might appear that way; but, caution must be taken not to draw that conclusion too quickly.

The four varnas are hereditarily passed patrilineally, and typically refer to a general class of people who perform certain functions within the society. The members of each varna, however, are not restricted to only those occupations associated with their varna. For example, India has become a major supplier of IT (information technology or computing) to the world. A very large percentage of these specialists belong to the Brahmin varna; but, technically, this occupational jati would be a better match for the Vaishya varna.

Some sources refer to the varnas as being "psychological categories". That is, they refer to a person's frame of mind, and attest to their *karmic* status (the result of their actions in past lives). In any case, the four varnas are usually described as:

- ◆ **Brahmin** – priests; teachers; educators; advisors;
- ◆ **Kshatriya** – kings; princes; warriors; nobility;
- ◆ **Vaishya** – merchants; craftsmen; skilled workers; businessmen; and,
- ◆ **Shudra** – unskilled workers; farmers.

Below these four varnas, as a sort of foundation stone for them, is the group commonly known as the "untouchables". Historically, there have been several different terms used to name this group: the Aryans, 4000 years ago, called them *dasas* ("slaves"); members of the group prefer the term *dalit* ("the oppressed"); and, Mohandas Gandhi insisted on calling them the *harijan* ("the children of God"). So, whatever they're called, what is this group?

When fairer-skinned Aryans emerged in northern India nearly 5,000 years ago, they differed from the darker-skinned Dravidians. The earliest caste system thus appears to have been a means for the fair Aryans to avoid assimilation with the darker Dravidians. As time passed, the indigenous dasas developed numerous occupationally based jati; and, these jati became highly protectionist – *i.e.* carpenters wanted to protect their occupational knowledge from being usurped, and others (blacksmiths, potters, *et cetera*) wanted the same thing. As a result, informal rules began to evolve that restricted entry into these jati, the marriage of children in each jati, and so forth. At this point, the jati were virtually identical in form, structure, and goals with the craft guilds of mediæval Europe.

Gradually, the jati system merged with the Aryan caste system to form the four major varnas known today. Although there are alternative theories, the most likely source for the word *varna* is the Indo-European root *var-*, meaning "color". All of the recognized occupations were represented by a specific jati; and, groupings of these jati were collectively assigned to particular varnas.

What had never been organized into one of the nascent craft guilds were the most offensive of the tasks that must be done in any society: the removal and handling of human waste, the removal and disposal of dead animal carcasses, the processing of animal waste into fuel packets, *et cetera.* These tasks still must be done today. For example, fresh cow manure and straw are mixed, formed into bricks, sun

dried, and sold as a fuel source to local householders – *by the harijan!**

It is widely believed that the "untouchableness" of these people resulted from the fact that their community gradually developed an immunity to many of the bacteria and diseases associated with the tasks they were performing, while the general population had no such immunity. In an age prior to antiseptics, antibacterial compounds, and antibiotics, contact with these people could lead to illness or death. As a result, they were severely restricted from contact with the general population. It was believed that even their shadow falling on you could result in illness. Actually, this was quite possibly true, as a human sneeze is approximately coterminal with a human shadow.

Local rules and laws regarding the mixing and integration of the various jati (and their superstructure, the varnas) became commonplace. Always on the outside of these legal systems were the untouchables – the *dasas*; the *dalits*; the *harijan*. As foreigners entered India, they were gradually enmeshed into the existing social structure following a period in which they were assessed and evaluated. This was not a formal practice, but an informal process that simply evolved over time. During the period of exclusion and evaluation, non-caste individuals were considered *malecha*.

Actually, the caste system initially provided a stratified and hierarchical socio-economic organization to society that gave their racially and ethnically complex society a sense of order and stability, with people classified according to their profession, societal role, economic place, and heritage. The Aryans had introduced a whole new range of professions and roles unfamiliar to the Dravidians. No longer was everyone a farmer. In fact, it was impossible to be a farmer, priest, merchant and warrior all at the same time. The caste system provided structure and discipline to this social chaos. This very rigidity, however, also led to its problems.

---

* The photo (page 191), taken by the author, is of a young Harijan boy taking a load of "manure bricks" into Agra to be sold to a distributor. Most of the homes in Agra use these bricks to heat their homes and fuel their stoves. He will walk about 6 hours in each direction to make the sale, and then repeats this task every day of the week.

By the end of the second century CE, most of the rules associated with the system had become universally accepted throughout the society. It was at this point that the *Muni Smriti* was written, documenting just what these rules were, and how they were to be observed.

Unquestionably, the caste system is not an egalitarian social construct. It recognizes an innate difference in people, blames the individual for membership in an inferior varna (as a result of past life *karma*), and then codifies it for all to observe. Nevertheless, it provided India and Nepal with a means to confront the most devilish of social problems: social inequality, blatant racial divisions, and perhaps even invader–inhabitant co-existence.

In 1950, the Constitution of the newly independent Republic of India removed the legal basis for the caste system. In many parts of the country, prior to the new Constitution, untouchables had been required to wear a bell to warn others of their approach, to live outside the town, to use a separate well for water, never to enter higher caste homes or businesses, and to restrict their roles to the jobs that nobody else would do (such as molding fresh manure into blocks for fuel). Gandhi had forced the leadership to rename the untouchables as children of God (*harijan*); but, that did little to help, for the harijan preferred to call attention to their plight by using the more descriptive term *dalit* ("the oppressed").

Illegal for more than half a century; actively discouraged by leaders of the Hindu religion; forcibly undermined by the government (by enacting mandatory affirmative action quotas in jobs, colleges, and other civil functions); and, yet, the system flourishes. Pick up any major newspaper in India, and there are pages dedicated to finding suitable mates for their sons and daughters – *broken down by caste!* It is believed that perhaps up to ¾ of all marriages in India are still arranged by the parents; and, to these parents, these caste divisions are so ingrained in their thought that virtually nothing will alter it. It is the ultimate closed class system.

The Basic Race / Ethnicity Concept

It seems fairly common for anthropology and sociology texts to sort of gloss over the underlying concept behind the ideas of race and ethnicity. What is usually missing is the underlying concept of "the other". Too often, people concentrate on some of the various ways in which we *identify* and *classify* these others, rather than look at the basic reasoning behind why humans have such an obvious issue with others in the first place.

It is a natural tendency for all humans (and many animals) to divide the world population into us and them. *Us* includes all of those individuals whom we consider to belong to the same group to which we belong; *them* is everybody else. In other words, there is 'our group and everyone in it', and there are all the 'others, those who belong to some other group'.

There are several terms which are used to define membership in these groups. At this point, those that are of immediate interest are *race* and *ethnicity*. When a group of any kind is established, there needs to be some measure by which it can be determined whether or not someone "belongs" in that group. These are not always crystal clear, and may overlap; but, there are some clearly predominant methods that are used. For example:

When people are categorized by:	we tend to rely primarily on:
◆ **RACE**	physical features, biological characteristics, ancestry, and earliest region of origin.
◆ **ETHNICITY**	more recent region of origin, ancestry, language, or culture.

These categories can overlap, and occasionally the same term is used in multiple contexts. For example, *Franco-American* is used to describe an American, but is modified by "Franco", which may apply to either nationality (someone whose family came from France), ethnicity (*e.g.* someone whose family is from Québec), or even linguistically (someone who speaks French, such as someone from Geneva, Switzerland).

These groupings are neither good nor bad in and of themselves. Although they tend to isolate people by turning them into others, they also tend to reinforce family and social bonds in a climate in which the gradual deterioration of these bonds is highly likely. What we need to understand is which of these groupings are actually what they claim to be, and which of them are essentially smokescreens that have been adopted for the primary purpose of identifying and excluding others.

What do we mean by smokescreen? Consider two of the better known organizations in the black–white continuum: the NAACP, and NO-FEAR.

- African-Americans founded and generally support the NAACP (the *National Association for the Advancement of Colored People*). This organization first met in February, 1909 to provide a means of advancing both individual and collective social stand-

  ing for people of color. One of the founding members (and first editor of their magazine, <u>Crisis</u>) was William Edward Burghardt DuBois (the first African-American to ever earn a Ph.D. from Harvard). Better known as WEB DuBois [right], Dr. DuBois recognized that it would be impractical to have a Nigerian-American Club, or a Ghanian-American Club to parallel existing Caucasian groups (*e.g.* Italian-American or Irish-American) because, unlike whites, a majority of African-Americans have no concrete knowledge of their actual heritage – having been forcibly relocated by the slave trade just a few centuries earlier, and having had all records of their background systematically and deliberately destroyed.

- Another race-focused organization was known as N.O.F.E.A.R. (the *National Organization For European-American Rights*). This organization claimed to stand for the protection and res-

  toration of what they perceived as the erosion of Caucasian rights in the United States. The group was forced by a trademark infringement lawsuit (from the *No Fear* clothing company) to change its name – to EURO (the *European-American Unity and Rights Organization*). Under either name, it is simply a later incarnation of the NAAWP (the *National Association for the Advancement of White People*) founded in

1980 by David Duke [photo]. Duke (the one-time Grand Wizard of the Knights of the Ku Klux Klan, and 1988 Populist Party presidential candidate) founded the group specifically to support "white rights" at the expense of minority rights. In fact, Dr. Duke, as he likes to be called (the degree is an honorary one from a correspondence school in Ukraine) was quoted by a doctoral candidate who traveled with him as saying "We don't want Negroes around. We don't want Negroes around. ... That's in no way exploitive at all. We want our own society, our own nation."

It should appear obvious to all but perhaps the most bigoted observer that the NAACP is a legitimate, productive organization; and, that the NAAWP – NOFEAR – EURO is little more than an organizational smokescreen to provide a forum for a racist platform. When encountering any organization that seems to focus on the concept of other, make the effort to determine if it has a history of "reinforcing family and social bonds in a climate in which the gradual deterioration of these bonds is highly likely", or whether it has demonstrated a knack for simply "isolating people and turning them into others".

Race

It is not uncommon for genetic variation to often be greater within a specific race than it is between races. Let's make this as clear as possible: *race is a social invention; there is absolutely no genetic or biological basis for it.* That is not to say that skin color is a social invention; obviously, there are differences in the color of people's skin. But, this does not indicate any fundamental biological or genetic difference between the two people. It is merely an easy way to be able to identify who belongs to the other group. It is no more significant than categorizing people by hair color or eye color.

It is a well established maxim of science that genetic discontinuities do not occur across human populations. In other words, skin color tends to change progressively as one moves about the globe – there is no magic line on one side of which people are white, and the other side of which people are black. In point of fact, everybody is blue and orange! Artists (particularly water colorists)

Even if there are provable genetic differences, the question has to be asked as to whether those differences are sufficient to label a group as a separate race; and, this raises the question of "just what is a *race*?". This is not as easy an answer as some would want you to believe.

Webster defines *race* as "the descendants of a common ancestor; a family, tribe, people, or nation, believed to belong to the same stock." This is far too broad and encompassing to be useful to an anthropologist; under that definition, you could belong to the Smith race, the New England race, or the Apache race. It might work for the layman, but nobody within the scientific community would ever accept such a broad definition.

Webster also offers a *biological* definition for the term: "a group within a species, having similar characteristics which do not sufficiently distinguish from the specific type to form a separate species." On a cursory basis, this appears to be a much more restrictive definition; but, it really isn't. It is still a frustratingly broad definition.

Having blue eyes and blond hair (which the "typical" Swede has) are "similar characteristics which do not sufficiently distinguish from the specific type to form a separate species". In other words, blue eyes and blond hair may be genetic differences, but they don't rise to the level of creating a separate *species*; *i.e.* they are still human. So, by Webster's biological definition, Swedes could be considered a separate race. It is doubtful, however, that you would ever find a scientist (nor layman) who would agree.

You might, however, find a politician to agree. The US Census is an official product of the United States federal government; so, it should serve as an indicator of the official government position regarding race. And, it does. What it shows is that the US is remarkably inconsistent regarding this subject. In the 1930 census, Americans were provided with a list of 13 different races to which they might belong! These races* were:

---

* ------- *Fifteenth Census of the United States* (1930) (Washington, DC: United States Government Printing Office).

- White
- Chinese
- Hindu
- Malay
- Indian (*i.e.* Native American)

- Negro
- Japanese
- Korean
- Siamese

- Mexican
- Filipino
- Hawai'ian
- Samoan

By the most common current standards, this list of 13 "races" actually includes 2 races, 6 nationalities, 2 island isolates, 2 regions, and a religion.

In 1977, the OMB (Office of Management and Budget) issued Statistical Policy Directive #15. This directive collapsed the racial listing (which had varied from census to census) to just 4. In addition, they added 2 new ethnicity categories. As a result, the census taken in 1980 (and again in 1990) offered the following choices:

- White
- Hispanic

- Black
- Non-Hispanic

- Asian or Pacific Islander
- American Indian or Alaskan Native

In 1997, the OMB organized workshops, convened public hearings, appointed the *Interagency Committee for the Review of Racial and Ethnic Standards*, and funded several independent research projects – all to consider what to do about Directive #15. Later that year, they adopted nearly all of the committee recommendations, and established 5 racial and 2 ethnic categories for the 2000 census. This time, they were:

- White
- Hispanic
  or Latino

- Asian
- Non-Hispanic
  or Non-Latino

- Native Hawai'ian or Other Pacific Islander
- American Indian or Alaskan Native
- Black or African-American

The major change (in addition to separating Pacific Islanders from the Asian category and grouping Native Hawai'ians with them) was that citizens were asked to "self-identify" (rather than have the Census Bureau agent guess), and respondents were allowed to check multiple boxes in cases of mixed heritage.

If the United States government can't decide what the human races are (or even how many of them there are), what seems to be the problem? The answer to that was summed up by Luigi Luca Cavalli-Sforza, Professor Emeritus of Genetics at Stanford University Medical School. Dr. Cavalli-Sforza wrote that "The idea of race in the human species serves no purpose. The structure of human populations is extremely complex and changes from area to area; there are always nuances deriving from continual migration across and within the borders of every nation, which make clear distinctions impossible."* He also points out that so-called experts have identified the number of races as being anywhere from three to more than a thousand.

Dr. Cavalli-Sforza was being diplomatic when he said it serves no purpose, for he knows very well that it does. It enables us to marginalize people that don't belong with *us* as *them*. It makes it possible for us to isolate these *others*. In fact, later in the same text, he indirectly acknowledges this when he states that "Various elements combine to make racism a form of deviancy, which is not at all unexpected. Racism is just one manifestation of a broader syndrome, xenophobia, the fear or hatred of foreigners, and more generally of those who are different. Misogyny falls into the latter category, but we may need to coin a new word – misoandry – for the opposite phobia, women who hate men, as well as others for the hatred of homosexuals, priests, blacks, Jews, and the rest." Race may be a convenient statistical and political convention, but it is of little or no value in scientific terms.

Ethnicity

In most cases, ethnicity is related to national borders; but, not always. As we just saw, the 2000 US Census asked people to identify their race, and then gave them the opportunity to check off *Hispanic*. Although the OMB acknowledges that this information is to identify "race or ethnicity", lumping them together blurs the distinction. Hispanic is not a race; it is an ethnicity. It is generally defined as being that group which consider their traditional family language to be Spanish, and whose forbears came from Central or South America. But, the government even confuses that: Brazilians speak a form of Portuguese, not Spanish; but, they are generally classified for government purposes as Hispanic. In the narrowest possible definition, the term should refer only to those people who trace their heritage to the island of Hispaniola (the source of the term 'Hispanic'); but, that would only include

---

* Cavalli-Sforza, Luigi Luca, and Cavalli-Sforza, Francesco (1995). <u>The Great Human Diasporas</u> (Reading, Massachusetts: Addison-Wesley Publishing Company).

Dominicans and Haitians – and Haitians speak French!   People from Belize are also classified Hispanic, and they speak English!

We had trouble identifying the number of races; but, how many ethnicities are there? Believe it or not, this answer is actually much more straight-forward – hundreds, perhaps thousands. White (*i.e.* Caucasoid) Americans may refer to themselves as Italian, German, Polish, English, Spanish, Greek, *et cetera*. Native Americans are likely to specify that they are Seminole, Cherokee, Passamaquoddy, Abnaki, Mohawk, Cheyenne, Navajo, Hopi, *et cetera*. African-Americans who are able to trace their regional origins may refer to themselves as Yoruban, Zulu, Congolese, Nigerian, *et cetera*. Americans, tracing their origin from nearly every continent, usually do this. In many cases, these divisions fall along national lines (*e.g.* French, Italian, Polish). In other cases, they follow tribal divisions that may or may not still exist. Other ethnicities may refer to a particular region (*e.g.* Provençal) or an island isolate (*e.g.* Puerto Rican, Faröese). With so many options from which to choose, what purpose, what value is there in ethnicity?

Where are you from ?

This may seem an innocent question; but, the response may be quite exotic. From the beaches of Hawaii, to the Yucatan coast of México; from the majestic cities of Canada to the open desert of Egypt; Americans come from all corners of the world.

Often, the answer given is not correct, because many Americans don't respond to this question by answering where *they* were born, but by explaining what it is they consider to be their *roots*. How do they identify themselves? With what social subgroup do they identify? Typically, an ethnic group is a subgroup of a larger society, and is distinguished by some form of shared bond. These bonds may be racial (at least perceived as such), linguistic (*e.g.* the Census Bureau's "Hispanic" category), historical (a shared history is a powerful bond), or behavioral.

Ethnicity is just one of the cultural complexities which every individual must confront. It is natural for people, when in a chaotic environment, to try to attain some reasonable level of stability or security. The most common way of doing this is to find others who share something meaningful, and bond with them. This is the essence of ethnicity – a group of individuals who believe that they share something meaningful that society, as a whole, does not.

Fundamentally, ethnic identification and nationalism are diametrically opposed. The goal of a nation, a political state, is to unify all citizens under a common banner — one which recognizes the nation as the only worthy recipient of their admiration and loyalty; however, the role of ethnicity is to provide an alternative focus for this loyalty – one which, since most of society does not share the same bonds, tends to divide rather than unify. Nations have tried different means of dealing with this apparent dichotomy:

- elimination of those whose bonds society fears may be stronger than the national bond (often through violence – *e.g.* Jews and Gypsies in Nazi Germany);

- forced removal of those whose solidarity poses a potential threat (*e.g.* Muslims and Jews from late 15th century Spain);

- legislated assimilation of groups into the larger culture, with the associated destruction of the former ethnic bonds (*e.g.* the French legislative advancement of the French language, and corresponding suppression of the Breton language in Brittany, Provençal around Nice, and Corsican on the island of Corsica);

- induced acculturation of ethnicities through dilution to the point of dissolution (*e.g.* massive relocation of ethnic Chinese to Tibet to dilute the traditional Tibetan ethnic community to the point of extinction);

- absorption through an offer of potential reward (*e.g.* the "melting pot" of American society, which reduces ethnic expressions to mere symbolism by offering assimilation as the means to "achieve the American dream", and thus attain economic advancement); and,

- so-called *ethnic cleansing* (*i.e.* genocide – a word actually invented in the late 1940s to describe what Hitler had done to the Jews) by the ruthless, physical elimination of an ethnic group through extermination (*e.g.* Bosnians and Croatians by Serbia, Armenians by Turkey, and the Hutu by the Tutsi in Burundi).

Apparently, one of the better methods of dealing with cases of pronounced ethnic diversity (*i.e.* not the usually more benign symbolic diversity often found in the US) is what is known as *ethnic pluralism*. This is basically a nationalistic recognition of the diversity, along with a scheme to share power. Examples of this can be seen in Switzerland (with ethnically oriented cantons, and 4 official languages), India (with 15 official languages and an impressive number of distinct ethnicities), and Canada (with 2 official languages, and nearly all of the provinces being ethnically oriented toward one or the other).

This does not always work for the long term, however (as it appears to have done in Switzerland). In some cases, populations gradually shift, and competing ethnic groups soon become uncomfortable with power sharing arrangements (whether formal or informal). New groups may also be introduced – groups which want the same considerations that they see were given to others in the past. In Canada, both of these changes have occurred, and it has caused serious difficulties for the maintenance of the Canadian confederation. The large, populous, ethnically French province of Québec wants either more power within the confederation, or complete independence from it; most of the other provinces (primarily those with ethnically English populations) want to see Québec assimilate, and dissolve their Franco-Canadian heritage. At the same time, the First Peoples (a term used to refer to the native Inuit and other Native Canadians) want the same provincial recognition and power that they perceive was granted to the Franco-Canadians. Finally, for a variety of reasons (perhaps the greatest being the reabsorption of Hong Kong by China), the largest cohesive ethnic group in the western province of British Columbia is now Chinese; and, they are also clamoring for ethnic recognition and power.

In the United States, ethnic diversity is primarily seen by the average citizen when:

- ◆ Irish-Americans have a Saint Patrick's Day parade through Boston's South End;

- Italian-Americans hold street parties in the Fall in Boston's North End;
- Native Americans meet in a national *pow-wow* in Durango,Colorado);
- Mexican restaurants price margaritas 'two-for-one' on Cinco de Mayo;
- East Indian shops in Chicago become ablaze with color for Holi;
- Chinese New Year is celebrated in the streets of San Francisco; *et cetera.*

It only becomes ugly in the US when one ethnic group (or set of groups) feels threatened by the solidarity of another ethnic group. Caucasians fear that Affirmative Action is, or will become, a formal quota system that will entitle African-Americans to things they have not earned. Government programs such as 'minority owned business' contracts in the defense industry measure contractors on the percentage of work sub-contracted to businesses owned by minorities. It appears that this program has managed to worry just about everyone: Caucasian-owned businesses fear they are disadvantaged by preferences given to African-American firms; African-American businesses fear that Asian and East Indian firms will steal the program out from under them, when it was designed specifically to level the playing field for African-American businesses; and, the Asian and East Indian businesses fear that they will be marginalized by being treated as Caucasians rather than minorities (to their significant disadvantage).

In other parts of the world, however, ethnic diversity can be even more divisive, and far more violent. As the European colonial empires fell, and Asian and African colonies won their independence, the Europeans often established new national boundaries that bear no resemblance whatsoever to linguistic, historical, ethnic, racial or religious groupings. The result has been a large number of newly independent nations whose first order of business is to find a means to diminish internal tensions and move forward together. Yugoslavia was formed after World War I by Europeans who had no regard for the fact that the only shared history of several of the component Balkan states was hundreds of years of mutual hatred and warfare. The resulting multi-ethnic country spoke several different languages: wrote with three distinct and different alphabets: had widely divergent histories; regionally practiced Islam, Christianity and Judaism; and, often held social and ethical views completely different from their countrymen. The country held together primarily on the back of an effective, but ruthless, dictator by the name of Josip Broz Tito.   Tito ruled for over 40 years; but, only a decade after his death, Yugoslavia fell into ethnic animosity, resentment, fear, and open warfare. The result is that what was formerly Yugoslavia is today Slovenia, Bosnia-Herzegovina, Croatia, Macedonia, Serbia, and Montenegro.

Basque: An Ethnic Case Study

Perhaps one of the best examples of ethnicity is the people known as the Basques. The reason they are such a good example is that they are <u>clearly</u> an ethnicity – by anyone's definition of the term. Consider a few Basque facts:

- the Basque language (known to native speakers as *Euskara*) is not known to be related to any other human language – current or extinct:

- Euskara is the native language of roughly 600,000 people in what is commonly known as *Basque Country*;

- Euskara is one of 2 official languages (the other is Spanish) of the *Euskal Autonomia Erkidegoa* (Autonomous Basque Region in Spain);

- the flag of the autonomous region [right] shows a white cross over a green X on a red background;

- most Basques consider the Spanish autonomous region to be only one part of the larger Basque Country *(Euskal Herria)*;

- Basque Country is considered by Basques to consist of 7 regions – 4 in northern Spain, and 3 in southern France;

- genetic studies conducted by Dr. Cavalli-Sforza indicate that the Basque people are almost certainly not related to the Indo-Europeans (who settled Europe about 4,000 years ago) – and are most likely a remnant of the first human migration into what is now Europe (*i.e.* the Cro-Magnon arrival about 40,000 years ago);

- albeit France has always tried to assimilate Basques (*e.g.* banning the use of their language) and Spain persecuted them during the reign of General Francisco Franco, Euskara has flourished, and it is estimated that better than 90% of Basque children attend Euskara-medium schools (speaking Spanish, if at all, as a second language);

- culturally, women hold many high positions and respect within Basque society;

- Basques are an extremely tight community – so tied to their roots that virtually all family names are derived from a physical description of the place of their earliest known homestead (equivalent to English surnames such as Hill, Rivers, Wells, *etc.*);

- the economy of the Autonomous Basque region in Spain is roughly 10% better than that of the European Community as a whole (and the rest of Basque Country is comparable);

- most Basques (there are well over two million of them in Basque Country) are fiercely nationalist, holding much greater allegiance to the Basque ethnic community than to either France or Spain; and,

- genetically, the Basques are different (having abnormally high percentages of Rh-negative and Type-O blood, and abnormally low levels of Type-B and Type-AB compared to the rest of Europe).

All of these factors combine to make the Basques a strong, vibrant, healthy, expanding ethnic community. They also make them an increasingly destabilizing factor in southern France and northern Spain. Basque communities in America and other countries have unusually strong ties back to their homeland, and thus often provide funds for the paramilitary ETA (*Euskadi Ta Askatasuna*, or "Basque Fatherland and Liberty", a Basque nationalist group founded in 1959 to press for Basque independence, and often utilizing terrorist methods; somewhat equivalent to the IRA in Northern Ireland).

Diversity, Ethnocentrism, and Changes in Meaning

In 1948, Webster's first definition of *ethnic* was "neither Jewish not Christian". With that definition, not only would Jews not be considered an ethnic community, but neither would most Europeans. Nearly 40 years later, the American Heritage Dictionary broadened the definition of *ethnic* to "pertaining to a religious, racial, national, or cultural group." This same dictionary defines a *culture* as "products of work and thought characteristic of a community or population", and a *group* as "a number of individuals considered together because of similarities." When these pieces are put together, you arrive at an understanding of ethnicity today: 'a number of people with similar thoughts or work products'. This is a much broader definition than Webster's 1948 version, and is virtually identical to the criterion of 'having a shared bond' of some sort (offered above).

In this sense, the concept of *diversity* is virtually synonymous with the concept of *ethnicity*, and ethnicity – in this broader sense – can be viewed as encompassing all of the different forms in which diversity is often considered:

- gender – although one-half of the world is male, and the other half female, most small group environments (*e.g.* at work, at church, your neighborhood, *et cetera*) tend to be highly skewed one way or the other;

- race – even the definition of ethnic includes race as one of the four areas where ethnicity may be established;

- nationality – again, this is one of the four areas, and is actually the criterion upon which Americans most often base their understanding of ethnicity;

- religion – one of the four areas, this would consider people of a common religion (who share common beliefs and thoughts) to effectively constitute an ethnic group, or ethnicity (*e.g.* Catholic, Eastern Orthodox, Jewish, Muslim, Hindu, Buddhist, *et cetera*);

- age – the *American Association of Retired Persons* (AARP) has created a huge organizational structure based on the fact that many older Americans share similar thoughts, concerns and circumstances;

- sexual orientation – if there actually is such a thing as a *gay community*, then they constitute an ethnic group;

- class – as discussed when the subject of class was covered, humans tend to group in line with perceived social strata (*i.e.* classes); and,

- disabilities – those who are either handicapped or physically challenged share common experiences in dealing with society, regardless of whether or not they share the same physical challenge.

So, the meaning of *ethnic* changed during the latter half of the 20th century (becoming much broader and more inclusive); and, *ethnicity* and *diversity* became nearly synonymous. Whether or not that diversity is a good thing depends largely on evaluating whether it is valued, appreciated and utilized to advantage, or whether it is systematically eliminated, oppressed, or abused.

The final area of ethnicity to be considered is that of *ethnocentrism*. This is a word that has been constructed specifically from Greek roots to mean "to place a particular people (ethnic group) at the center". American schools teach world history from a *eurocentric* perspective – assuming that history "has revolved around the Europeans". Teaching it this way has some justification, since a large majority of Americans trace their heritage back to European roots; but, although Europeans had a major impact on world history, it certainly never revolved solely around them. How much do American schools teach about Parthia (the rival and peer of Rome), the Egyptian dynasties, or the Chinese dynasties and their many contributions to modern life (*e.g.* gunpowder, rockets, paper, and wine)?

American foreign policy has been criticized and accused of being *Americentric*, assuming what's good for America is good for the world. In fact, virtually all ethnic organizations are *ethnocentric* to some degree. It is the belief that their world revolves around their collective identity that forms the bonds that are so important to the continuation of their language, their culture, and their community.

Most often, the word *ethnocentric* is used disparagingly, to indicate a *tunnel vision* view of the world. To a degree, this is correct; but, it is not necessarily bad. It also is not necessarily good. Consider the issue of American slavery.

- White abolitionists (*e.g.* the Religious Society of Friends, *a.k.a.* Quakers) were highly inclusive and non-ethnocentric in fighting for freedom for African-Americans; but,

- Black slaves were clearly being self-centered, or ethnocentric, in wanting their freedom from slavery.

In moral and ethical retrospect, both groups were correct; but, one was being ethnocentric, while the other was being broadly inclusive. The key in determining whether or not ethnocentrism is a good thing is to assess the ethical impact that it has on a surrounding population or non-included ethnicities.

Chapter 19
The Other: Nationality, Legal Status

Nationality

There is no mystery to nationality. At a time in history when we divide the world into various *nations*, it is relatively easy to identify the heritage, traditional home, or original source of a specific person or family. If we choose to determine group identities on the basis of this national origination, then nationality falls into place easily. The only dangers are when: (a) the same term is used for both nationality and some other grouping format (*e.g.* French – the nationality, the heritage, or the language); or, (b) when nationality is being used covertly to disguise other motives (*e.g.* EURO, page 195). Most often, when nationality is used to group people, any biases which do occur result from political differences originating at the leadership level.

For example, many citizens in European, African and Asian societies tend to group all Americans together by nationality; and, there is often a bias attached. This bias results primarily from political differences with the foreign policy of the US administration (Clinton,
Bush, Obama, *etc.*);   it is not anti-Americanism *per se* (*i.e.* they have nothing against the individual American citizen). This is similar to the anti-Soviet attitude that many Americans held during the Cold War. Americans didn't dislike Russian nationals as people; they disliked the Soviet-era government policies.

"In an age when it is so common for progressive, cosmopolitan intellectuals (particularly in Europe) to insist on the near pathological character of nationalism, its roots in fear and hatred of the Other, and its affinities with racism, it is useful to remind ourselves that nations inspire love, and often profoundly self-sacrificing love."* (Benedict Anderson)

As was written above, although nationality may "tend to isolate people and turn them into 'others', it also tends to reinforce family and social bonds in a climate in which the gradual deterioration of these bonds is highly likely."

Legal Status

Illegal aliens. The very phrase is designed to foster an emotional reaction. These two simple words are what is known in psychological circles as an *emotional trigger phrase.* Schroth, Bain-Chekal and Caldwell identified three categories of emotional trigger phrases: negative labeling, commanding, and power phrases. Under this labeling scheme, *illegal alien* constitutes negative labeling. They found that the most common response, by far, to negative labeling was anger. So, who is using this phrase; and, is it inadvertent, or are they deliberately trying to evoke anger?

Aliens

The term *alien* is defined as belonging to, or characteristic of, another place. Science fiction books and movies have made aliens virtually synonymous with creatures from another planet, solar system, or galaxy. Although these are sometimes today portrayed as somewhat foolish (top), they are often intended to portray characters with less than positive intentions (bottom, the Ferengi bartender Quark from *Star Trek: Deep Space Nine* – played by Armin Shimerman). Although the legal use of the term alien has been used for centuries, the common use of it to describe people from another area has only recently become commonplace with the public.

The legal definition of alien under US federal statute is "any person not a citizen or national of the United States", which includes virtually everyone who is from 'someplace else'. At one time, more descriptive terms would have been more likely to have been used by the public: visitor, tourist, student, guest worker, *et cetera.* The problem, however, is that none of these terms evokes an emotional reaction; none of them is an emotional trigger phrase. And, there are a large number of people who are concern-

---

* Anderson, Benedict (1983) <u>Imagined Communities</u> (New York: Verso).

ed about non-US nationals. They fear that these people may be an *enemy alien* (a less obvious, and therefore even more dangerous, version of an *enemy combatant*).

Technically, US immigration law never uses the phrase *illegal alien*. It does, however, frequently call people *illegal immigrants* – people who have immigrated to the United States without legal permission to do so. The influx of these illegal immigrants (particularly from México) has become an irritant to the conservative talk show hosts in the media – believing that they are "taking the jobs of real Americans". Although this is undoubtedly true in some instances, studies have shown that they are, more often than not, taking jobs that most Americans would not do. They are employed in positions and roles where most Americans would prefer to accept welfare than perform.

Does this make them legal? Absolutely not. Does this make them non-dangerous? No. Does it make them less threatening? Perhaps. And, that offends these paragons of media virtue. So, the term *illegal aliens* is used as an emotional trigger to anger Americans into having no sympathy or empathy for these individuals. Supporters often attempt to dilute the negative labeling by euphemistically calling them *undocumented workers*. This whole battle of labels is similar to the politico-religious fight tover *Roe v. Wade*: the two sides each preferring a positive phrase (Pro-Life or Pro-Choice) rather than the negative ones attached by their opponents (Anti-Women or Pro-Abortion).

Despite all of the public debate that surrounds the issue politically, cultural anthropologists have a different interest in the issue. The fact is that these *illegal aliens / illegal immigrants / undocumented workers* collectively form a unique group of 'others'. They are often unable to participate in much of public society (*e.g.* sending their kids to public schools, going to an emergency room, reporting a crime to the police, and so on) for fear of discovery and deportation. As a result, they are significantly more likely to become victims of crimes (they can't report), and victims of poverty (which they can't escape through education).

No, this is not some liberal plea on behalf of these people; and, it is not intended to elicit sympathy for them. It is simply a statement of the sociological facts. By virtue of their not being in the US legally, they have unintentionally marginalized themselves as *others* in our society. However the federal government attempts to resolve the issue, it will not be a simple solution. There are problems with all of the simplistic answers:

- *Send them all back.*   Although this might work from one perspective, many will face severe hardships, punishments, or even death upon their return. In addition, many of the functions that they perform would likely go wanting – ultimately potentially raising the cost of food, clothing, and numerous other items.

- *Offer them a path to citizenship.* This also might work to a degree, although it appears to critics to be a reward for initially violating US law. There is also a fear this approach might encourage, rather than discourage, future violations.

- *Seal the borders.*   This would have the current number of illegal immigrants gradually decline, and the problem would be self-limiting. This solution would preclude future illegal entry, but has both limitations and undesirable consequences. For example, the border with México is 1,969 miles long and cuts across deserts, mountains, cities, and even runs 1,254 miles along the center of a river (the *Rio Grande*). Building any meaningful barrier or wall would be an intimidating venture – both financially and technically. The US–Mexican border has the second most border crossings (both legal and illegal) of any international border in the world. Even if it could be sealed, that would only put more pressure on the US–Canadian border (the world's longest international border, and the one with the most border crossings). Sealing that border would be even more difficult: 5,525 miles across mountains, forests, rivers, and the world's largest fresh water lake. Even if that could be done, there is still the problem of illegal immigration by sea – with the US having a tidal coastline of 88,633 miles! Although some of that would be relatively easy to monitor (such as New York City, Boston, *et cetera*), most of it is quite remote.

- *Strictly enforce employment documentation.* This might succeed in preventing the illegal immigrants from obtaining employment; but, that would only lead to other problems. People will not voluntarily starve to death. Some work; others will commit crimes to survive. If employment is removed as an option, the likelihood is that the crime rate would skyrocket.

This does not mean that there are no solutions. It only means that there are no <u>easy</u> solutions. All simplistic answers have either extraordinary costs associated, or have undesirable and unintended negative consequences. As an *other*, this group *of illegal aliens / illegal immigrants / undocumented workers* is an interesting, intriguing, and extremely complex cultural grouping. It even spans multiple ethnic and national groups; it is not entirely Mexican, or even Central American. It also includes Chinese, Ukrainians, Russians, Haitians, and many, many others.

Chapter 20
Gender, Psychology & Personality

Sex

Sex and gender are not necessarily what you think they are. Most people equate them; but, Webster's definition of gender qualifies this with: "*Colloquial.* Sex, male or female." There is also an "*Archaic.* Kind, sort", and a "*Grammatical.* That characteristic of a word ... which requires that other words ... agree with it according to which of three (or two) classes it belongs". That's it; no other definitions for gender.

In other words, the only common usage of the word is actually a colloquial use. It is typically used in this fashion because the word *sex* may refer to either the biological class of the individual (based on certain specific anatomical attributes) or the physical actions "pertaining to the distinctive function of the male or female in reproduction." The way that most anthropologists use these two words is to distinguish between biological (*i.e.* sex) and social (*i.e.* gender) categorizations.

As a result of her research, Dr. Anne Fausto-Sterling described what she came to believe are <u>five</u> biological sexes*. For most students, these are not truly 5 different biological sexes, but 2 biological sexes with 3 other, defective combinations thereof. Whether it is truly 5 different sexes or 2 sexes with biological defects depends largely on the view of the person doing the classifying. These five "sexes" (all of which are defined by specific anatomical attributes) are:

- *male*   a human with male genitalia and two testes;
- *female*   a human with female genitalia and two ovaries;

---

* Dr. Anne Fausto-Sterling is Professor of Biology and Gender Studies at Brown University in Rhode Island. She is a renowned researcher and writer in the fields of gender identity, gender roles, and sexology. She was married in 2004 in Massachusetts to Pulitzer Prize winning playright, and Yale professor, Paula Vogel.

- *hermaphrodite**   a human with one testis, one ovary, and a mix of male and female genitalia;
- *male pseudohermaphrodite**   a human born with two testes, no ovaries, and a mix of male and female genitalia; and,
- *female pseudohermaphrodite** a human born with two ovaries, no testes, and a mix of male and female genitalia.

Students often find this material disturbing, because it involves what is often only whispered or snickered about; and, this makes it seem somehow inappropriate. This is far from the truth, however. Anthropology is the study (*ology*) of humanity (*anthropos*); and, there is perhaps nothing more basic to humanity than human sexuality. That does not, however, make it any easier to talk about. This reluctance is, in fact, an example of the cultural limitations which we have placed on certain areas.

Dr. Fausto-Sterling's research has also generated a good deal of controversy, as the more fundamentalist religious groups try to marginalize her work, while some transgender groups want to enshrine it. Dr. Fausto-Sterling may not get the final say in this area; but, she certainly has the credentials necessary to be heard. She has written that:

> "Complete maleness and complete femaleness represent the extreme ends of a spectrum of possible body types. That these extreme ends are the most frequent has lent credence to the idea that they are not only natural (that is, produced by nature) but normal (that is, they represent both a statistical and social ideal). Knowledge of biological variation, however, allows us to conceptualize the less frequent middle spaces as natural, although statistically unusual."#

This is a controversial view of human sexuality; but, she is neither uninformed nor alone in her thinking. There are many

---

* although Dr. Fausto-Sterling considers these distinct sexes, it should be noted that the US National Institute of Health considers them "ambiguous genitalia", and declares an individual's sex to be determined genetically (*i.e.* 2 X chromosomes make you female, and, an X and a Y chromosome make you male; if the reproductive organs are not consistent with this, it is classified as some form of dysfunctional syndrome). The NIH thus classifies all hermaphrodites and pseudohermaphrodites as dysfunctional males or females.

Fausto-Sterling, Anne (2000) <u>Sexing the Body: Gender Politics and the Construction of Sexuality</u> (Philadelphia: Basic Books, a division of Perseus; p76)

highly respected biologists and anthropologists who agree whole-heartedly. Again, this doesn't necessarily make her correct; but, it does mean that what she has proposed must be judged openly, and without any preconceived bias by the scientific community.

At the opposite end of the academic spectrum from Dr Fausto-Sterling are some so-called feminist anthropologists who maintain that there is really only one sex: female. Their claim is that the Y chromosome (which delineates maleness) is just a deformed, incomplete X chromosome; and, that simply makes all males defective females! That may fit a radical feminist agenda, but is also highly academically controversial.

Homosexuality

Another so-called "hot button" issue is homosexuality. Most religious teachings consider this to be a choice, and to be clearly forbidden by God – *i.e.* a sin. And yet, the twin studies that were referenced in Chapter 4 seem to indicate otherwise. To add some detail to what was listed in the discussion on page 31, consider the results of research conducted by JM Bailey: first, with RC Pillard[*], and then with DS Benishay[#]:

- ◆ if one male identical twin (*i.e.* monozygotic) is homosexual, his brother is homosexual 52% of the time;

- ◆ if one male fraternal twin (*i.e.* dizygotic) is homosexual, his brother is homosexual 22% of the time;

- ◆ if a family's male biological child is homosexual, his adoptive brother is homosexual 11% of the time; and,

- ◆ approximately 6% of all males are homosexual.

Similarly,

- ◆ if one female identical twin (*i.e.* monozygotic) is homo-sexual, her sister is homosexual 48% of the time;

---

[*] JM Bailey and RC Pillard, "A genetic study of male sexual orientation" *Archives of General Psychiatry* vol. 48:1089-1096, December 1991.

[#] JM Bailey and DS Benishay, "Familial aggregation of female sexual orientation" *American Journal of Psychiatry* 150(2):272-277, 1993.

♦ if one female sororal twin (*i.e.* dizygotic) is homosexual, her sister is homosexual 16% of the time;

♦ if a family's female biological child is homosexual, her adoptive sister is homosexual 6% of the time; and,

♦ approximately 3% of all females are homosexual.

What does this all mean? Well, it says that what makes a male homosexual is most likely about ½ nature and ½ nurture. This can be seen in the fact that the likelihood that a male is homosexual nearly doubles (from 6% to 11%) when he is raised by parents who also raised another homosexual male.

How much is biological? How much is genetic? How much is environmental? Consider this analysis of Bailey's data regarding male twins (the same logic applies equally well to female homosexuality, although the percentages are slightly different):

♦ Identical twins (*i.e.* monozygotic) have identical genetic codes. Other than a rare gene mutation, they are two exact copies of the same human being.

♦ Fraternal twins (*i.e.* dizygotic) evolve from two simultaneously fertilized eggs. As a result, about 50% of their genetic codes are identical (the same as it would be for any two siblings). But, they share something that other siblings (with the exception of identical twins) do not share: a common gestational biological environment.

♦ A fraternal twin (as does an identical twin) grows in the same amniotic fluid, receives the same nutritional support from mother, endures the same hormonal events, and develops in the same close-proximity environment as their twin. When we say that something is biological, we are referring to these biological – but non-genetic – factors.

♦ About 6% of all human males are homosexual. Assuming that we have absolutely no idea what causes this, we will need to exclude this from further data.

♦ Bailey found that, if their adopted sibling is gay, 11% of males are gay. We account for the 5% that this exceeds the global norm by attributing it to the effect of their nurturing (*i.e.* the way in which they were raised).

♦ In the case of fraternal twins, when one brother is gay, the other is also gay 22% of the time. We already know that 6% is the global norm, and 5% can be attributed to their upbringing. That leaves 11% as a result of their shared gestational environment and ½ shared genetic code.

♦ Finally, in the case of identical twins, when one brother is gay, the other is gay 52% of the time. 6% is the global norm; 5% is upbringing; so, 41% arises from the fact that they are genetically identical with identical gestational factors.

♦ If we assume that the physical, gestational environment is a major factor in (or, the primary cause of) homosexuality, this does not account for the observation that a fraternal twin (who shared gestational conditions, but only ~50% of the genetic coding) is less than half as likely to turn out homosexual as an identical twin (who shared both identical genetic coding and gestational conditions).

Dr. Deborah Blum (a Professor at the University of Wisconsin at Madison, and a Pulitzer Prize winning science writer) wrote that "homosexuality has been around for countless generations without its non-reproductive aspect making a dent in the unbelievable flood of humanity across the planet. In fact, considering the march of human population – some six billion and counting – I could make the argument that the planet would be a little healthier if we had more same-sex couples and fewer heterosexual couples busy pursuing their reproductive potential."[*] But, is it really genetic? Blum goes on to quote Dr. Bailey who, when commenting on his results, said that "the essential genetics may not directly code for homosexuality at all, but something correlated with it." In other words, Bailey is taking a very cautious approach to interpreting the data, as it clearly conflicts with the religious views of numerous major religions; but, the data are clear – there's something that causes ho-

---

[*] Blum, Deborah (1997) <u>Sex on the Brain: The Biological Differences Between Men and Women</u> (New York: Viking Press), pp 132-133.

mosexuality. It is not a conclusive, statistical proof of a genetic link; but, it certainly appears to meet the criteria for being seen as a *sufficiency of evidence* proof that there is at least a genetic predisposition to homosexuality, and that it is not simply a "choice".

Gender

Moving from sexuality to gender (remember, they are not the same thing), we discover that virtually all societies have established a *gender hierarchy*, and gender specific roles. Some roles tend to be typically male or typically female regardless of where you are in the world; other roles shift between male and female as you travel. Roles that appear to remain nearly universal include:

Universally male societal roles	Universally female societal roles
• Hunting, fishing, trapping food	• Gathering food
• Working wood, stone, metal, bone, and other materials	• Working dairy production (cheese,cream, butter, *etc.*)
• Fabrication (*e.g.* houses, boats)	• Fabrication (*e.g.* clothing, blankets)
• Butchering & meat preparation	• Vegetable, fruit & grain prep.
• Clearing and preparing land	• Crop gathering
• Creating and tending fire	• Gathering firewood
• Making leather products	• Milking domesticated mammals
• Training and discipline of older children	• Care and discipline of infants and toddlers
• Protection (of the group, tribe, nation)	• Protection (of the family)
• Generating family assets	• Dispersing family assets

Placing males and females on an hierarchal scale requires assigning value or worth to each of these roles, and then determining which set of roles has greater overall value and importance to the society. Even when the specific roles are the same, this assignment of worth can vary greatly from society to society.

Gender hierarchies   When we talk about a hierarchy, we are talking about a recognized ranking or ordering of something. In the case of a gender hierarchy, it is a ranking of the male and female genders; and, many anthropologists thus refer to a culture's *gender hierarchy*. The problem is that life is not that simple. We all know of situations where the male "takes the lead" and makes the decisions; but, we also know of situations where the female is in charge and makes the decisions. Car salesmen are notorious for expecting the male to choose the vehicle, and the female to select the color. Similarly, many real estate agents appear to accept without question the premise that the woman will choose which house the couple wants, and that the man's role is to then "inspect" the house and affirm its structural integrity and value. In reality, neither of these stereotypes is accurate; but, they do occur. The difficulty in establishing a social ranking, or hierarchy, is in determining what factors and what situations will be used to determine who is in control. This is not always obvious.

Consider a situation that arose in India in the 1980s in the rural areas of Madhya Pradesh and Maharashtra (two large central and north-central states).

> The so-called *Green Revolution* was a global drive to increase crop yields by replacing traditional seed stocks with seeds that were hardier, more productive, and disease resistant. When the seed suppliers went to these Indian states, they were accompanied by government agricultural officers. These Indian agricultural officers would convene a meeting for all of the adult males – *i.e.* all the farmers – in a local village. At the meeting, the seed rep would then explain what they had done, illustrate the improved yield per acre, extol the virtues of the new seed variety, and provide free samples for them to take home and try. Much to the bewilderment of the seed companies, the farmers would order the same seed variety the next year that they had always used – ignoring the new and improved variety. It took them quite a while to determine what went wrong.

> In rural India, traditional male roles include clearing the land, plowing the soil, planting the crops, and harvesting the yield. But, tending the crops during

the growing season is usually left to the females. It is also the female role to feed the family. Traditional Indian families equate tending the crops with putting food on the table. Since it is a female responsibility to feed the family, it thus becomes a female responsibility to ensure a good harvest; so, it is the female who gets to decide which seed they will plant. But, they were not invited to the meetings and never saw the advantages of the new variety.

The men would go to the meeting and become convinced of the wisdom of switching to the new seed variety. They would then go home and explain what they had heard to their wives. The wives would then say "No, we're not going to experiment and take chances". It was culturally inappropriate to have the women attend evening meetings without their husbands; and, there would be nobody home to care for the children if they both went. As a result, the seed suppliers resorted to going door-to-door during the day to contact the women; and, this eventually worked.

What had gone wrong in this example in India was that the seed suppliers and agricultural agents had adopted an *etic* approach to the local culture; but, their observations failed to adequately represent the *emic* views of the local people. In other words, they assumed their own gender hierarchy also applied in rural India; but, it didn't.

Stratification Just how rigid the gender hierarchy is depends on a number of factors, as does the relative status of females within the society. Researchers have discovered that:

patrifocal societies tend to predominate where an ability to fight wars is critical (*e.g.* if there is a shortage of resources, or where forcible defense of one's resources is essential). These circumstances tend to produce warfare that is "close to home" (defending one's home, fields, and resources). This benefits from the fact that a patrifocal society forms clusters of related males – males who form bonds, ties, and familial alliances that benefit them in war or defense. This creates a strong public–domestic dichotomy, where men tend to dominate the public arena and women the domestic arena. In a society where survival itself often depends on the society's ability to wage war, the public arena achieves a much greater prestige status. Often, males use this public prestige to devalue the domestic role of women. The consequence of this is often the perceived elevation of males, the suppression and oppression of females, and fairly rigid stratification of the gender hierarchy.

matrifocal societies tend to predominate where localized warfare is rare, and resources are relatively abundant. In these societies, it is the women who tend to form clusters of solidarity. When warfare does occur, it usually results from some source other than conflict over resources. It is almost always remote – at some distant site – and warriors must go there to participate. With the women bonding in localized clusters, and the males leaving home – sometimes for protracted periods of time – to do battle, the perceived status of females is elevated, the social contribution and prestige of males is minimized, and the gender hierarchy tends to become quite fluid.

Shifting Status

In very broad terms, gender hierarchies tend to follow along with the evolution of a society from foraging and horticulture – to agriculture – to industrialization – to technology.

- in foraging cultures, males and females both gather wild food, and the roles of the genders are virtually identical and interchangeable.

- in horticultural cultures, the crop work tends to be small scale, and physical strength rarely becomes an issue. As a result, women do as much of the horticultural work as men.

- so, in both foraging and horticultural cultures, neither the role of the male nor the female has greater prestige, and gender hierarchies tend to be relatively balanced and fluid.

- in agricultural cultures, physical strength begins to become a consideration. Land must be plowed, animals must be controlled, and so forth. This favors the males, who generally have greater body strength. Similar considerations apply in cultures that turn to pastoralism. The result is often a shift toward a more rigid gender hierarchy, with men gaining additional prestige from their roles.

- industrialization created many jobs where physical strength became a major criterion. Operating large equipment, lifting and handling large loads, *etc.* all require greater body strength. Again, this creates a shift toward a more rigid gender hierarchy, and more prestigious male societal roles.

- technology has converted much of industrial society into one which relies more on brains than brawn. That may seem rather glib; but, it's true that modern technological cultures have removed physical strength as a primary attribute for workers in many (if not most) jobs. The result has been a shift back toward a less rigid gender hierarchy, and a more balanced level of prestige between the genders. This last shift can be seen in the rapid increase of women in the American job market (chart below). In 1960, in the early years of the *computer age*, they accounted for just 19% of American employment outside the home. By 1970, it had become 30%; in 1980, it was 45%; in 1990, it was 59%; and, by 2000 had leveled off around 60%. Anthropologists generally expect that a more fluid gender hierarchy and less male-role prestige will automatically follow.

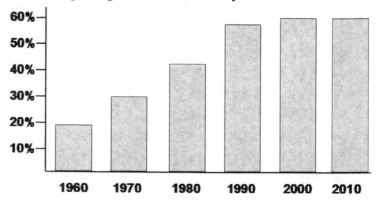

Despite this rise in female representation within the workforce, America is facing what is known as the *feminization of poverty*. This refers to the growing trend toward poor families being headed by women: in 1960, about ¼ of America's poor; just 40 years later (2000), this had doubled to account for about ½ of America's poor.

Psychology

The big question in this area is "which came first, the chicken or the egg?" To be more specific, since culture and personality are each unique social patterns, the question is actually: "Is culture the collective of individual societal personalities, or do individual societal personalities evolve along lines pre-established by the culture?" Say what?

Let's use a hypothetical example as a way of trying to make this a little clearer. Statistically, it would be highly improbable that everyone in a given community (for example: Palm Bay, Florida) would be left handed. This is because only about 15% of the world is left-handed, and there is no practical reason why Palm Bay would differ from that statistical norm. Although highly improbable, it is nonetheless possible that Palm Bay could be entirely left-handed.

If that were to happen, Palm Bay organizational responses would likely follow. For instance, the traditional elementary grade desk (right) was designed to facilitate the 85% of the world that is right-handed. If the entire population were left-handed, however, Palm Bay school administrators might opt for a desk that would be more user friendly for their now strangely left-handed student body (left). In

Right-hand Desk

addition, they might want to reverse the hot and cold handles on the faucets in the restrooms. After all, as any ergonomics engineer could explain, having the cold handle on the right makes that the handle someone is most likely to

Left-hand Desk use when they don't have a valid reason for selecting one or the other (*e.g.* when all they want is a little water to wet a toothbrush, dampen a comb, or rinse their hands). Hot water requires more energy than cold water even if the water is not run long enough to get the hot water to the faucet. Even that little bit of water used in these circumstances can create a huge energy demand if done millions of times a day in homes, offices and schools across America. Realizing this, the Palm Bay officials might also have the handles and piping reversed so that their left-handed students would not increase energy demand by automatically using the hot water faucet.

Other changes which could result from a "handed anomaly" in Palm Bay might include:

- Installation of slot machines on gambling boats and in local mini-casinos with the arm (and button) on the left side of the machine, and coin slots on the right;

- putting the ENTER key on computer keyboards at the left end of the keyboard rather than the right (with the less frequently used CAPS LOCK and TAB moved to the right);

- reversing the placement of the knife, fork and spoon at local restaurants (*i.e.* real restaurants that actually know where they belong, not those that give you a clump of flatware gift-wrapped in a paper napkin or those that reward your patronage with a plastic *spork*);

- theaters (at least those few with double arm rests) with cup holders built in to the left arm-rest rather than the right;

- clothing that buttons on the opposite side from that found in the rest of the world (men's and women's clothing already button on opposite sides for totally different reasons); *etc.*

In this example, a "left handed culture" would arise as a result of the collective attributes of the included individuals. Because everyone in Palm Bay was left-handed, the societal norm for the area would be for society to accommodate their left handed residents in preference to right handed visitors.

By contrast, if Fellsmere administrators were to add their order to that of Palm Bay (to save money on volume) with a traditional population (one predominantly right handed), the students in Fellsmere would learn to adapt. They would learn to use their left hand; would cross their hands to turn, strike or pick up items; or, would find other ways to adapt to this left-handed world (in practice, this is what left handed people are forced to do in typical cultures every day). *In this case, culture would dictate individual personality traits.* The left-handed culture would dictate norms, and individuals would learn to adapt to them.

Now, back to the question. Were a stranger to arrive in either Palm Bay or Fellsmere after they had done this for a few generations, it would be impossible for them to determine which scenario had been the cause of the strange behavior. Did society establish behavioral norms to which the residents learned to adapt? Did society alter their behavioral norms to facilitate their residents' biological anomaly? The fact is that the visitor would be totally unable to say, for certain, which it was. This is true at all levels for culture – it may be the collective of individual personalities or attributes; or, these individual personalities and attributes may have been molded by the proscribed culture. In fact, it appears to anthropologists that most cultures are actually a combination of both.

Mental Disorders

This *culture molding individuals* versus *individuals evolving culture* argument goes much further than just left and right handedness or other physical attributes. Consider what are often classified as "mental disorders".

- ♦ *amok* is described by Webster as "a murderous frenzy that occurs chiefly among Malays." The American expression "to run amuck" (or "to run amok") is derived from the Malay word *amok* that describes this phenomenon. It is a state of delirium that follows a bout of depression, and appears to be culturally specific to Malaysia, Singapore and New Guinea.

- ♦ *schizophrenia* is "a psychic disorder characterized by loss of contact with the environment, by noticeable deterioration in the level of functioning in everyday life, and by disintegration of personality expressed as disorder of feeling, thought (as in hallucinations and delusions), and conduct – called also *dementia præcox*." Although this disease is diagnosed in most of the world's societies, it usually accounts for only a small percentage of total psychiatric diagnoses, and typically amounts to a hospitalization rate of less than 50 per million citizens. But, in Ireland, it accounts for more than half of all psychiatric diagnoses, and typically amounts to a hospitalization rate in excess of 3,500 per million citizens (70 times that of the rest of the world).

♦ ***susto*** describes a severe, prolonged depression brought about by the "kidnapping" of the soul by evil spirits – at least that is the traditional, native explanation in Central and South America.

♦ ***spirit possession*** is related to susto (above), and is a person's assumption by an alien spirit (not necessarily evil). This phenomenon, and its associated behavioral patterns, is diagnosed as "dissociation" in the United States. Changing the name, however, does not alter the fact that it is rare in the US, but fairly common in Haiti, the Dominican Republic, and other Caribbean cultures.

♦ ***addiction*** — the "persistent compulsive use of a substance known by the user to be harmful" is often highly culturally specific. Heroin addiction rates in Western Europe and North America (*i.e.* societies that exhibit high degrees of social mobility) are approximately 8 per thousand. By contrast, even though their governments rely on far more forcible means to restrict and control addiction, Iran and Pakistan (where social mobility is highly restricted) are believed to have addiction rates closer to 85 per thousand.

♦ ***anorexia nervosa (and bulimia nervosa)*** are both generally categorized as being obsessive–compulsive disorders. Although a relatively even global dispersion of victims might be expected, incidents in North America and Western Europe far out strip those of anyplace else in the world.

♦ ***attention deficit disorder and attention deficit hyperactivity disorder***, known as ADD and ADHD, are at epidemic proportions in the United States, but are neither recognized nor diagnosed in over half of the world's societies.

Just as we could expect any sizable population to be roughly 85% right handed, we have every reason to expect that any of these mental disorders would be relatively evenly distributed around the globe. But, they aren't. Americans suffer much higher rates of obsessive-compulsive disorder, lower rates of addiction, and no reported cases of amok. The Irish are being hospitalized for schizophrenia at a frequency roughly 70 times that of the rest of the world. The UN reports that the rate of alcoholism is less than 2.2% world wide; but, it is more than 4.6% in the UK (more than double the world average). And so on.

Why does this happen? Do cultures look for (and report) certain disorders so often because so many of their citizens legitimately suffer from them? Or, are citizens diagnosed with these disorders because society has created a culture in which finding an unusually high incidence of the disorder is the norm? Regardless of which came first, these disorders – with distinctive symptoms, and found in only a very few cultures – are known to anthropologists as *culture specific psychoses*.

Cultural Configurations

Clearly, physical differences (*e.g.* handedness) and mental differences (*e.g.* psychoses) can differ from culture to culture. But, it is much more extensive, and much more subtle, than just these examples. In fact, humans construct a mental and emotional template which is then used by them to forecast, interpret, and evaluate the events in their lives. These are constructed individually by every person on earth; but, experience shows that they are highly culturally sensitive and specific.

These templates are actually formalized *cultural configurations*. Most anthropologists refer to one of these configurations as a *schema*. If we liken life to a movie, the schema is the storyboard that outlines the key events, actions and premise of the movie. Just as a movie writer will work from this storyboard to generate a script, humans work from their own personal schema to develop their own *script*. This is not a script that tells them what to say, but a script that outlines what to expect, how to respond, and how to interpret what we experience.

have traditionally mixed blue and orange in different ratios and with varying intensity to produce skin color in their works – regardless of whether the subject was Caucasian, Negroid, Asian, or whatever. All that changes is the ratio and the intensity; and, the changes occur relatively gradually as one travels around the globe. There are no discrete breaks which make it readily apparent based on skin color as to whether someone should be classified in one race or another (*e.g.* nearly all Americans know, or know of, light skinned African-Americans and dark skinned Caucasians).

Thomas Sowell, a senior fellow at the Hoover Institute (Stanford University), author and journalist, warned Americans that "all differences between groups that are genetically different are not genetic differences. … There are … numerous … non-genetic differences between groups who differ genetically."* What Sowell was pointing out is actually pretty obvious; but, that doesn't mean that everyone sees the distinction. For example, there have been IQ tests given which indicate that Jewish children are smarter than Mormon children. Does this indicate that there is a Jewish race? Is there a Mormon race? Are Jews genetically more intelligent than Mormons?

Jews and Mormons are genetically different (*e.g.* group vulnerability to *sickle cell anemia* – a genetic blood anomaly); and, intelligence may be genetic. Jews and Mormons differ in this measurement. On the surface, one might jump to the conclusion that this means that intelligence is a genetic difference between the two groups; but, there is another, more insidious explanation. Numerous studies have shown that children from large families generally score lower on IQ tests than children from small families. Mormons typically have large families; Jews typically have small families. These are choices they each make based on cultural – not genetic – factors. Knowing this, one should expect the average Jewish child to score higher on an IQ test than the average Mormon child; but, it does not indicate that intelligence is a genetic difference between Jews and Mormons.

---

* Sowell, Thomas (1994) <u>Race and Culture</u> (New York: BasicBooks).

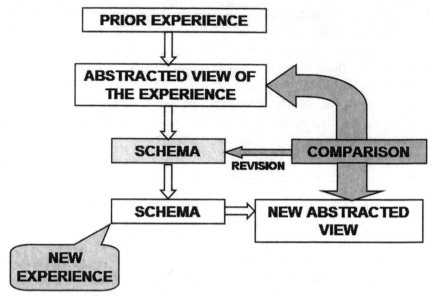

This diagram (above) provides a simple flow chart of the typical cultural configuration process. Humans – all humans – experience things. As we grow and age, the list of what we have experienced also grows. As this list becomes extensive, we innately gather those experiences that we consider to have been similar. For example, on different occasions while being raised in eastern Tennessee:

- you saw lightning, and then heard thunder;
- the sky darkened, and you heard thunder;
- you heard thunder, and then felt rain;
- you saw lightning, and felt rain;
- you felt rain, and noticed that the sky had darkened;
- *et cetera.*

Mentally, you then develop an abstract view of these various experiences. You recognize there is a connection between the dark clouds, thunder, lightning, and rain; and, you form an abstracted conception of how these experiences are related. You then formalize this abstraction into a schema – a storyboard that enables you to apply this abstracted view, and may even offer an hypothesis as to why this is so. This hypothesis may be technical, philosophical, mythical, or another form altogether.

- ♦ In a scientifically-oriented culture, you relate the gathering of the clouds to visible moisture in the atmosphere, postulate that this moisture generates electrical charges in the immediate area, and discharges an electrical release between areas of positive and negative energy (*i.e.* cloud to cloud, or cloud to ground). This discharge "cuts through" the air, which then 'collapses back together' with a huge bang (*i.e.* thunder). Moisture begins to solidify around microscopic dust particles, and these heavier than air bundles of moisture fall to the ground as rain.

- ♦ In a mythically-oriented culture, you may relate the gathering of the clouds to the arrival of the storm god and his mistress, consider the lightning to be bolts of electricity angrily hurled at the earth by this god, his booming voice ringing out as the thunder, and the rain as the tears of the goddess who weeps for the humans who have done nothing to merit such anger from her mate.

Regardless of the format in which the hypothesis occurs, it is inherently designed to enable us to understand our experiences; and, to allow us to forecast future experiences based on preliminary information. This is our schema.

Based on our schema, we evolve a *script* – a set of expectations and projections that instruct us on what to expect, and how they will impact us based on our former experiences. In the example of the storm, our script might, among other things, inform us that when clouds gather and the sky darkens, that rain is likely to follow. In addition, when the sky looks a certain way, that thunder and lightning are also likely to follow.

In late July 2004, you moved from Tennessee to Florida. You got there just in time to get settled in before you had a new set of experiences – experiences that went by the names of Charley, Frances, Jeanne, and Ivan. As we all do with every new experience, you compared them to your script – to see how well your script outlined what you should expect from certain experiences. You then use that comparison to determine if your script is working very well (which only reinforces your faith in the script), or if it needs to be "tweaked" (*i.e.* revised to incorporate this new information). In our example, you discover that:

♦   it grew very quiet just as the clouds began to gather; and,

♦   it got very windy about the same time that the rain began.

When this new information is compared to your script, you find that your script was either incomplete or inaccurate. Nothing in your Tennessee experiences prepared you for a hurricane. You did have another script that prepared you for a tornado; but, nothing prepared you for a hurricane. As a result, you use the new experiences to provide additional input to develop a modified abstract view. This modified abstract is then compared to your basic schema; and, if warranted, your schema is revised to improve its usefulness to you.

This seems very complex; and, we know that we don't really do all this stuff. Right? Wrong! We do, in fact, do all of it; we just don't do it consciously. What is interesting is that although every person develops their own, internal schema by which they live their life, people from a common community share remarkably similar schemata [note: *schemata* is the plural of *schema*]. It is unlikely that anyone born and raised in eastern Tennessee would have sufficient personal experience with hurricanes to have integrated them into their schema; it is equally unlikely that anyone in Florida would not have done so.

Schemata are culturally sensitive – not just to the geography of the society's area, but to any aspect of the culture. In fact, as very young children, we don't simply begin to write on a blank slate; we receive and accept a well-developed slate from our parents, relatives, friends, and the community, and then begin to revise it based on our own experiences. In other words, we accept the cultural schemata *a priori*, and then modify them as required.

What do these schemata do for us? Well, they:

- determine how we will act in certain circumstances;
- establish how we will interpret events in our world as they occur;
- provide us with goals;
- serve as a model for our behavior;
- color our expectations;
- give meaning to new experiences;
- motivate our actions and reactions in society;
- *et cetera.*

This may seem somewhat academic or philosophical; but, it has a very practical side to it. Schemata actually provide us with a way of understanding why it is that foreign visitors behave so differently when certain circumstances present themselves. For example, it may appear to you that the Indian, Chinese, French, or German tourist that you see while at Disney World® is making what you consider to be unreasonable demands on their children. But, what they expect for behavior from their children is based on their personal–cultural schema, and that is based on, and has been formulated by, their cultural experiences – experiences which you have not had.

People sometimes refer to the "Americanization" of new immigrants to the United States – referring to the gradual adaptation process of the new US resident to "the way things are done here". The Hispanic community in Orlando began organizing what they call *Latino Leadership*, an annual festival that provides newer immigrants an opportunity to interact with residents, city officials, and vendors – to aid their *Americanization*. In reality, what they are doing is providing these new immigrants with additional experiences and information which they then incorporate into their schema – helping them to interpret, evaluate and understand similar experiences when they occur.

What Should You Expect?

A person from a different background, with different cultural conditioning, having lived different experiences, and who has thus developed a different set of schemata on which to base their life —

> *will* act differently, interpret events differently, have different goals in life, behave differently, have different expectations, be motivated by some different things, react to societal incidents differently, and assign different meanings and understanding to what they experience.

They're not wrong!   You're not wrong!   You are just using different *schemata*.

Section V
Applied Anthropology Research

Applied Anthropology is sometimes regarded as a fifth field (*i.e.* in addition to Linguistics, Archæology, Physical Anthropology and Cultural Anthropology) by many colleges and universities; but, these academics are not the best judge of whether or not it is truly a fifth field – because few, if any, of them are applied anthropologists! The author is. And, what quickly becomes apparent to anyone who is employed as an applied anthropologist is that it is not a different field, but simply the application of knowledge and information from the four fields to the world "outside academia".

Sometimes, data gathered to support the theoretical advancement of a science is not the same data that would be of most value to someone trying to apply that science commercially, industrially, governmentally, convincingly, educationally, or charitably. Institutions engaged in commerce (*e.g.* the New England Dairy Promotion Board), industry (*e.g.* Ford Motor Company), government (*e.g.* the United Nations), advocacy (*e.g.* Greenpeace), education (such as Oxford University), or charity (*e.g.* Oxfam International) often need specific information not typically available in theoretical formulations.

As a result of these needs, there are a number of researchers who have conducted extensive research into the specifics of how the four basic fields can be applied in our everyday world. This is *Applied Anthropology Research*, and some of the leading researchers in this area have been:

- Dr. Shuming Zhao (China)
- Dr. Lisa Marie Ilola (Finland)
- Dr. Marcel Mauss (France)
- Dr. Janak Pandey (India)
- Dr. C Harry Hui (Hong Kong)
- *Dr. Kwok Leung (Hong Kong)*

- ◆ Dr. Uichol Kim (Korea)
- ◆ Dr. D. P. S. Bhawuk (Nepal)
- ◆ *Dr. Geert Hofstede (Netherlands)*
- ◆ Dr. Vladimir Karabatic (Poland)
- ◆ Dr. Jean-Claude Usunier (Switzerland)
- ◆ Dr. Çigdem Kâgitçibasi (Turkey)
- ◆ Dr. Douglas White (US – California)
- ◆ Dr. George Murdock (US – Connecticut)
- ◆ *Dr. Richard Brislin (US – Hawai'i)*
- ◆ Dr. Paul Farmer (US – Massachusetts)
- ◆ *Dr. Edward T. Hall (US - New Mexico)*
- ◆ Dr. Ruth Benedict (US – NewYork)
- ◆ Dr. Margaret Mead (US – New York)
- ◆ Dr. Walter J. Lonner (US – Washington)

From this list, we'll take a look a closer look at the work of four of these researchers (the four in *italics*: Drs. Leung, Hofstede, Brislin, and Hall). We'll begin with Drs. Hall and Hofstede (Chapters 21 to 23), and return to Drs. Leung and Brislin in Chapter 26.

Chapter 21
Research of Dr. Edward T Hall (part 1)

Dr. Edward T. Hall [1914 – 2009]

There are probably few, if any, anthropologists more closely tied to the concept of communication than Dr. Edward T. Hall. Dr. Hall earned his doctorate from Columbia, and quickly became a recognized expert in how humans learn to communicate. Dr Hall was instrumental in identifying many of the unique aspects of human communication, and then, believing that culture not only colors this communication, but is transmitted by it, looked to see what we can learn from the observation of it. Most of the material in this chapter was either developed by Dr. Hall (several of whose books are still in print), or evolved from research by other anthropologists who owe their inspiration to him.

Often called the "father of cross-cultural communication", Dr. Hall was instrumental in introducing a number of key concepts in the field. Key cultural concepts first identified and introduced by Hall include:

♦ the high context – low context continuum;

♦ the monochronic – polychronic continuum; and,

♦ the field of proxemics.

From 1933 to 1937, Dr. Hall (right) worked on government projects on the Navajo and Hopi reservations in northwestern Arizona. It was this experience that led him to an instrumental role in creating *code talkers* during World War II – the soldiers who used generally unknown native languages to transmit tactical information for the US military to  avoid German or Japanese cryptanalysts from breaking American codes. Soldiers used in this effort were drawn from those who spoke Navajo, Hopi, Choctaw, Comanche, Cherokee, and Basque. It was Hall's familiarity with the Navajo and Hopi languages that got him involved in the early stages of this effort.

Communication

Communication is not verbal. Well, it is; but, there is so much more to it than that. Communication is, literally, a "transfer of information from one person to another"; and, this is accomplished in several ways in addition to speech. As a result of Hall's work, we find a list of 9 additional 'forms or attibutes of communication' beyond the obvious verbal transmission. These are:

+ **Spatial** – how cultures view "spatial relativity" differently;

+ **Temporal** – how different cultures "manage" time;

+ **Context** – how much information is "built in" by different cultures, not needing explicit declaration;

+ **Interface Patterns** – the concept of "fit", or how well two parties interface based largely on the patterns that they have culturally adopted for general communication interface;

+ **Situational Dialects** – situation- or culture-specific shorthands;

+ **Action Chains** – sequences of communication events that cultures employ in an attempt to culminate in the attainment of some objective;

+ **Message Speed** – the culturally determined transfer speed of information, based on content, medium, *et cetera*;

+ **Synchrony** – the culturally dependent degree of "harmony" that exists between the sender and receiver of a communication; and,

+ **P.A.G.E.** – **P**ositions, **A**ctions, **G**estures and **E**xpressions that are often summarized colloquially as 'body language', and which can differ markedly from one culture to another.

Spatial

Hall coined the term *proxemics* for the study of how culture influences interpersonal space constraints. In addition to proxemics, there are 2 other areas where a culture's spatial sense makes itself apparent: these are *territorial space*; and, their *sensory screening horizon*. These are not common terms, so definitions are in order.

Territorial Space – humans appear to have an innate, well developed need to claim ownership of certain spaces as "theirs". This can vary widely in both intensity and societal impact.

♦ Infants are known to declare their ownership of particular toys, and to refuse to share them with a sibling or playmate;

♦ food preparation, whether at home or in a 5-star restaurant, is often done on a specific counter or surface peremptorily claimed by the cook or chef;

♦ the television-watching "couch potato" may lay claim to a particular chair or spot on the sofa (*e.g.* Archie Bunker on *All in the Family*); and,

♦ organized societal groups often may claim control over specific regions or land (*e.g.* Nazi Germany claiming all adjacent German-speaking regions as part of "the Fatherland").

The degree to which this territorialism occurs varies widely across cultures: Germans and Americans usually display it almost blatantly, while Asians usually display very little of it. All of these modern areas are state societies; and, it generally appears that the intensity of territorial claims is weaker in small-scale societies than it is in state societies.

Proxemics — the space that surrounds a human being (like a bubble) was referred to as *proxemics* by Hall. This space consists of four concentric circular regions, none of which is a constant size, but can vary widely depending on such things as their relationship with nearby people (*i.e.* their level of intimacy), their emotional state at the moment (*e.g.* happy, angry, melancholy, stressed, caring, *et cetera*), the activity being performed, and cultural training.

In 1966, Hall published the results of his research into proxemics. He also detailed what he had found to be the "standard" distances involved – for American culture. He divided this into four distinct regions or circles.

♦ ***Intimate Space*** is that space which is typically reserved for family, very close friends, and pets. This is that region where acts of affection or comfort are typically performed. He found that the only people comfortably allowed within this range other than family or close friends were health care professionals (nurses, doctors, *etc*). For Americans, Hall found the radius of this circle to be about 18 inches.

♦ ***Personal Space*** is reserved for acquaintances and more casual friends. When strangers are introduced, the most common action in American culture is a handshake. At this point, the stranger has become an acquaintance, and this physical act tends to place this new acquaintance in the outer band of the personal space. For Americans, the personal band ranges from about 18 inches to 4 feet, with the handshake typically placing the new acquaintance someplace between 2 and 4 feet away.

♦ ***Social space*** is used for more formal activities. This is typically the region where business is conducted, formal functions take place, and generally impersonal interactions (*e.g.* meeting a client) occur. This space ranges in the US from 4 feet to about 12 feet.

♦ ***Public space*** is everything beyond the 12 foot outer boundary of social space. This area is considered beyond an individual's control, and is typically not secured. By secured, we mean that we make no real attempt to control who is in that region, as it is considered beyond our concern. Interestingly, the US Secret Service is trained to maintain control of the 12 foot bubble around their subject; they are aware of what is going on beyond that distance, but they rarely make any attempt to secure or control it.

Occasionally, personal space and social space are grouped as ***conversational space***, and this is defined as half the outer distance of social space (*i.e.* 6 feet). People want conversational spaces to overlap: to ensure the attention of the person with whom they are talking, and enable them to focus more easily on what the other person is saying. The relative sizes of the various spaces delineated by Dr. Hall is shown at the right.

When people get together, they may come close enough to each other where more than just conversational space overlaps, and intimate space also overlaps (right).
In these situations, people may become irritable or uncomfortable. Culture and relationship are the primary determining factors in establishing these *proxemic* requirements.

As cultural differences get injected into a conversation, what one party considers acceptable conversational space may appear to be intimate space to the other – resulting in feelings of discomfort; and, modern societies hold very different ideas of what constitutes an appropriate distance for conversational and intimate space.

Societies with relatively small conversation space regions	Societies with relatively large conversational space regions
• China	• France
• Pakistan	• Canada
• India	• Italy
• Lebanon	• United States
• Latin American countries	• Nordic countries

The fact that a society appears to want a small conversation space does not necessarily mean that it also wants a very small space for increased intimacy (*i.e.* intimate space). In fact, societal norms can be graphed as shown here (below).

Small Conv Small Int	Small Conv Large Int	Large Conv Large Int	Large Conv Small Int

Societies with relatively small intimate space requirements	Societies with relatively large intimate space requirements
• India	• United States
• China	• Canada
• México	• Germany

As you can see from the diagrams (at the bottom of the previous page), there are 4 possible combinations of size requirements involving conversational space and intimate space. Perhaps the best means of illustrating this is to observe what might happen if someone who follows Indian norms tries to hold a conversation with someone who follows American norms.

> To hold a meaningful conversation, an Indian feels a need to be fairly close to the American in order to feel "connected". This is not a problem, as they also have a very small intimate space boundary. Thus, coming close to the American (to engage their conversational region) does not risk putting them inside their intimate region.

> A problem arises, however, because the American typically has a much larger spatial boudary for both conversational and intimate distances. In order for the Indian to get comfortable and be within their conversational region, they inadvertently get so close to the American that the American feels that they are within his intimate region.

> The resulting dance can actually be comical to observe. The Indian leans in (to engage in conversation), so the American leans back (to clear his intimate region). The Indian, now conversationally disconnected from the American, takes a step forward to reestablish conversational connection. This again penetrates the American's intimate region, who responds by stepping back. The dance then continues as the Indian repeatedly steps forward or leans in, while the American steps back or leans out. If the conversation goes on long enough, the two of them may work their way all the way across the room.

Sensory Screening Horizon – many cultures do not like to screen out surrounding sensory inputs, whereas others have no problem  with it. This sensory screening usually refers to auditory input (*i.e.* sound), visual input (*i.e.* sight), or olfactory input (*i.e.* smell). A person's constraints for this sort of input refers to the level of input which a person can tolerate before it becomes an intolerable interference to communication. Typically, this has a very high cultural sensitivity: *e.g.* French, Italians, and Indians have a far higher tolerance of *sensory overlap* than do Americans, British, Scandinavians and Germans. To offer an example: are you uncomfortable with the loud cell-phone conversation (above left), strong perfume or body odor, or constant movement and jumping around of a person sitting at the next table at a fast food restaurant? If so, then that input (auditory, olfactory, or visual) has exceeded your personal *screening horizon*.

Temporal

There are multiple ways of looking at time; but, the way that relates most closely to cultural communication styles is to look at the nature of time. What is it?

♦ *Monochronic time* is what one encounters when we experience time as a strictly linear phenomenon. In this context, time becomes virtually *tangible* – *e.g.* it becomes possible for a person to spend time, save time, waste time, lose time, find time, have time, or simply enjoy the time one has.

♦ *Polychronic time* is the way anthropologists describe the nature of time which one experiences when they view time more holistically. In this context, time tends to be pervasive; it is everywhere, wrapped up in everything (*e.g.* time may move quickly when partying with your friends, but seem to crawl while reading this book – sorry about that). Time is, in this context, *intangible*.

Perhaps these are best understood by example, so:

Traits of a *monochronic* society	Traits of a *polychronic* society
People:	People:
• perform one function at a time;	• may perform tasks simultaneously;
• concentrate on the job at hand;	• are easily distracted or interrupted;
• take time constraints seriously;	• consider commitments as goals;
• commit to the job;	• commit to people and relationships;
• adhere religiously to plans;	• change plans easily and often;
• worry about not disturbing others;	• are more concerned about friends and family than privacy;
• have a great respect for private property (things are rarely either borrowed or lent);	• see property in communal terms (and easily borrowed or lent)
• emphasize promptness; and,	• base promptness on relation; and,
• people are generally accustomed to short-term relationships	• have a strong tendency to build life-time relationships.

How a person views time is a function of childhood training, parental example, and numerous other factors; so, each person may have their own peculiar view of the nature of time. However, temporal views often tend to share a high degree of similarity within a given society. When we look at some of the modern, state societies (below), we find that the United States is about as *monochronic* as a culture can get, while Latin American cultures tend to be about as *polychronic* as possible.

We see this difference very clearly when the television news reports some large meeting (*e.g.* negotiations to expand NAFTA to include additional Latin American countries). The American delegation will be sitting at the conference table thoroughly engrossed in the presentation at hand; by contrast, the Latin delegations will be watching the presentation, reading from a printed proposal on their desk, talking quietly amongst themselves, writing notes to their assistants, and accepting telephone calls — *all at the same time!*

USA	Switzerland, Bavaria, Austria	China, Japan	India, Pakistan	Latin American Countries
Monochronic		**TIME**		**Polychronic**
UK	Scandinavia, Germany, Netherlands	Arab Countries		France, Italy, Spain

Context

Context is, in Dr. Hall's words, "the information that surrounds … an event; it is inextricably bound up with the meaning of that event." This is information that is understood by all parties to the event, and therefore does not appear to need to be explicitly stated. Messages and communications may thus be classified as being *high context* or *low context* – depending on the degree to which there is unstated, but understood, meaning. American parents may tell their teenager to "please take out the rubbish". Your employer may ask you to "please get them the O'Reilly file". There is no need, in either example, for them to explicitly state that ignoring them is not an option; it is simply understood (the "please" is being used as a courtesy, and is not providing the option to decline). It is, in fact, part of the *context* of the message – in an American cultural environment. This is not necessarily so for other cultural settings. In India, for example, "please" might be more properly rendered as "if it pleases you", similar to the French *s'il vous plaît*; in other words, in India and in France there is an option to decline. Not knowing the culture in which this expression was uttered means that we don't know the *context level* of the message; we don't know what additional information may be included.

All communication has some level of context; and, societies are classified as *high context* or *low context* on the basis of how much hidden meaning is typically embedded in a communication.

For example, the French have a wealth of cultural information that is simply understood by all Frenchmen (and, therefore, does not need to be included in every communication); Americans trace their heritage to all corners of the world, and virtually all of the world's cultures, so they usually provide a great deal of detailed, surrounding information in the message itself (fearing it will be misunderstand if not stated explicitly). Here, France is a *high context* culture, while America is a *low context* culture. This typically would only cause a problem when they attempt to communicate with each other: with the result that Americans complain that the French are arrogant – leaving out valuable information, and then expecting everyone else to "guess" what they mean; the French also complain – that Americans are long-winded and juvenile, incessantly stating the obvious to the point of frustration.

Consider the difficulty that an alien (from another planet, not another country) might have communicating with us after they land (even though they have been monitoring our communications and have learned English very well). Consider the problems that would arise if we started using phrases such as the following:

- "like Romeo and Juliet"   – *a literary simile*
- "like Grant and Lee"   – *an historical simile*
- "that's strike one"   – *a baseball simile*
- "need to punt"   – *a football simile*
- "on your knees"   – *a religious simile*
- "down on one knee"   – *a romantic simile*
- "until all the votes are counted" – *a political simile*
- *et cetera*

Each of these can be described as a simile (not the same as a metaphor – look them up); but, when we use them in our everyday speech, they become more than that. They become an assumed *context*. If the person with whom we are talking knows no American history, never played American sports, knows no US history, *et cetera*, they will quickly get lost in the conversation.

If you tell your English pen pal something, and they respond with "I don't mean to be a Thursday morning tippy tappy, but that was a real knock for six", would you understand? Probably not – because both expressions come from popular English sports that are not as popular in the US. Essentially, he said that "I don't mean to criticize after the fact [a soccer simile], but that shocked me [a cricket simile]." The problem is *context!*

Chapter 22
Research of Dr. Edward T Hall (part 2)

Interface Protocol

In order for your Personal Computer (PC) to communicate with a mainframe system at Google® or Yahoo! ®, the two computers must establish an agreed-upon interface protocol. Usually, on the internet, this is the *Hyper-Text Transfer Protocol* (http). People are no different. When you call someone in another country on the telephone, and want to communicate, the first step in establishing this interface protocol is to determine what language you will use.

> At one time, the author was in Gruyère, Switzerland at a small, Swiss hotel. His daughter, trying to reach him, called the hotel from the US. When the desk answered, no interface protocol could be established: the Swiss desk attendant spoke French and German, but she only spoke English. Knowing that the author was American, but also fluent in French (we had been talking at the desk), the desk attendant brought the wireless phone out to the patio to ask if he could determine what this girl wanted. Although they were surprised when informed that what she wanted was the author, an interface protocol had now been established.

Language, however, is just one aspect of establishing an interface protocol for communication between people; and, it is probably one of the simplest. Some of the components which enter into establishing an interface protocol include:

- ◆ *Language* – a common structural basis for communication; in lay terms, it may be English, French, Japanese, *et cetera*. In the case of children, it may even be an invented protocol language such as *Pig Latin* or *Double Dutch*.

- ◆ *Context* – as the degree of context rises, the degree of difficulty encountered in establishing an interface increases; the context gap may be cultural (as described above), social (*e.g.* an 18 year old girl attempting to discuss politics with her 78 year old grandfather), or industrial (*e.g.* a NASA aeronautical engineer trying to explain rocket navigation systems to the salad chef at Olive Garden®).

♦ ***Complexity*** – when the communication involves a higher degree of complexity, the interface must be more robust. Pidgins developed, and worked well, to facilitate cross-cultural trade; but, they would be unsuitable for people exchanging biomedical research results.

♦ ***Generic Culture*** – the further apart two cultures are (in general terms), the more likely something will complicate successful interface (*e.g.* communication between the US and Germany would be fairly straight-forward; but, communication between the US and the isolated tribes living on the Andaman Islands in the Indian Ocean would be far more difficult).

♦ ***Levels*** – human systems all involve multiple *levels*. This can involve their understanding of time, space, politeness, diet (it's difficult to hold a long conversation with a hungry cannibal), and numerous other factors. The more levels in a planned communication, the more difficult the interface is likely to be; and,

♦ ***Technical Evolution*** – human societies have become very technically evolved, and this can significantly complicate interface processes. If you were to find yourself in downtown Rome, and unable to speak any Italian, it still would not be terribly difficult to communicate the idea that you were hungry (*e.g.* try rubbing your stomach, pointing at your mouth, and looking pathetic). Beggars all over the world manage to communicate this idea to tourists without even having any idea what language the tourist speaks. Now, try telling the same Italians that you need to find an internet café that allows file uploads from USB 2.0 flash memory with a minimum telecommunication bandwidth of 8 mps. Good luck.

Situational Dialects

Dr. Hall defined *situational dialects* as "non–standard, specialized vocabularies associated with a wide variety of activities and situations [that] perform various functions." Typically, they are a kind of linguistic shorthand that frequently embodies a significant increase in context. The classic example is that used by waitresses and waiters to place orders with the short order cook in a diner for most of the 20th century (it's dying out now courtesy of fast food restaurants that have standardized everything with cash register buttons and kitchen video displays). Virtually every item on the menu once had a colorful shorthand to describe it.

> "Two chicks on a raft - wreck 'em, shingle with a shimmy and a shake in the alley, Zeppelin in a fog, city juice, 86 the hail, drag one through Georgia and sweep the kitchen floor!"

This can be translated into standard American English as:

> "Scrambled eggs on toast, side order toast with butter and jam, sausage and mash, a glass of water with no ice, Coca-Cola with chocolate syrup, and an order of hash."

Common Diner Slang (Situational Dialect)

Bow-wow	*hot dog*	Breath	*onion*
Burn one	*hamburger*	Bullets	*baked beans*
Burn the British	*toasted English muffin*	Crowd	*three of anything*
Drag	*add chocolate*	Draw one	*cup of coffee*
Frog sticks	*french fries*	Georgia	*Coco-cola*
High and Dry	*without mayonnaise*	In the alley	*side dish*
Italian perfume	*garlic*	Paint it red	*add ketchup*
Sweep the floor	*hash*	Warts	*olives*

Sports also often use their own form of specialized shorthand, or *situational dialect*. Every sports-minded teenager in America could translate the following line:

> Jon Lester   7.2 IP, 0 ER, 8 K, 1 BB, 1 HBP

This is simply a situational dialect that provides a more succinct way of communicating information that is critical to the subject at hand (in this case, the pitcher's line in a baseball game).

Industries also rely on situational dialects to communicate industry-specific data with a minimum of verbosity. The author was employed in the Aircraft Engine business for nearly 30 years. In reviewing an incident status report, someone in this industry might be told:

DL114: B777 on circle for ETOPS –P3/E1. ETA +2.0

This is an industrial shorthand, or situational dialect, that says:

> Delta Airlines flight #114 from Barcelona, Spain to Atlanta,
> Georgia, with Boeing 777 equipment has taken the more cir-
> cuitous route over Scotland, Iceland, Greenland, and New-
> foundland rather than the shorter, scheduled route across the
> North Atlantic. Flight 114 has lost its Extended Twin Opera-
> tions rating as a result of a low Stage 3 pressure reading on
> Engine 1. [This rating allows twin engine commercial aircraft
> to be up to 3 hours from any airport that can accept that air-
> craft. Without an Extended Twin Operations – *i.e.* ETOPS –
> rating, the plane must remain within 1 hour of such an airport
> – forcing it to take the longer route that keeps it closer to land
> throughout the trip.] The Expected Time of Arrival (ETA) is
> now 2 hours later than scheduled.

Clearly, situational dialects – whether they are based on a specific industry, service, sport, *et cetera* – may be used to speed communication or reduce the chance of confusion, but will certainly increase the difficulty of successfully establishing this communication.

Action Chains

The original (and still the most common) use of the term *action chain* is in the field of ethology, or animal behavior. In this setting, it refers to a series of actions which spawn, or interact with, one another in a regulated, patterned process. One of the more complex, but nevertheless better understood, ethological action chains is that of mating. Virtually every animal species (including humans) has a well-defined mating process that consists of an intricate series of steps each leading to another until it finally culminates in the actual act of mating (*i.e.* copulation). When any step in the process is left out, minimized, added, or exaggerated (*i.e.* the 'action chain' is broken or distorted), the entire process must begin again in order to reach its conclusion (many teenage males can attest to this).

The term, however, is also used to refer to a *series of situational frames* – *i.e.* a set sequence of events which are linked to ensure a particular outcome. For example, consider going to the store to buy a can of soda:

- Walk to the door;
- Open the door;
- Walk through the door;
- Close the door;
- Lock the door;
- Walk to the car;
- Open the car door;
- Get into the car;
- Close the car door;
- Insert the key in the ignition;
- Turn the ignition;
- Depress the brake pedal;
- Shift the car into Drive;
- Release the brake pedal;
- Depress the accelerator;
- Use the steering wheel to navigate the road to the store;
- *et cetera.*

In fact, this long sequence of actions only gets you to the store. You have yet to stop there, and you're not even close to actually having the soda. But, you get the idea. And, there are millions of action chains (such as this) that we go through every single day. Communication comprises a sub-set of our daily activities, and includes a large number of action chains. When these chains are broken or distorted, however, they often (in many cultures) must begin again to achieve success – *i.e.* communication fails.

Unfortunately, different societies have evolved different communication action chains. One of the major differences between societal action chains is the degree to which they are inviolate. An example that Dr. Hall uses in <u>Beyond Culture</u> is that of a cat that has been trained to kill mice. He describes the major steps in the action chain:

- The cat sees the mouse,
- stalks it,
- pounces on it at precisely the right moment,
- pins the mouse down,
- rotates it (if necessary), and
- breaks its neck with a swift bite just below the base of the skull.

Through observation, this is a well established action chain; but, it is not entirely inviolate. There are modifications that are

allowed to occur. A cat that is neither hungry nor expecting a reward for capturing and killing the mouse (such as when no human
is around to witness the act) is often likely to avoid hurting its prey
during the capture, and will play with it rather than kill it. There
are also certain action chains played out by humans, and many of
these are not as straight-forward as the feline hunger motivation
and are even less inviolate than that is.

Typically, high context cultures tend to be strongly committed
to the completion of action chains once begun, while low context
cultures appear much more willing to see them broken or altered.
Anthropologists have speculated that this linkage is based on the
fact that high context societies have a highly integrated, cohesive,
interpersonal social structure, while low context societies more often have a fractured, independent, individualistic society.   The
thought is that this increased context level and interpersonal connection tends to demand more consistent, predictable social patterns;   and, these demand that action chains – once begun – get
played out to their natural conclusions.

Message Speed

Still another aspect of communication is what has been called
message speed or *content velocity*. This is the relative speed with
which information is dispensed in a communication; and, all societies appear to have a very uniform adherence to this speed. By
that, I don't mean that all societies are the same; I mean that every
society tends to closely congregate its members around a very well
established point on a *message speed continuum* (or, as Dr. Hall
terms it, the *message velocity spectrum*).

People appear to be somewhat similar to a radio or television
set – *i.e.* they are tuned to a particular frequency (message speed).
Just as your television ignores, or fails to receive and process, all
of the stations other than the one to which it is tuned, human beings fail to receive and process information delivered at a frequency or message speed other than that to which they have become
culturally attuned. You may think this is foolish; after all, would-
n't you be aware of these other information channels if they really
existed? Not necessarily. You know there are many television

stations; but, your TV doesn't know that. It only knows the one to which it was tuned.

One of the more surprising attributes of this communication aspect is that virtually anything that a human being considers (plus most things they don't) can be located at some point on this message speed continuum. Even the so-called *great questions of life* fall on this continuum. Dr. Hall, in <u>The Dance of Life</u>, notes that "the meaning of life is a message that releases itself very slowly over a period of years. Sometimes there aren't enough years for the message to unfold." Perhaps one of the better ways of illustrating this concept is to provide a brief list of sample communication (information dispersal) formats, and identify on which end of the message speed continuum they tend to fall.

<u>High Speed Message Formats</u>	<u>Low Speed Message Formats</u>
• Newspaper headlines	• Books
• Cartoons	• Etchings
• Lust	• Love
• Photography	• Water color painting
• TV commercials	• TV mini-series
• Film short subject	• Full length movie
• Situation comedy	• Documentary
• Propaganda	• Research paper
• Sporting events	• History
• Prose	• Poetry
• McDonald's jingle	• Beethoven's 9th Symphony

The list could go on and on; it is, literally, endless. What is of greater importance to students of Cultural Anthropology, however, is that different cultures orient themselves at different points on this continuum. As an illustration, consider two common human interests: friendship, and sex.

> **Friendship** is something that generally forms pretty quickly in the United States. It is not unusual for people to consider their acquaintances at school, work, or church to be their "friends". This may happen even if they have only gone to that school, worked at that job, or attended that church for a matter of months. In that short period of time, it is highly doubtful that a person can get to know very much about another person; and yet, Webster says a friend is someone who becomes "attached to another by esteem, respect, and affection." Achieving this esteem and respect in such a short time demands very high

message velocity (in this case the message being a person's character). If American friends find themselves separated by great distance for a prolonged time period, the friendship often suffers as a consequence.

In France, China, Japan, Korea, Latin America, and many other areas, friendship does not occur in less than a period of several years. People in these societies expect to know a great deal about a person before deciding to consider them worthy of their esteem and respect. However, once friendship has been declared, it appears that these friends are very capable of weathering separation, strain, and time.

Sex is another area where Americans tend to fall on the high side of the speed continuum. There is no question that sex is a virtually universal, biological drive for humans; but, that does not mean that all humans will experience it (living is also a universal, biological drive for humans; but, people die). The question becomes whether sex is something that occurs quickly within a relationship, or whether it is something that takes a great deal of time before it is considered. Although it may be true that it does occur in every society, research consistently shows that sex occurs faster (*i.e.* earlier in a relationship) and more often in some societies (*e.g.* the United States) than it does in many others (*e.g.* China).

Examples of modern societies and where they generally fall on the *message speed continuum* is as follows.

Low message speed cultures	High message speed cultures
• India	• United States
• China	• Canada
• France	• Germany
• Latin America	• Norway
• Korea	• Austria

Synchrony

Synchrony is that aspect of communication which enables two people to exchange information on a continuing basis. As we saw above, an *interface protocol* must be established before any meaningful communication can begin; but, that is not enough to ensure that information continues to flow.

In the review of interface protocol (pages 249-250), the example of a computer protocol was used to illustrate the point. Part of this initial connection between computers is to establish the *trans-*

fer rate between processors; but, if one of the systems has a 'bad clock', and the transfer rate begins to drift or cycle, the second system will soon find that it can no longer communicate with the first. What is required is a continuing degree of *synchrony*.

Perhaps an even better illustration of synchrony than computers is – are you ready for this? – ballroom dancing! The ability of two people to engage in ballroom dancing, moving around the dance floor in total harmony with each other, is synchrony.

> *Tempo* can be likened to the drum beat of the music to which they are dancing. For computers, it is the transfer rate; but, it occurs in many places within society. It is simply a fact that different cultures tend to move at different speeds. This is frequently seen by tourists when they visit a restaurant in a different area – either feeling that they are being rushed, or fearing that their meal will take the entire evening. For example, native Floridians who visit New York City or Boston often report, upon arriving home, that they felt the waiters were rushing them out the door. Conversely, native New Yorkers and Bostonians often find, when visiting the theme parks and other Florida tourist destinations, that Floridian waiters all drag their feet on their way to and from the kitchen – wondering if they are that slow in everything they do.
>
> This is more than just a perception difference. People from New York and Boston actually do move faster than people in Florida. This difference is the tempo of their lives. Do you know anyone who, when you ask a question, would respond slowly enough for you to go out for coffee and not miss any of their answer? Tempo!!
>
> *Rhythm* is "the beat". In ballroom dancing, a couple could dance two waltzes one after the other; but, one of them may be much faster than the other. It is the *tempo* that determines how fast the music moves; but, it is the *rhythm* that makes it a waltz. In the popular Broadway musical *The Music Man* by Robert Meredith Willson, there is a very well known piece called *Seventy Six Trombones* (a Sousa-style march that begins "Seventy Six Trombones led the big parade, with a hundred and ten cornets close at hand ..."). As Willson was preparing his musical for Broadway, it became apparent that he needed another song to fill out the show.
>
> Willson didn't have time to compose an all new song; so, he revised *Seventy Six Trombones* to be sung as a waltz, wrote new lyrics for it, and it became *Goodnight, My Someone*. This

is an ideal example of the difference between rhythm and tempo. Tempo is the speed at which each song is presented; and, they are extremely close. Rhythm is what makes *Seventy Six Trombones* a march, but makes *Goodnight, My Someone* – the exact same melody – a waltz.

Other aspects of communication also have distinct rhythms. One communication may consist of an extended presentation of material followed by a brief interlude, and then an equally extensive response by the other party, *etc.* Another communication may be almost entirely composed of short bursts of information – first from one party, and then the other. These patterns, or *rhythms*, are not arbitrary. They tend to follow predictable modes based on subject matter, age of participants, culture, *et cetera.*

Lead Time is the amount of time required to introduce certain things into a communication. In the case of our example (ballroom dancing), it might include such decisions as how much advance notice the woman needs before the male introduces a particular step (assuming that the male is leading). If the male decides during a Tango he is going to spin and dip his partner at the end of a step sequence, she needs to know that before they reach the end of the sequence. The question is: "how much notice does she need?" In ballroom dancing, partners occasionally (rarely) verbally tell each other what is coming. Partners learn instead to "read" their partner's moves, and to thus anticipate the upcoming step. Partners that have only recently begun dancing together will almost always need more lead time than partners who have been together for years.

Communication works exactly the same way. Transferring information from one party to another is a give and take process, and these participants also rely on a certain degree of anticipation in order to be able to keep communication progressing.

Dr. Edward T. Hall (he always used the middle initial) gained some of his fame within the field of cultural anthropology by doing something that, today, would most likely have had him arrested by the local police on suspicion of pedophilia: he hid in the bushes across from an elementary school playground, and filmed the children at recess. Hall, however, was not some well-educated pervert. He was exploring *synchrony*.

After the filming, Hall took the film, isolated exchanges between pairs of children, and set it all to music! What he discovered was that these exchanges – between children of closely matched ages, and common cultural backgrounds – could all be set to the same piece of music without having to make any major modifications to tempo, rhythm, lead time, *et cetera*. Once the music had been put to the first pairing, all of the others merely had to be queued up to begin on the beat. After that, they all matched perfectly.

France, Spain, Italy, Greece	China, Japan, India, Pakistan	Austria, Hungary, Czech Republic	USA, Canada, Switzerland, Germany
Low Speed, Broad Spacing, Long Leads, Schedules Flexible	**SYNCHRONY**		High Speed, Quick Spacing, Short Leads, Schedules Sacred

P.A.G.E.

PAGE is the acronym we'll use to try and capture what is commonly known as *body language* – in the broadest possible usage. And, although the human body may be essentially the same in different societies around the world, how we use it, and what we communicate with it, is not.

Postures refers to the various positions into which the human body may be placed. Such positions might include: sitting with one leg in an open cross (right); sitting with the legs in a tight cross (*i.e.* with the back of one knee on top of, and pressing against, the top of the other); arms open (right); arms tightly crossed over the chest; standing with arms akimbo (*i.e.* the hands resting on the tops of the hips, and elbows out to the side – the arms looking like handles on a sugar bowl); standing, with weight constantly shifting from foot to foot; military at ease position (with hands behind back); sitting at the dinner table with hands in lap; sitting at the dinner table with hands (or elbows) resting on the table; *et cetera*.

These postures are highly culturally sensitive. For example, consider the two options for placement of the hands while sitting at the dinner table. American culture maintains (and parents in the United States routinely teach their children) that hands should be kept in the lap (except while eating); to place them on the table is considered a sign of rudeness to your host.

In contrast to this, Japanese culture maintains (and parents in Japan routinely teach their children) that hands should be kept on the table; to hide them by placing them on your lap is considered a sign of rudeness. So, what's rude? Hands on table? Hands on lap? It depends entirely on whether you are in Tokyo or Orlando.

Other postures also work this way; but, in many instances, the differences are much more subtle than the hands on the dinner table example. For example, standing (or sitting) with your arms crossed does <u>not</u> always mean you are being defensive.

Actions is used to refer to any of the numerous things that a person does. The social acceptability and understanding of what is meant by these actions is also highly dependent on the culture within which they occur. For example, it would be considered extremely rude for an American to spit on the street as they walk down the sidewalk on Disney World's® Main Street; but, this most certainly happens frequently. This is because there are people from all over the world who come to Florida specifically to visit Disney World®; and, this clientele often comes from cultures where this action wouldn't even raise an eyebrow. They consider the need to spit to be a perfectly natural bodily function; and, how can something so natural be considered offensive? Typically, these are the same societies that have no problem with belching at Wendy's®, hacking/coughing in church, or farting at a movie. These are natural bodily functions; so, how can society declare them unacceptable? These societies might equate this with posting "no breathing" signs in a museum, or a portrait photographer instructing clients not to blink.

Other human actions may also be highly influenced by culture. What does a head movement mean? Up and down; side to side; in a mixed sort of 'lazy eight' – actually, all of these could mean pretty much the same thing if the people were from the right cultures. Or, they could have diametrically opposite meanings. It all depends on the cultures involved.

Common human activities that can have a variety of interpretations include, among many, many others:

• spitting	• farting	• burping
• head movements	• whistling	• doodling
• finger tapping	• shrugging	• *et cetera*

Gestures includes all those "motion[s] of the limbs or body made to express or help express thought or to emphasize speech." This definition (again, from Webster) probably nowhere applies as directly and succinctly as it does to *the* gesture. Every North American, and much of the rest of the world, understands the expressed thought intended by a closed fist, palm facing the body, with a raised middle finger pointing upward. Commonly known as "giving the finger", "flipping the bird", or any one of a number of other rather colorful, colloquial names, it is an unequivocally obscene hand gesture that is almost always exercised in anger. But, this gesture is not universal; there are many societies who would never use this gesture, for it has no such meaning for them. All societies, however, have something that is at least somewhat comparable. This family of obscene gestures includes:

- raised middle finger
- the "OK" sign
- pointing at someone with the index finger and little finger simultaneously (with the other two fingers folded down)
- the "fig hand"

- pointed index finger
- the "thumbs up" sign
- wiping the back of the hand against the throat toward someone (with the fingers pointing to the throat) with a flip
- the "V for Victory" sign with tha palm facing in

and several others.

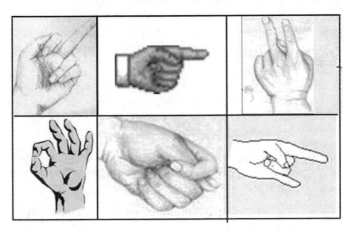

Other gestures (not just obscenity) may also be interpreted differently in different situations or by different cultures. For example, the raised, clenched fist salute could indicate:

- anger;
- solidarity; or,
- that the runner is out at home.

Be very cautious in assuming that someone from another culture is expressing the same thought by their gesture as you would if you were making that gesture.

Expressions are "indicative of character ... also, facial aspect or intonation as indicative of feeling." In other words, expressions are the means we have of indicating both our character and our emotions through facial contortions. But, in order to convey information – *i.e.* to communicate between humans – both parties must have a comparable interpretation of the contortions used. It is a scientific fact that, barring a genetic flaw, all humans have the ability to smile. It is also an anthropological fact that people from every cultural entity ever known do smile. But, do they all mean the same thing by it? Typically, we think that they must; but, do they? [Hint: they don't]

What does a 'furrowed brow' mean? How about 'raised eyebrows'? Consider an illustration for an example. American parents teach their children that maintaining eye contact is an indication of honesty, sincerity, *et cetera*. If their child goes to a job interview, the parents remind their child to "keep eye contact during the interview so they won't think you are hiding anything." Does this actually indicate sincerity and honesty, or is that just the cultural interpretation that the American culture has assigned to this expression/practice?

In India, parents teach their children that maintaining eye contact is an indication of aggressiveness, and is rude. If their child goes to a job interview, the parents remind their child to avoid prolonged eye contact during the interview so they won't think they are being challenged.

Who's right? They both are – in their respective cultures. This can actually become somewhat comical when an Indian is interviewing with an American manager, or an American is interviewing with an Indian manager:

- The Indian invariably focuses their attention on an imaginary spot about three inches above the top of the American's head;

- the American, trying to maintain eye contact, sits up straighter in their chair;

- the Indian, still trying to avoid direct eye contact, readjusts the spot to remain three inches above them;

- the American, persistently seeking to make direct eye contact, actually begins to rise up out of the chair;

- the Indian adjusts; and,

- the game goes on and on until the American simply can't get any higher up.

Foolish? Silly? Perhaps; but, each of them is trying to put their cultural interpretation of facial eye contact into actual practice. The problem arises because they each have their own, unique interpretation of what it means to maintain direct, prolonged, eye contact.

Japanese are almost never smiling in a photograph. Americans nearly always are. Why? Americans think smiling indicates a general satisfaction or contentment with what is happening. Japanese think that the smile indicates that they are either: (a) oblivious to the world, or (b) mentally or emotionally challenged. As a result, a Japanese family may be all laughing and smiling as they talk amongst themselves; but, as soon as the photographer indicates that he is about to take their portait, they all become very somber – the exact opposite of what would happen in an American portrait studio.

Chapter 23
Research of Dr. Geert Hofstede

How it all began

Dr. Geert Hofstede [photo; b. 1928 in Haarlem, Netherlands as Gerard Hendrik Hofstede] is a psychologist who was educated and trained in his native country of the Netherlands.  It was there that he received his MS in Mechanical Engineering (1953; Delft Technical University), and later followed that with his PhD in Social Science (1967; Groningen University). In the interim, he had worked on the factory floor, and moved into management – holding jobs at various times ranging from foreman to plant manager. Our interest rests primarily in his tour as the Chief Psychologist for IBM-Europe™ (1965-1971), a post from which he founded and developed the IBM™ Personnel Research Department. While in this position, Dr. Hofstede began to collect responses to a cultural questionnaire he had developed. His position gave him access to a very large and culturally diverse population. His findings (after analysis) had broad implications. After leaving IBM™, Dr. Hofstede: taught and lectured at universities in France, Belgium, Switzerland, the Netherlands, and Hong Kong; founded research institutes, think tanks, consulting firms; and, later became Human Resources Director for Fasson™ Europe.

As a result of this early work, he established a large database of cultural responses. Dr. Hofstede has said this was not a planned career move, and has written that "in the late 1960s, I accidentally became interested in cultural differences". As businesses, colleges, and universities asked for permission to use his findings and his questionnaire, he wisely agreed – asking only that they provide him with the responses that they got, so that he could add them to his growing database. In retrospect, this had two direct consequences: (1) he soon had the largest cultural data set ever assembled in the world; and, (2) this new data served as a basis for the growth, refinement and expansion of his findings. Based primarily on this work, Dr. Hofstede has become:

♦ the author of five books, and contributor to five more;

♦ a lecturer who has spoken all over the world (roughly two dozen countries);

♦ the editor for two other books on cultural theory;

♦ the published author of more than sixty articles on related subjects of interest to him (culture, organization, and management);

♦ Professor Emeritus at Maastricht University (Netherlands); and,

♦ Cultural consultant to the World Bank, OECD (Organization for Economic Coöperation and Development), and the European Union.

The Over-all Concept

The concept that Dr. Hofstede formulated revolves around the fact that cultural trends mathematically correlate with regional and national groups. Although there is wide variance across the world, specific population groups (political states, ethnic groupings) were found to have a high level of agreement on certain cultural traits. When Dr. Hofstede ran correlation tests on the collected data (literally, tens of thousands of responses), he found what appeared to be four distinct *cultural categories* with high levels of correlation. After he revised his questionnaire (with help from students and faculty while at the University of Hong Kong), he uncovered a fifth category that also correlated well. Dr. Hofstede later documented his work in interesting, unusually readable form (for an academic) in several books; so, we'll limit discussion here to very brief summaries. For details of his work and findings, his published work should be consulted (see Reading List, Appendix A).

The five areas where Dr. Hofstede found a significant population correlation (and his names for them) were:

♦ *Power-Distance*   The general responses of an individual to perceived inequities in authority, power and perquisites.

♦ *Individualism*   How the typical individual in a society relates to that society. Are they primarily focused on what is best for them? Or, are they primarily focused on what is best for their family or community, even if not best for them personally?

♦ *Masculinity*   The expected roles of males and females as defined by society. How does gender affect how society normally assigns functions?

♦ *Uncertainty Avoidance*   A measure of the comfort level associated with unknown, uncertain results; how society reacts to not knowing what is to come.

♦ *Long Term Horizon*   The "temporal horizon" of a culture. Do they generally plan, and look for results, in terms of hours, days, weeks, months, years, decades, or centuries? How do past events color their expectations of the world of today?

It must be stressed that Dr. Hofstede is not stereotyping people through his research. If you were born and raised in the United States, American cultural norms will likely have been thoroughly imprinted on you. Hofstede notes that Americans are the single most individualistic cultural grouping on earth; but, that does not mean that you are. What it means is that Americans – on average – are more individualistic than other cultures; and, that there is a high likelihood that individual Americans are such. But, there are always exceptions, and specific individuals may or may not align with the predominant norm for any category in their culture. Critics of Dr. Hofstede's work maintain he is treating cultural norms as static states, while they are actually constantly in flux. Although that is true, all applied cultural research deals with a specific point in time. Hofstede is not denying that these norms may have shifted, currently be shifting, or will shift in the future; he is merely reporting on what he has found currently to be the case.

In each of the five reviews that follow (one for each of his defined cultural categories), all quotes are attributable to Dr. Hofstede's summary work, <u>Cultures and Organizations</u> (1991; London: McGraw-Hill International).

Power Distance Continuum

Power Distance (PD) is how Hofstede chose to describe the response of a culture to a perception of inequality in society. Not everyone appears to have access to the same level PD benefits and rewards, and some people always seem to struggle to attain what others seem to receive with little effort. He noted that different societies respond to these observations with different attitudes. He saw this attitude as being formed first within the family, and then carrying over into academia, the workplace, health care, and society in general. Dr. Hofstede postulated that the family generates a particular view of social inequality based on the traditional family roles, those that children see while growing up; and, they then apply, or superimpose, this onto other areas of life. The differences that are observed result from the fact that the form the family itself takes is not consistent across the globe. As a result, traditional family roles vary widely from culture to culture, and children are socialized with very different views of social inequality.

Hofstede measures this as the *PD-factor*, and his data indicate that in cultures with a large PD-factor, superiors and subordinates (in virtually all situations) mutually consider each other as fundamentally and existentially unequal; and, a strong hierarchical system usually results. Usually, it appears that the attitude one holds toward parents is extended to managers, educators, health care professionals, and leaders; and, the attitude taken toward children is repeated toward employees, students, patients, and followers.

By contrast, a review of cultures with a small PD-factor revealed that superiors and subordinates mutually consider each other as fundamentally and existentially equal – *i.e.* they're all individuals who simply have different roles to play. Any hierarchical system that does develop is based on roles and functions, and not on individuals. Salary difference between the most prestigious and least important roles is usually relatively small, and organizations (business, schools, hospitals, *etc.*) are decentralized and empowered.

Examples of attitudes in societies with a high PD-factor would include:
- expecting (even desiring) inequalities among people;
- expecting that power or authority is subject to the constraint of good and evil (*i.e.* those with power exercise it fairly);

- parents teaching children obedience, respect, and discipline;
- children treating parents with respect and deference;
- more educated persons typically holding less authoritarian values than the less educated;
- subordinates expecting to be told what to do, rather than being consulted, or acting independently; and,
- the ideal leader being a sort of benevolent autocrat (somewhat like a "good father").

By contrast, examples of attitudes in societies with a low PD-factor would include:

- minimizing inequalities through active efforts to do so;
- acknowledging that might makes right (*i.e.* having power legitimizes its use, regardless of what may be perceived as right or wrong);
- parents treating children as equals;
- children treating parents as equals;
- people with more and less education holding similar values;
- subordinates expecting to be consulted for their view on a matter; and,
- the ideal leader being a resourceful democrat (like a wise brother).

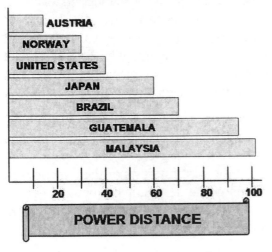

Keep these attitudes in mind as you review where some representatives societies fall on Dr. Hofstede's continuum. Relative strengths for their PD-factor are shown proportionately (*i.e.* roughly to scale)

Individualism – Collectivism

Different cultures hold different views on the role of the individual within society, and Dr. Hofstede's research showed that "the vast majority of people in our world live in societies in which the interest of the group prevails over the interest of the individual"; however, "a minority of people in our world live in societies in which the interests of the individual prevail over the interests of the group". He links this latter view to the small, so-called nuclear family – those where children typically grow up thinking in terms of "I". By contrast, most of the world's societies rely on extended families – those where children mature thinking in terms of "we". That may or may not be a causal relationship; but, the empirical data clearly do support the idea that there is a relationship present.

Dr. Hofstede measures this tendency by his so-called *I-factor*; and, in cultures with a large I-factor, individuals are expected to act in their own best interests. So, the goal for managers, teachers, health care providers, government, *etc.* is to ensure that their interests and those of the individual are aligned. In these societies, individuals see themselves as independent agents who have contracts with the various social groups – contracts that can be broken by either party if this contract no longer meets their needs.

By contrast, for individuals from cultures with a small I-factor, groups never actually hire, educate, treat, or govern individuals as such, but as members of particular social groups. It is expected the individual will act according to the best interests of their group – regardless of whether or not this coincides with his or her own individual best interests. Often, benefits must be shared with others in the group, and sacrifice in the interest of the group is common.

Examples of attitudes in societies with a high I-factor include:
- growing up looking after themselves and their immediate family;
- basing personal identity on the individual;
- speaking one's mind as a common social goal;
- operating in a low context environment (one of Dr. Hall's measures);
- all relationships being seen as mutual-value contracts;
- using individual merit and skills to determine hiring and promotion;
- expecting tasks to prevail over relationships when in conflict; and,
- viewing management, instruction, care, or governance as being primarily exercised over individuals.

By contrast, examples of attitudes in societies with a low I-factor would include:

- people being born into extended families or groups which continue to protect them in exchange for their loyalty;
- individuals basing identity on the social network to which they belong;
- maintaining community harmony as the greatest social goal;
- operating in a high context environment;
- viewing relationships in moral terms (like a family link);
- using consideration of an individual's social or cultural group as one of the primary factors in hiring and promotion decisions;
- expecting relationships to prevail over tasks when in conflict; and,
- viewing management, instruction, care, or governance as being primarily exercised over groups, or social collectives.

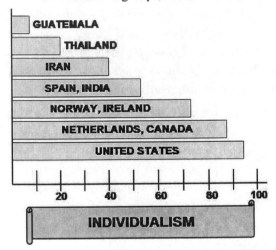

Recall these attitudes as you review the following world societies, and where they fall on Dr. Hofstede's continuum. Their relative strengths for this measure (their I-factor) are again shown proportionately (*i.e.* roughly to scale).

Masculine – Feminine

Dr. Hofstede begins by acknowledging that some functions related to conception, pregnancy, birth, and the initial time following birth (*e.g.* nursing) are biologically predetermined; but, he states that apart from those, the physical differences between the genders is "not absolute, but statistical." In other words, we note statistical differences in the genders, but not absolutes. With this approach, Hofstede strives diligently to avoid being sexist. Nevertheless, it is a fact that every society raises their young (both male and female) with certain attributes they consider to be more culturally "acceptable" than others – basic social modes of behavior that are seen to be desirable, to be the norm. Hofstede classifies these traits *masculine* or *feminine* on the basis of how they would likely be seen in the US, Canada or Western Europe; however, he emphasizes repeatedly that this is solely because he has to use some classification scheme, not because this view is inherently more accurate.

He points out that in cultures with a large M-factor (*i.e.* masculinity), children are socialized by their parents and community to stress assertiveness, ambition, competition, and success (however they may be measured). Employers, schools, health care facilities, and even government bodies stress results, and are most likely to reward or compensate on the basis of performance.

However, in those cultures with a small M-factor, children are socialized to stress modesty, fairness, harmony and solidarity. Employers, schools, health care facilities, and governments stress process, and are more likely to reward or compensate on the basis of equality rather than equity – *i.e.* according to need, not merit.

Examples of attitudes in societies with a high M-factor include:
- making good performance a societal ideal;
- considering failure (in school, work, *et cetera*) to be a disaster;
- viewing the role of society as being corrective when there are differences;
- expecting men to be assertive, ambitious, and tough, while women are expected to tend toward tenderness, kindness, and nurturing;
- giving the highest possible priority to maintaining economic growth;
- often resolving conflicts through violence, force, or a show of strength;
- girls are allowed to cry, and expected to avoid physical confrontations, while boys are expected to fight back, and are not expected to cry; and,

- understanding the concept of *Women's Liberation* to mean that women and men should hold equal shares in virtually all areas of society.

By contrast, examples of attitudes in societies with a low M-factor would include:

- identifying the ideal society as one that provides for the social welfare;
- considering failure to be little more than a minor incident;
- viewing the role of society as being tolerant or even permissive when there are differences;
- expecting both men and women to be tender, kind, and nurturing;
- giving the highest possible priority to preservation of the environment;
- generally attempting to resolve conflicts through negotiation, mediation, and compromise;
- allowing both boys and girls to cry, with neither expected to fight; and,
- understanding *Women's Liberation* to mean that women often get to hold positions formerly only held by men.

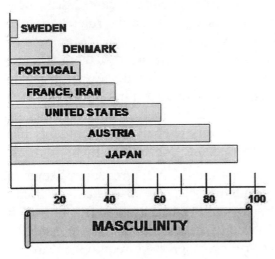

These expectations should be kept in mind as you review these representatives of the world's societies, and where they fall on Dr. Hofstede's continuum.

Uncertainty Avoidance – Acceptance

It is inevitable that, as human beings, we must periodically face uncertain or ambiguous situations. And, every cultural group has developed their own unique ways to deal with this uncertainty. In general, extreme uncertainty creates an intolerable level of anxiety; however, Hofstede proposes that "the essence of uncertainty is that it is a subjective experience, a feeling." Thus, the level to which we allow uncertainty to influence our behavior, and the methods developed to cope with it, all belong to the cultural norms of our society. They essentially become collective patterns of behavior which, as observed by Hofstede, "may seem aberrant and incomprehensible to members of other societies."

Dr. Hofstede noted, in cultures with a large UA-factor, there appears to be a societal need for rules. In many cases, such societies establish rule-oriented behavior even when the rules appear rationally nonsensical, inconsistent or dysfunctional. Members of these societies seem to take solace in knowing that there is something which governs and is in control in virtually every instance. These rules provide an orderliness to life that life, on its own, does not possess. They provide a rigid structure where uncertainty becomes a virtual impossibility, as every conceivable eventuality has already been considered, addressed, and constrained by these rules.

By contrast, in cultures with a small UA-factor, "there seems to be an emotional horror of formal rules". Rules are established only in cases where failure to do so would be catastrophic (*e.g.* on which side of the road you are allowed to drive). For society to establish rules where there is no over-riding, oppressive requirement to protect the lives of the citizens would be viewed as an unnecessary intrusion into their daily lives. Interestingly, Hofstede noticed that there is frequently an inverse relationship with public conventions – *i.e.* low UA-societies, where rules are rare, were often found to be unemotional, patient, courteous, accepting, and highly disciplined. Logic seems to imply that it is a lack of these very traits that most rules are intended to address. So, low UA-factor societies often exhibit highly defined public conventions, while high UA-factor societies are more often lacking in these.

Examples of attitudes where there is a high UA-factor include:
- high stress, and a general feeling of anxiety;

- feeling that the general uncertainty inherent in life is a constant threat;
- understanding that which is different is highly likely to be dangerous;
- believing that time is money;
- having a resistance to innovation – seeking to suppress deviant ideas or behavior, and preferring the 'tried and true';
- employees and students motivated by stability, respect, or esteem;
- a general preference for experts and specialization; and,
- very tight rules for children on what is obscene, taboo, or unacceptable.

By contrast, examples of attitudes in societies with a low UA-factor would include:

- low stress, and a general feeling of well being;
- viewing uncertainty as a normal feature of life – one that makes each new day a pleasant surprise to see what it brings;
- seeing that which is different as curious;
- considering time to be just a framework for orientation;
- encouraging innovation, and thus having a predisposition to tolerance for deviant ideas or behavior;
- employees and students more often motivated by achievement, reward, appreciation, or recognition;
- a general preference for generalists and common sense; and,
- very lenient rules for children on what is obscene, taboo, or unacceptable.

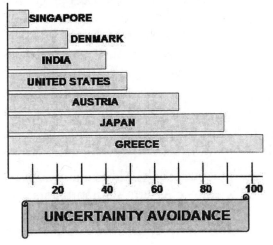

Think about these factors and the attitudes (and how your culture responds) as you review where several representatives of the world's societies fall on the continuum developed by Dr. Hofstede.

Long Term Horizon

Humans have widely divergent views with regard to time, and how their lives interact with it. This is the cultural trait that focuses on the extent to which the group invests for the future, is persevering, and is patient in waiting for results. It is the degree a society embraces or rejects long-term devotion to traditional, forward thinking values. Some societies have even constructed their native languages with little or no regard for the categories of past, present and future (this was, in fact, one of the revelations that drove Benjamin Whorf to formulate his hypothesis on language – the *Sapir-Whorf Hypothesis* discussed earlier in the course).

Although not identified in the earlier work of Dr. Hofstede, it was during his tenure at the University of Hong Kong that he was approached by students and faculty peers who claimed that there was another cultural dynamic, another category, that the questionnaire had failed to reveal. Hofstede recognized that his questionnaire had limitations, and that it might not be asking the questions necessary to expose this correlation. After revising his questionnaire appropriately, the data revealed a fifth cultural category that exhibited high levels of correlation. At first, Hofstede labeled this new category *Confucian Dynamism*; but, the fact that high levels in this field were not limited to Confucian societies eventually led him to adopt the title *Long Term Horizon*.

Discovery of this trait initially acknowledged the reality that it not only aligns with the teachings of Confucius, but also correlates extremely well with those cultures where Confucianism has traditionally had a significant impact on the cultural development.

The expanded analysis of the data revealed that cultures with a large LTH-factor typically adhere to long-term commitments and respect for tradition. This is thought by Dr. Hofstede to support a strong work ethic – one where long-term rewards are expected as a result of today's hard work. However, activities may take longer to develop in this type of society (particularly for an outsider), and extreme patience is often required to realize any benefit from the endeavor. This applies equally well to business, education, health, and government-social reforms.

At the opposite end of the continuum, cultures with a small LTH-factor typically do not reinforce the concept of long-term, traditional orientation, but prefer situations in which quick rewards result from action. This has been described (derived from the fast food restaurant chain) as the *Jack-in-the-Box*™ response: speak into the clown's mouth, tell him what you want, drive around the corner of the building, and someone gives it to you. In these cultures, change often occurs rapidly, as traditions and commitments never become impediments to change.

Examples of attitudes when there is a high LTH-factor include:
- a strong work ethic seeking long range compensation;
- business and social relationships building slowly;
- weak detailed planning (since most goals are long term);
- great patience, although grudges and resentment may evolve into feuds;
- rewards and benefits not being of supreme importance; and,
- people rarely showing anger or intemperance.

By contrast, examples of attitudes in societies with a low LTH-factor would include:
- an opportunistic work ethic focused on quick rewards;
- relationships that form quickly based on 'mutual interests';
- detailed planning being common, as goals are mostly near term;
- very little patience, with anger and resentment generally passing quickly;
- rewards and benefits being of the utmost importance; and,
- people often being described as being hot tempered.

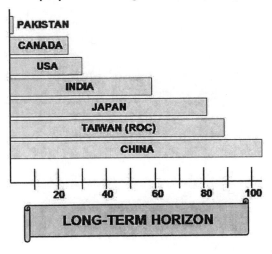

Note on this final category that "Confucian" cultures are not the only ones to score relatively high. Also, notice the difference between the neighboring countries of India and Pakistan.

Chapter 24
Research into Cross-Cultural Motivation

Motivation

Although they may not seem to be related, *motivation*, *happiness* and *stress* share a very basic trait: none of them is something that you can buy, rent, own, possess, or have given to you. Self-help gurus have long espoused the view that happiness comes from within, not from the external world. Similarly, stress has more to do with the basic personality type of the individual (the infamous *A personality* and *B personality*) than it does with what is going on around them. Donald Trump appears to seek out, and thrive on, situations that are so stressful that they would put most of us into a psychiatric care facility. Similarly, there are people who are perpetually happy in circumstances that would cripple or stunt the spirits of most people. There are also people who are energized and motivated by situations that would depress or disgust others.

Does this mean that you're either happy or you're not, and there is nothing anyone can do about it? Does it mean that if you are stressed, there is nothing a friend can do to help relieve it? If you are responsible for a group of workers who are distant and disengaged, is there nothing that you can do to motivate them? Sure there is; but, you need to remember – you can't make someone happy; you can't make a situation tension free; and, you can't motivate someone to succeed. Isn't that a contradiction? Not at all. You can't do these things; but, they can. And, what you can do is to ensure that the circumstances are those that are most supportive, and least obstructive, to their efforts and, ideally, success.

Research has revealed that, although there are cultural tendencies present, happiness and the ability to respond positively to stress are primarily individual characteristics. There are happy and unhappy people in every culture; there are stressed and relaxed people in every culture; and, albeit stress and happiness appear to be individual personality traits, motivation does appear from the research to be largely culturally influenced. What follows are the 6 predominant motivational theories in use today.

Needs Hierarchy

Abraham Maslow [1908-1970] (left) was born in Brooklyn; and, after studying law at both City College of New York (CCNY)  and Cornell (not doing very well at either school), he married his first cousin and moved west to attend the University of Wisconsin. Shifting his major to psychology, married life, the change in focus, and the change in location all combined to make him an exceptional student – earning his BA, MA, and PhD (all in psychology) over just the next six years. His greatest impact on the world of psychology was his introduction of what he called a *hierarchy of needs*. The hierarchy was presented in the form of a pyramid of 5 layers (below). The lower 4 layers were identified by Maslow as *deficit needs*, and the top layer as *being needs*.

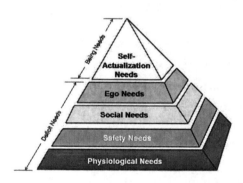

Deficit needs are those that when there is a lack (*i.e.* you have a deficit), you feel a need; but, once there is an adequate supply, you feel nothing. They only motivate by their absence, never by their excess. There is an old blues song that sings "you don't miss your water 'til your well runs dry", and this is the concept behind deficit needs. Example: if you were to find yourself trapped in a submarine a thousand feet below the surface, you would only have a discreet supply of oxygen. When it begins to run out, you will feel a distinct *deficit need* for air. By comparison, if you were to find yourself in a cool, green valley in North Carolina with all the fresh air that has to offer, you would feel nothing for the excess air available to you. Air is only a motivator – a physiological need – when there is a deficit of it.

Maslow believed that people work their way up the pyramid, not worrying about any layer until the earlier layers have been satisfied. In ascending order, Maslow identified these various layers of the pyramid (with specific examples) as being:

Deficit Needs
- Physiological Needs
  - Food
  - Salt
  - Water
  - Air
  - Warmth
  - Sex
  - Sleep
  - *etc.*
- Safety Needs
  - Job security
  - Physical safety
  - Insurance
  - Safe home
  - Retirement provisions
  - Stability
- Social Needs
  - Friends
  - Sense of community
  - Children
  - Affection
  - *etc.*
  - Mate
- Ego Needs
  - Status
  - Confidence
  - Respect from others
  - Appreciation
  - Independence
  - Recognition
  - Freedom
  - *etc.*
  - Fame
  - Dignity

Being Needs
- Self-Actualization Needs
  - Truth
  - Simplicity
  - Goodness
  - Justice
  - Uniqueness
  - Order
  - Beauty
  - *etc.*

Maslow first introduced this in the 1940s, and his *needs hierarchy* is often referred to simply as the *Maslow Theory*. The first four layers (the deficit needs) were called the *D-needs* by Maslow; and, by contrast, he called the fifth layer the *B-needs*. Dr. Maslow believed that these provided a person with *deficit motivation* and *growth motivation*, respectively.

Maslow's theory was considered the premier method of assessing human motivation for nearly 40 years. And, during this entire period, it was considered to be a virtually universal method. In other words, it was thought that it didn't matter whether the people being assessed were English, French, German, Chinese, Japanese, or whatever.

This all changed with the work of Edwin C. Nevis. For seventeen years, Dr. Nevis served on the faculty at MIT's Sloan School 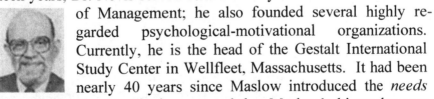 of Management; he also founded several highly regarded psychological-motivational organizations. Currently, he is the head of the Gestalt International Study Center in Wellfleet, Massachusetts. It had been nearly 40 years since Maslow introduced the *needs hierarchy* when Dr. Nevis proposed that Maslow's hierarchy was built upon American and West European definitions of which needs were critical, and a revised pyramid would be more appropriate for China (specifically) and collectivist societies (in general). In other words, Dr. Nevis challenged the idea that Maslow's *Needs Hierarchy* was a culturally independent theory.

Dr. Nevis realized that collectivist societies (*i.e.* those with low Hofstede I-factors) such as China, India, and Japan placed a more critical valuation on their social role – their family and community responsibilities – than they did their own personal, physical needs. As a result, he dropped the social needs to the bottom level (*i.e.* most important), and moved the others up. In addition, he found that many cultures were unable to distinguish between Maslow's fourth and fifth layers (Ego Needs and Self-Actualization); so, he combined these two into a single layer, and called that layer the *Esteem Needs*.

Perhaps most importantly, Dr. Nevis made no claim that his new, revised model was any more universal than Maslow's original pyramid. In fact, he maintained that the cultural differences between societies might have corresponding impacts on the *Needs Pyramid* whenever cultures differed.

Two-Factor (*aka* Motivation-Hygiene Theory)

Frederick Irving Herzberg [1923-2000] earned his PhD from the University of Pittsburgh, but spent most of his academic career at the University of Utah. Herzberg approached motivation differently than Maslow. Herzberg approached motivation / satisfaction by evaluating what he thought was the normal human response to a variety of factors as predominantly either negative or positive. For example, in a job situation, company policies can easily generate negative reactions, but are virtually powerless to create a positive motive force. The nature of the work is the opposite: positive (*e.g.* making it interesting), but never negative.

Dr. Herzberg proposed the *Two Factor theory* (also known as the *Motivation-Hygiene theory*) of human motivation. According to his theory, people are influenced by just two factors. Personal satisfaction and psychological growth were the result of *motivation factors*, while dissatisfaction and stagnation resulted from *hygiene factors*. In order to motivate someone into higher performance, motivation factors are needed. This was not without criticism: anthropologists and psychologists often disagreed with Herzberg, and argued that his research methodology was faulty.

Herzberg identified numerous hygiene factors. These include:
- working (or living) conditions;
- finances;
- interpersonal relations.
- status;
- security; and,

He also identified a number of motivation factors, including:
- achievement;
- recognition;
- growth.
- responsibility;
- advancement; and,

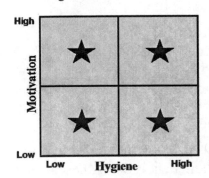

Although Dr. Herzberg's research on motivation focused on employment issues, his findings (if you accept his methodology) apply generally to all areas of motivation (not just work). He found that the combination of hygiene and motivation factors result in four possible conditions:

■ High Hygiene / High Motivation
This is the ideal situation where people are both highly motivated and have very few complaints (upper right quadrant in figure).

■ High Hygiene / Low Motivation
These people have few complaints, but are not highly motivated. For work, the job is just a check; in life, these people just ride it out (lower right quadrant).

■ Low Hygiene / High Motivation
Motivated, but a lot of complaints – often a situation where things are challenging, but the rewards just don't appear to be what is warranted (upper left).

■ Low Hygiene / Low Motivation
This is, without question, the worst of the four possible situations. These are unmotivated people with lots of complaints. (lower left quadrant).

Even if we accept his methodology, agree with his interpretation of the data, and concur with all of his findings, Dr. Herzberg's work was based on North American – West European standards. Just as Nevis pointed out regarding Maslow's work, Herzberg's findings are based on his classifications being universal; they're not. For example, recognition is not only not a motivator, it can actually be a hygiene factor in some societies (*e.g.* in India and China, where individual recognition is often seen as a perceived failure to place the family and the community – one's highest responsibilites – ahead of any self-aggrandizement).

Achievement Motivation

David C. McClelland [1917-1998] took a different approach to understanding humans. After earning his BA at Wesleyan University, his MA at the University of Missouri, and his PhD at Yale, he joined the faculty at Harvard – remaining there for 30 years before joining Boston University as the Distinguished Research Professor of Psychology for the final 11 years of his life.

Dr. McClelland (right) had a radical idea: people are internally driven to achieve; that drive is intrinsic. He posited that humans are innately driven to succeed, to accomplish, *something*. He left it open as to what it was that a particular individual was seeking, so his approach is the first one that appears, at least on the surface, to be culturally neutral.

He proposed that if you "fed that innate desire to achieve, you could motivate" people. Dr. McClelland believed that those people who rated high on his test for nAch (a sort of achievement desirability measure) preferred tasks with an intermediate level of difficulty – easy enough to minimize the risk of failure, but challenging enough to stimulate their desire to succeed. However, McClelland readily admitted the culturally biased view this could give – having found substantial indirect evidence that both organizational and national factors have a direct relationship to the nAch (his 'desire to achieve'). In other words, he proposed that a desire to achieve was innate, biological, and universal; but, there was no universal, culturally neutral means to measure that drive. Since McClelland was primarily concerned with job motivation, this lack of a universal test was clearly a problem for him.

What McClelland never addressed was the very real fact that success and achievement are almost always defined in cultural terms. This, combined with the lack of a culturally neutral test, made his work of questionable value. For example, while a job promotion which brings with it more responsibility and longer work hours may be thought to indicate success in one culture, a state of security that enables more time off to be with the family may be more widely regarded as success in another.

Equity

Charles A. Kiesler [1934-2002] served as the Dean of the College of Humanities and Social Sciences at Carnegie Mellon, Provost at Vanderbilt, Chancellor at the University of Missouri – Columbia, Founding President of the American Psychological Society, and the Chief Executive Officer of the American Psychological  Association. Despite these impressive credentials, his thoughts on human motivation were deceptively simple: he believed people make internal assessments of what is fair and equitable, and then respond in accord with that assessment.

Dr. Kiesler (and many others) maintain that individuals want (and expect) life to be fair. The oft–heard sarcastic response "whoever said life was fair" might certainly be relevant in a discussion of Kiesler's theory; and, any attempt to measure personal satisfaction that you're being treated fairly inevitably relies on social psychology and the state generally known as *cognitive dissonance*.

Essentially, Kiesler proposed that people try to be consistent in their thinking, and make subconscious adjustments to their belief system whenever new data are acquired. These adjustments are made to maintain a state of *cognitive consonance – i.e.* what you see and what you understand are in agreement If data are acquired that are inconsistent with existing beliefs, a state of dissonance arises. And, something must be adjusted to eliminate this dissonance.

> Example You live next door to a couple that you admire immensely. You respect them as people and hold them up to your children as role models of what good people can accomplish. When they bought a hybrid-engine car, you bought one; when they started the neighborhood watch group, you joined;

et cetera. Then, one night, you turn on the local news to see that your neighbor has been arrested for embezzling $200,000 from the insurance company where he works.

This creates a state of *cognitive dissonance*: someone that you respect, admire, and often emulate has committed a crime. Your expectations and beliefs are suddenly in conflict with this new data.

Dr Kiesler's *Equity Theory* maintains that you will not – can not – maintain this state of cognitive dissonance; adjustments must be made. You may decide that:

- embezzling from an insurance company isn't really a terrible crime since they "stole" that money from hard working souls like you;

- the television station is always getting things mixed up, and it was probably somebody else who stole the money;

- the police were "out to get him" because they resented it when he started the neighborhood watch; or,

- he was always a little funny, and there was always something about him that you didn't trust, but, you never could put your finger on what it was – until now.

Each of these adjustments would delay, minimize, or totally eliminate the dissonance that arose from learning of his arrest; and, you may accept any of them (or a combination of them) to resolve your discomfort.

Perceived equity (since it is the perception that matters, not necessarily reality) is attained when an individual believes that the *ratio* of their efforts to their rewards is in accord with some preconceived norm. When it is not, the assumption is that the individual will find some way to bring the two dissonant perceptions into agreement. This can be done through mentally adjusting the norm, changing input (effort), or altering the perceived output (results).

> Example Your employer has informed you that she needs you to work a 12 hour shift, 7 days a week, for the next 4 months while they send one of the other people at work to a management training course. You are now being asked to work 84 hours a week with no days off. Your pay, based on 32 hours at 'time and a half', and 12 hours at 'double time' will be nearly three times your normal week's pay.
>
> If you consider your job to be just the way you make money to feed your family, this may be fine. Although your effort

has more than doubled (from 40 to 84 hours per week), your reward (*i.e.* compensation) has nearly tripled (from $800 to $2,240 per week).

If, however, you consider your job to be a stepping stone to promotion, you may not find this to be acceptable. Although you will be paid a lot more money, you are doing it so that somebody else gets trained to be ready for that next promotion – not you.

Cultural factors also play a major role in determining *perceived equity* in the change. In Japan, a great deal of value is placed on the socialization aspects of a job. Being there twice as much, and integrating yourself into a situation where the company needs you is a good thing to do. In France, though, your extra compensation comes at the price of less time with your family and friends, and would be a terrible imposition.

As can be seen from the first example, *equity theory* applies to virtually all facets of life, and not just employment. Dr. Kiesler made an academic presentation of what may appear to be common sense to others: *everyone simply wants to believe life is fair*.

Goal–Setting

Dr. Edwin A. Locke [b.1938] became a professor at the University of Maryland after being awarded a PhD from Cornell. Dr. Locke emphasized that people have internal, conscious *intentions* with regard to life; and, as much as conditions permit, act in accord with those intentions.

Dr. Locke assumed that people always act in accord with these internal intentions (at least as far as reality permits), and that they self-measure their success on the basis of how well results match what was desired. In other words, people are satisfied to the extent that things turn out the way that they intended them to turn out. He accounted for all of the other factors by relating them to the *goals* that people establish for themselves (which are, in essence, simply the final embodiment of their intentions).

- Offering a worker more money to produce more parts does not motivate someone directly; however, offering more money may make them set their aim higher (*i.e.* revise their goals). And, since they work to achieve their intentions (to meet this new goal) , it is this that ultimately provides the necessary motivation.

- Promising a teen-age son or daughter a new car for their birthday if they earn straight A's from school will not motivate them to study harder; but, offering the car will encourage them to raise their sights. And, when they work harder to meet this new goal, they inevitably achieve higher grades.

Again, however, we must account for the cultural aspects of this approach. In determining what factors induce an individual to alter their goals, we must factor in their cultural predispositions.

- Offering college tuition reimbursement for good High School grades in an Arab Emirate (where college is free) would not be an enticement to alter one's goals – in the United States, however, it probably would.

- Promising more money for longer work hours in a culture that places its highest value on spending time with family may actually lower goals.

- Advertising an engineering scholarship open to the children of employees who voluntarily participate in a company program will have no impact on an employee who has two daughters if it is a culture in which only men work outside the home.

Valence–Expectancy

Finally, we come to Dr. Edward E. Lawler, III (a professor at the University of Southern California's Marshall School of Busi-

ness). Dr. Lawler was instrumental in formulating a much more detailed, more complex theory that combines parts of Kiesler's *Equity Theory* with Locke's *Goal Setting*. Dr. Lawler maintains that people subconsciously evaluate any potential action in terms of the reward one might receive for that action and the likelihood that this reward will become available; they then act accordingly.

Lawler was a leader in the field developing this highly complex method of balancing and assessing motivation and satisfaction. His theory is often known as *Expectancy Theory*, but is also frequently referenced as *Valence–Expectancy*. What this theory does is to relate an individual's expectancy of a certain outcome and the value of that outcome with the likelihood of any possible alternative outcomes and the relative values of those alternatives. Dr. Lawler's theory states that individuals assess:

a) the likelihood an increased effort on their part will result in better performance (expectancy);

b) the likelihood this improved performance will pay off as some form of reward (instrumentality); and,

c) the positive or negative weighting (valence) assigned to the anticipated outcome.

This approach is absolutely loaded with cultural implications that bear consideration. Let's consider just a few:

♦ First, the likelihood that an increased effort will probably translate into an improved performance has educational, cultural, and economic aspects (as well as others).

   • An 8-year old can put as much effort as he wants into driving the family car. Any expectation that this will result in better driving is almost certainly misguided.

   • The daughter of a Saudi sheikh can go to the UK to acquire the necessary education to become a brilliant military strategist. The hope that this will generate a successful career for her in the Army when she returns home is foolish.

   • A butcher in Tel Aviv, Israel can learn to slice bacon so thin that it will fry in the sun and melt in your mouth. The idea that this will lead to business success in overwhelmingly kosher Israel is ridiculous.

♦ Second, the likelihood that any improvement in performance will pay off in some reward is often a function of things other than performance in many societies (*e.g.* membership in an in–group).

   • You may excel at work by comparison to the son of the owner; but, who is likely to gain a promotion?

   • If you are African-American, do you believe that outstanding performance could ever get you selected as Grand Dragon of the Knights of the Ku Klux Klan?

   • If you're female, do you think having grades that are a full grade better than your brother's grades will get you accepted at Saint Patrick's University in Menlo Park, California? [Note: *Saint Patrick's is a Roman Catholic seminary that trains future priests.*]

♦ Finally, the weighting is culturally influenced by what is considered the actual value of a particular reward.

- Fresh water has a much higher value in Aruba (where all drinkable water comes from a government run desalination plant) than it does in Bangalore, India (which gets nearly 40 feet of rain a year).

- $10,000 cash is likely to be more highly valued in Orlando than it would in rural Papua New Guinea, where there is no place to spend it.

- A full four-year scholarship to Grambling State University in Louisiana would probably be of more value to a poor, inner-city, African-American youth than it would be to a rich, suburban, Caucasian [Note: *Grambling U. is a highly rated HBCU – Historically Black College or University*].

Bottom Line on Motivation

Business people often only think of motivation in terms of employee motivation – how to get a worker to improve quality, try harder, or do more. But, in fact, motivation is what makes anyone decide to do anything. This chapter has very briefly introduced six different theories as to how we can evaluate and assess motivation. Actually, every one of these methods is used by a number of businesses, governments, schools, churches, community groups, *etc.* There is no right way to assess a person's motivation; there is also no way for anyone to motivate someone else. All that can be done is to provide an incentive, an understanding, or an opportunity to someone that encourages them to self motivate.

In every such instance, however, educational, geographical, economic, and yes, cultural factors ensure that no method is universal. Don't assume that what might seem highly desirable to you will necessarily seem desirable to someone from another culture.

Although *motivational theory* began in the west, and was assumed to engage culturally neutral phenomena, modern research has shown that it is highly influenced by culture. The work of Drs. Hall and Hofstede and many others has shown that "job motivation" may be a major driver of this research, but it is not the only beneficiary of what gets discovered.

Section VI
Applied Anthropology

What is 'Applied Anthropology'?

Textbook after textbook attempts the daunting task of outlining the numerous fields in which *applied anthropologists* work; but, the task is hopeless. There is no way to succeed here where all of these others have fallen short. So, let's not even try. Dr. Marvin Harris (the late professor of anthropology at the University of Florida) wrote that *Applied Anthropology* "is a problem-oriented research in which anthropologists use their skills and knowledge to discover and explain factors that influence human behavior and solve practical problems." That is an excellent definition; but, let me offer a more colloquial definition. Together, these may help you to understand the field a little better.

> **Applied Anthropology** *compound noun phrase* [Latin: *applicare* to attach to; and, Greek *anthrōpos*, pertaining to humans + *logia*, discourse] **1.** The study of humans put to practical use.

In other words, *Applied Anthropology* is simply that point where the academic subject of anthropology meets the real world. In the above definition, the phrase "practical use" may refer to commercial, physical, social, political, emotional, or intellectual uses. If we consider a strictly commercial sense, how can anthropology be used to make a buck? The possibilities here alone are virtually innumerable. But, every four years, Americans are also exposed to the results of political use. In this sense, the question becomes 'how can anthropology be used to get so-and-so elected'? Or, perhaps, 'how can it be used to get a particular piece of legislation passed into law'? The possibilities here are also nearly endless; and, similar questions can be asked for all of the other areas where our knowledge and study of humans might be applied.

Theory is great; but, most students want to know if you can actually do anything with it. In the case of Applied Cultural Anthropology, the answer is a resounding yes. Before we spend a little time looking at some of the classic successes (and disasters) that have occurred, consider just a few of the ways in which Applied Anthropology theories might be of practical value.

♦ Hofstede's *Individualism* factor might be used to structure the parameters of a new job to entice more applications to find a superior candidate for the job – perhaps by offering subsidization of community projects in the employee's neighborhood (appealing to a more collectivist society);

♦ Understanding Hofstede's *Uncertainty Avoidance* factor might make it easier for a person relocating to Greece to take precautions to ensure no issues arise in the purchase of a house (realizing that anything unexpected could easily discourage a Greek from completing the transfer);

♦ Using Hall's *Polychronic* guide should encourage you, when doing business in Paris, to ignore what appears to be indifference on the part of your French partner as that partner takes phone calls, allows interruptions, and writes notes while you are trying to negotiate a price with them;

♦ American tourists should expect to find people from some of the places they visit to be "in their face" when they meet them (by understanding Hall's concept of proxemics);

♦ Understanding Lawler's *Valence–Expectancy* theory of motivation may come in handy if you are in danger of missing your flight and need to find ways to encourage a cab driver in Bangkok, Thailand to knowingly break the speed limit to ensure your making it to the airport in time;

♦ Sitting on a plane in São Paulo, Brazil, you see the baggage handler carefully loading your suitcase (filled with breakable gifts for the family back home) onto the conveyor. Grateful for his care, you throw him the OK sign to say thanks. He sees you and tosses your case 20 feet onto the tarmac. Hall's *PAGE* (body language) may help avoid that;

♦ and on, and on, and on …

Some of these may seem far fetched, but they're not. Others may seem trivial, but (as we'll soon see) multi-million dollar business deals and wartime peace treaties have sometimes hung in the balance when supposedly innocent mistakes were made.

But, are there any real jobs you could get if you specialized in Cultural Anthropology? Absolutely. Occasionally, the job titles for these jobs actually contain the word *anthropology*; but, usually, they don't. There are, in fact, very few positions outside academia where *cultural anthropologist* is the job title; but, there are a very large number of jobs for which this would constitute a clear advantage for the applicant and help determine who gets hired.

Chapter 25
Classic Examples of Practical AA

Introduction

Theory can be informative. It can be interesting. Nothing, however, brings home the value of ethnographic (*i.e.* cross-cultural) knowledge better than seeing what happens when that knowledge is needed, but missing. As a result, this chapter will appear much more informal than earlier ones; but, that does not make it less important. Quite the contrary. The examples provided in this chapter all serve to illustrate the often critical need for a sound cross-cultural knowledge base.

Cultural Ignorance

Ignorance of other cultures may at times appear funny. The humor often arises from the awkwardness in which someone has found themselves as a result of that ignorance. At times, this can have grave financial, political, or even international consequences.

Yes and No

Many cultures have great difficulty saying "no". They consider it rude, aggressive, or impolite. As a result, they either say "yes", say nothing, or avoid the question by changing the subject. And, "yes" may not mean what it means to you. It could mean:

- Yes (we can do that).
- Yes (it will be difficult, but we think we can do it).
- Yes (it's nearly impossible, but we'll try, and with luck it might happen).
- Yes (we totally understand what you want, but there's absolutely no way it will ever happen)

Substantive Questions

Since so many cultures have difficulty saying "no", cross cultural negotiators ask *substantive questions*. In other words, they never ask a question that begins "Can you ..." or "Will you ...", since the answer is always "yes". Why ask the question if you already know the answer? Instead, they use questions such as "When can you ..." or "What is needed to be able to ...".

Literal Interpretation

In most Western countries, people answer a question based on what they think the questioner intended, while others may answer what was actually asked. For example, if you were not in class on a Friday, this might follow:

- ◆ Were you here Friday?   No (US, UK)   /   No (Japan)

- ◆ Weren't you here Friday?   No (US, UK)   /   Yes (Japan)

The Japanese responder is literally correct – yes, you *were not here* Friday. This can cause confusion when translated. Note that Americans and British answered the same regardless of whether the question was worded in the positive or negative. They answer the implied question; the Japanese answer the literal question.

Examples

Consider a few examples where ignorance of another culture's history, goals, or realities caused tremendous embarrassment in an international political setting.

- Barbara Bush (right), along with her husband (then Vice President George H. W. Bush), was lunching with Emperor Hirohito at Tokyo's Imperial Palace. Sitting next to the Emperor, Mrs. Bush found conversation difficult. To all her efforts at verbal engagement, the Emperor would just smile and say "Yes" or "No," with an occasional "Thank You" tossed in for good measure. Looking around the elegant surroundings, she complimented Hirohito on his official residence. "Thank you," he said. "Is it new?" pressed Mrs. Bush. "Yes." he replied. "Was the old palace just so old that it was falling down?" asked Mrs. Bush. In his most charming, yet regal, manner, Hirohito replied, "No, I'm afraid that you bombed it."   [recounted in Barbara Bush's published memoirs]

- Early in 2008, French President Jacques Chirac (right) ended a 3 year moratorium on nuclear testing by exploding a nuclear bomb under the South Pacific – ignoring polls showing a majority of the French public opposed it. It also ignored his plea to non-nuclear nations to negotiate a permanent extension of the Nuclear Nonproliferation Treaty by promising a cessation of all testing. Throughout Southeast Asia and the Oceanic nations, this test led to widespread boycotts of French products, a ban on French companies bidding on major public contracts, and a general regional repudiation of all things French.

[reported by the *Associated Press*]

- In 1982, President Ronald Reagan (right) was asked whether his recent trip to Latin America had changed his impressions of the region. "Well, I learned a lot," Reagan replied. "I went down to Latin America to find out from them and [learn] their views. You'd be surprised. ... They're all separate countries in Central America."

  [reported online by *Salon.com*]

- While on an official visit to the United States in September of 2007, Iranian President Mahmoud Ahmadinejad (right) responded to a question at Columbia University on the treatment of homosexuals in Iran. President Ahmadinejad said: "In Iran, we don't have homosexuals like in your country. We don't have that in our country. In Iran, we do not have this phenomenon. I don't know who has told you that we have it."

  [Associated Press 9/26/2007]

- During the 2008 Presidential campaigns, Senator John McCain repeatedly referred to Czechoslovakia, a country that had not existed for 15 years (since 1993). Meanwhile, Sen. Obama told reporters he had visited 57 states and had just 1 more to go. Needless to say, both candidates were significantly embarrassed.   [reported online in *The Huffington Post*]

Another area where cultural ignorance can cause serious misunderstandings is in the area of gestures (one aspect of PAGE, reviewed in Chapter 22). Examples of where this has caused some potentially serious embarrassment or potential problems also often appear in political situations.

Thumbs up

Latin America, West Africa, Greece, Russia, Iran and a few other nations use the "thumbs up" sign as an equivalent of the middle finger. Westerners often don't realize this, and that can sometimes result in miscommunication of what was intended.

When Arkansas Governor Bill Clinton (right) was nominated for President by the Democratic Party in 1992, he came on stage at the convention to accept, and gave the assembled delegates two thumbs up. That was broadcast all over Europe and Asia – often bewildering these foreign viewers. Why would the man they had just nominated stand on stage in front of an international television audience and flip off the people who had selected him?

In October 2002, the American Services Press Office released a photo (left) taken in the Orgun Valley in Afghanistan. The photo  accompanied an article about how the soldiers who had just arrived in that area had already won the "hearts and minds" of the Afghani children. The problem was that several of the boys in the photo almost certainly thought they were flipping off the soldiers, not giving them the traditional American thumbs up.

V sign (bow finger)

The V sign with the palm facing out is a nearly global symbol for "Victory" or "Peace"; however, when reversed (with the back of the hand facing out), it is known in Ireland, Australia, New Zealand, and Great Britain as the *bow finger* or the *two finger salute*, and is comparable to "the finger" of most cultures.

In January 1992, while President George HW Bush was on a state visit to Australia, he was with Australian Prime Minister Paul Keating when he flashed the bow finger to Australian protesters along the route (apparently thinking it was the Victory sign). Unfortunately, this was printed in local papers, and the US was highly embarrassed for not having known the difference in meaning associated with the sign as he "flipped off" the local Aussies.

OK sign

In countries such as Brazil and Germany, "flipping someone off" is accomplished by giving the OK sign. Although considered somewhat rude by many Germans, it is in Brazil where it is generally seen as truly offensive.

When Richard Nixon (left) was Vice-President (January 1956), he paid an official visit to Brazil for the inauguration of Brazilian President Juscelino Kubitschek. With rampant anti-American sentiment  in Latin America at the time, his trip had been in doubt. As he disembarked the plane, the crowd cheered. Trying to convey "OK. Thank you.", he flashed them the OK sign with both hands. He was baffled when the cheers turned to jeers, and the crowd suddenly turned very ugly.

Dog Call

A crooked index finger, while meaning "come here" to most, has a different meaning in the Philippines, being so vulgar it can actually get you arrested; and, the punishment if convicted is to break your index finger so that you will never do it again.

Speech Acts

There are numerous instances where speech acts well known in many cultures get misunderstood, have different meanings, are not understood, or have homonyms with other meanings. The following are a few examples of each possible result.

Colloquial Expressions – Not Understood

"What's up?" – For foreign visitors to North America, this phrase is often baffling. What is it that is being referenced (*i.e.* what is the "what" in the question?), and "up where"?

"How's it going?" – Similarly, what is "it", and where is it supposed to be going?

Colloquial Expression – Misunderstood

"Punch Your Lights Out" – An American colloquial phrase that refers to a fist fight, there are instances where someone from another culture has inevitably been left wondering why the speaker would want to harm their home electric lighting.

Colloquial Terms or Expressions – Different Meanings

Boot – This term refers to a type of footwear in the United States and Canada; but, in Britain it refers to an automobile storage compartment (*i.e.* a "trunk" in North America).

Plaster – This may refer either to a chalky substance used to make walls (US), or an adhesive bandage such as Band-Aid© (UK).

Fanny Pack – This is an American term for the item called a *Bum Bag* in the UK. Fanny is considered rude,/obscene, and offensive in the UK, and is also a slang term for the vagina.

Vest – This may be either an undershirt (UK) or a clothing item worn as part of a "3-piece suit" (US; a *waistcoat* in the UK).

Cultural Blunders

Naming Conventions

In Western countries, John Smith consists of a family name (Smith) and a personal, given name (John) – given in that order. This is often not the naming system used in other cultures.

In a Vietnamese, Mien, Cambodian, or Chinese culture, his name would be Smith John – placing the family name first.

In the US, when Maria marries John, her name becomes Maria Smith. Again, this is not a universal system. In Cambodia, China, Korea, and Viet Nam, Maria would have retained her own family name, and continue to be known as Maria Lopez.

In 1995, US President Bill Clinton went to South Korea to dedicate a Korean War Memorial with South Korean President Kim

Young Sam [left]. He repeatedly called the Korean President's wife "Mrs. Kim" while in public, while her actual name was Sohn Myong Suk, or "Mrs. Sohn." This was embarrassing to the South Korean officials, and insulting to the Korean people – President Clinton had just come from Japan, and using the convention appropriate in Japan implied to them that Korea was less important to the US than Japan. Pres. Clinton later formally apologized for the slight. [Photo (left to right): President Kim Young Sam, General R Davis (ret), President Bill Clinton]

Mistranslations

American Airlines – When American Airlines introduced their new leather seats in Latin America, they translated their English "Fly in Leather" ads into Spanish. Unfortunately, the literal translation to the Spanish *Vuela en cuero* was understood by most Latin Americans with the colloquial meaning "Fly Naked."

Electrolux – The Swedish firm Electrolux marketed their vacuum cleaners in the UK with the advertising slogan that "Nothing sucks like an Electrolux." This was actually a deliberate *double entendre* (based on the connotation) intended to get their product noticed in the British market – and, it worked.

Clairol – The Clairol company decided to market their new curling iron, the Mist Stick©, in Germany. They chose not to rename it for sale in German speaking countries – with the unfortunate result that, in German, *Mist Stick* is understood as *Manure Stick*.

American Dairy Council – The ADC, in an attempt to broaden its market, began to advertise in México. They elected to simply have the American marketing slogan *Got Milk?* translated into Spanish, and not develop all new advertising; but, the meaning of the literal Spanish translation was *Are you lactating?*

Parker Pens – When marketing their highly reliable pens in Peru, Parker Pens emphasized that they wouldn't leak and leave a stain. In Peru, however, there is a colloquial meaning for the Spanish verb they used for "to stain". This resulted in their ads saying that "It won't leak in your pocket and make you pregnant."

Pepsi-cola – when the Pepsi company decided to use their American advertising slogan in China, they initially translated "Come alive with the Pepsi generation." into Chinese to get the unfortunate slogan "Pepsi brings your ancestors back from the grave."

Utilization

Middle finger

This is perhaps the most widely used obscene gesture found on earth; and, is generally understood nearly everywhere. That is nearly everywhere, not truly everywhere. Where it is not understood, that ignorance could by exploited.

Commander Lloyd M. "Pete" Bucher was Captain of the US Navy surveillance ship *USS Pueblo*. While monitoring North Korean activities, the ship and crew were seized on January 23, 1968 by the Democratic People's Republic of Korea (North Korea). Over the next eleven months, the Koreans staged numerous crew photos for propaganda use.

Although physically forced to participate in these photos, the crew wanted to find a way to let the outside world know what they really thought. As a result, the crew often displayed what they told their captors was the "Hawai'ian good luck sign" – a raised middle finger – to signal that they were healthy and being treated well

[photo, left, is one of these propaganda photos]. After their release in December, the crew reported that when the Koreans discovered the actual meaning of the gesture (reportedly reading it in *Time* magazine) they were severely beaten as punishment.

Similarly, ignorance of a language can cause severe difficulties with homophonic words (those that sound alike when spoken, but have different meanings).

Chinese & Japanese – Traditionally, the Chinese character for 4 (*si*) sounds very much like the word for death. This is also true in Japanese (*shi*). As a result, East Asian hotels often do not have a fourth floor; who would want to stay on the "death floor"? Again, in Chinese, the number eight sounds very much like "get rich quick". In Japanese, the words for bridge and chopsticks sound alike. There are literally hundreds of examples in Japanese, Chinese and Korean; and, these often either become an embarrassment or are used to one's advantage (particularly in advertising). It is reported that certain automobile license plates in China with unique homophonic misinterpretations can actually be more expensive than the car they identify.

When Commander Bucher (the USS Pueblo again) was told that his crew would be shot one at a time in front of him unless he "confessed" to being a spy, Bucher yielded. But, since none of the

Koreans spoke English well enough to write the confession, they had Bucher write it himself. They then checked it word by word to make sure they understood what he had written before they broadcast him reading the statement (left).

In this "confession", Commander Bucher told the whole world what the wishes of his crew were: "We paean the North Korean state. We paean their great leader Kim Il Sung." Since the definition of paean is "to honor", his captors approved the text, and left this in the broadcast. However, it is homophonic with "pee on" – an American idiom meaning "to urinate on" – that the Koreans did not recognize. When they learned of the deception from the Soviet Union after the broadcast, they were <u>not</u> happy.

Americans often assume – sometimes incorrectly – that a holiday is very special. They may even believe that it is nearly sacred. Although Americans ridicule the rigid line formations that were used by the British during the American Revolution, the American view of holidays is perhaps just as rigid and traditional. There are several instances in history where this cultural ignorance has been utilized to America's detriment.

Tet Offensive – On the Vietnamese *Tết Nguyên Đán* holiday, both North and South publicly announced on national radio a two day cease fire to celebrate the holiday (31 January 1968). However, during the early morning of the first day of the holiday, the Viet Cong [National Liberation Front for South Viet Nam] launched raids; on the second morning of the holiday, more than 80,000 Viet Cong troops attacked more than 100 South Vietnamese cities and towns.

Pearl Harbor – On Sunday, 7 December 1941, Japan launched Operation Z against the American naval forces in dock at Pearl Harbor, Hawai'i. A total of 2,402 were killed, and another 1,282 were wounded. The Americans were surprised; it was Sunday.

Greenland – Cultural ignorance can also be used to aid in advertising. In a classic example from history, Erik Thorvaldsson (better known by his nickname, Eric the Red) had been exiled from Iceland for 3 years for murder (His father, Thorvald Asvaldsson, had been exiled earlier from Norway to Iceland for "some killings"). Upon expulsion, Erik sailed northwest to find a reputed land, and settled there. According to an ancient Norse saga, he named it Greenland to make it sound as attractive as possible to potential colonists. It worked.

Conference Table Seating – Cultural preferences have a great deal to do with where we tend to sit at a table, and this can be effectively utilized by someone aware of another's preferences. For example, in the United States, the end of a rectangular table is called the *head of the table*, and sitting there is viewed as carrying some level of prestige. At Thanksgiving or some other auspicious meal, the "head of the family" is usually seated in that place. At negotiations, that is often reserved for the CEO or company president.

By contrast, many Asian cultures consider that to be an inferior position, and ascribe prestige to the center of the long side of the table. During peace negotiations to end the Korean War, the shape of the table and where everybody sat had to be negotiated before the issue of peace talks could even begin (*i.e.* they had to negotiate the negotiations). In business, there have been instances of American negotiators deliberately sitting in the center on both sides of the table, leaving only the ends open for their vendors.* This disrupts the protocol for some Asian companies (such as in India and Korea), and can actually provide a slight negotiating edge.

These have all been examples or illustrations of where Applied Cultural Anthropology has been utilized. There were commercial examples, personal examples, and political examples. In all cases, the advantages of having a solid cross-cultural knowledge base can be dramatic. The final three chapters (Chapters 26, 27 and 28) will look at how this impacts those areas with the greatest potential for either good or disaster:

- ◆ Cross-cultural Conflict Resolution;

- ◆ Commercial Applied Anthropology; and,

- ◆ Non-commercial Applied Anthropology.

---

* The author pleads guilty to having used this ploy on more than one occasion.

Chapter 26
Cross-cultural Conflict Resolution

Conflict Resolution

In the anthology <u>Applied Cross-Cultural Psychology</u>* the issues surrounding dispute processing were reviewed by Kwok Leung, Ph.D. and Pei–Guan Wu. At the time of publication, Dr. Leung was on the psychology faculty at Chinese University of Hong Kong, and Mr. Wu was pursuing his M.A. in psychology there – having earned his B.A. at Zhongshan University in Guang-zhou, China. Although they don't mention it, many of the ideas they present appear to have their basis in the studies of Drs. Hof-stede and Hall.

Types of Conflict, and their "solution"

Their first observation is that disputes and/or conflicts may be grouped into one of three general categories:

- severe (and massive), such as <u>between</u> countries;
- serious (and large), such as <u>within</u> a nation's structure; or,
- minor (and localized), such as <u>among</u> people.

Not only can conflicts be categorized into these three broad generalizations, but their potential resolution can also be cata-logued under general headings – *i.e.* two. And, in addition, these two general classifications can be sub-divided into numerous specific resolutions. Consider the following possible "resolutions" to conflict:

<u>Violent</u>	<u>Non–violent</u>
◆ war;	◆ negotiation;
◆ armed suppression;	◆ adversarial adjudication;
◆ riots;	◆ inquisitorial adjudication;
◆ armed rebellions;	◆ adversarial arbitration;

---

* Brislin, Richard [editor] (1990). <u>Applied Cross-Cultural Psychology</u> (Thou-sand Oaks, California: SAGE Publications)

- sabotage;
- enforced strikes;
- physical assault;
- random violence.

- inquisitorial arbitration;
- mediation;
- yielding through lumping;
- yielding through avoidance.

Resolution Options

Unfortunately, states often resort to the violent resolution methods (often with devastating effects through loss of life, economic costs, loss of confidence in leaders, declining public morale, *et cetera*). Fortunately, the resolution methods usually employed in individual or localized conflicts most often come from the non–violent list (albeit strikes and sabotage may occasionally occur in certain employment conflicts). Perhaps it might help to provide a clarifying description for each of these methods.

- **negotiation**: two parties attempt to work out their differences with a solution that is acceptable to both parties; this is usually most successful when the differences are subjective in nature (*e.g.* employment contracts, purchases, leases, *et cetera*);

- **adjudication**: a 3rd party acts as the decision maker for the disputing parties – frequently, with some level of legal force behind them, and often with little or no input from the disputees over selection of the 3rd party:

  - **adversarial adjudication**: each party gets to present their own case and to question the other's witnesses and experts (*e.g.* the American court system).

  - **inquisitorial adjudication**: the adjudicator asks the questions and determines when there is sufficient information to make a determination – the involved parties answer questions, but don't ask them (*e.g.* the British court system).

- **arbitration**: nearly identical to adjudication (and also exhibiting both types of process – adversarial and inquisitorial), but with the disputing parties mutually agreeing on the selection of the 3rd party (*e.g. Judge Judy*, and *The People's Court*).

- **mediation**: arbitration where the 3rd party is a facilitator, but has no power to enforce a particular solution (*e.g.* US government intervention in major strikes under the Taft-Hartley Act).

♦ **yielding**: one party simply stops dealing with the dispute (which usually happens in one of two ways):

- **lumping** is where one party no longer presses their case, but also does not acknowledge that they were wrong in any way (within the court system, this is often referred to as pleading *nolo contendere* – Latin for "I do not wish to contend", and accepting a negative ruling while reserving the right to deny any wrong doing in subsequent actions).

- **avoidance** is where one party attempts to resolve the issue by simply refusing to deal with it, and usually carefully avoids any contact with the other party which might bring up the issue (*e.g.* acquaintances at work or school might employ this "no-answer answer" to avoid a continuing or escalating disagreement).

Which method is preferable ?

Which resolution method is preferable usually depends on the type of conflict involved, the personalities of the parties concerned, and the cultural norms of those parties. As to the type of conflict, there are two basic types of conflict that frequently arise:

- ♦ objective conflicts; and,
- ♦ subjective conflicts.

Objective conflicts are usually over factual issues that are easily verified. These are often called "zero sum" situations: *i.e.* the total involved is inflexible, and one party loses to the same extent that the other party wins. If you were to sue someone for damages to your car as a result of an accident, the actual cost of repairs is easily verified (through estimates, receipts, expert testimony, *et cetera*). Once a decision is reached, if you are victorious, you win to the exact same degree that your adversary loses: if you can prove damages of $2,600 and your adversary is found responsible, they lose the same $2,600 that you win – hence the term *zero sum* ($2,600 – $2,600 = 0).

Subjective conflicts are generally over an interpretation of facts, and are highly culturally impacted. Subjective situations may be flexible, and often enable a so–called "win–win" solution. Suppose that you want to install an in-ground swimming pool, but your neighbor has a 3-year old who loves to play in water, but can't swim. They object to your pool plans. However, your neighbor wants to purchase a 120 pound Rottweiler, which is the same breed that bit you as a child, and of which you have been deathly afraid ever since. Installing a six-foot stockade fence between your property and the neighbor (and sharing the cost of installation) might be a "win-win" outcome. You win (no unexpectedly meeting the Rottie), and your neighbor wins (no unplanned toddler pool parties requiring EMTs).

Which resolution method is employed – out of all those listed above – is most often dependent on the nature of the conflict as well as the underlying personalities and culture of the parties. This is because it is culture that often defines the probable relationship of the parties. This relationship between the parties may be classified as *simplex* or *multiplex*.

Simplex relationships are those that are based on a single interest (*e.g.* doctor–patient, employer–employee, teacher–student). Disagreements, disputes, or conflicts may easily arise in this type of relationship without having any adverse impact on any other part of either party's life (*e.g.* you can fight with your dentist over his bill without it impacting your work, your home life, your family, *et cetera*). These conflicts usually respond best to adjudication, arbitration, yielding, or (in some cases) even one of the more violent solutions

Multiplex relationships are those that are based on multiple interests (*e.g.* having your nephew as your patient, working for your mother, or living next door to your teacher). Disputes which arise in this type of relationship can be tangled: if you were to live next door to your teacher, a nasty argument over damages caused when a tree falls during a storm could conceivably color the academic relationship as well as the financial issue around the tree. These conflicts generally respond better to mediation or negotiation (which more readily leave any other mutual interests intact).

In general terms, the likelihood of having simplex or multiplex relationships tends to be culturally biased. Some societies exhibit simplex relationships most often, while others more often exhibit multiplex relationships. Although this may seem strange at first, it appears to correlate very well to the individualism index developed by Hofstede. This can be seen by the fact that the United States (with an Individualism index in the 90s – the highest Dr. Hofstede found anywhere in the world) has 18 lawyers per 10,000 citizens (also the highest in the world). Germany and France (with I factors in the 60s & 70s) have 4 and 2 lawyers per 10,000 citizens, respectively. Japan (in the 40s) has only one, and China and India (in the 40s or below) have even fewer than that. In other words, the more individualistic a society, the more likely simplex relationships are the norm, and therefore more often a societal preference for conflict adjudication or arbitration (which require lawyers).

Multiplex relationships correlate inversely to Dr. Hofstede's Individualism factor: the less individualistic a culture tends to be (*i.e.* more collective), the greater the complexity of relationships. Everyone knows, interacts with, or is related to, everyone else in a massive *social network*; and, this tends to be a fertile source for multiplex relationships.

Other applications

In addition to conflict resolution, there are also some "related" areas in which the basic tools developed by Hall or Hofstede may be useful in the local environment. Among these are *persuasion, confrontation, negotiation,* and so-called *opening gambits.* These are "related" in that they may often serve to preclude an ensuing conflict.

Persuasion

There are 3 common *styles* of persuasion: Δ rational;
Δ affective; and,
Δ ideological.

Rational persuasion relies on facts and what is commonly known as "Aristotelian logic". This form of persuasion is almost always the form preferred by North Americans and West Europeans. In fact, this is so commonly used in these areas that it is often assumed to be the *only* valid form of persuasion.

> Example: You are discussing an upcoming national election with your neighbor. He believes you should vote for the Re-

publican; you believe he should vote for the Democrat. He points out that every major war in the 20th century was begun under a Democrat (WW1, WW2, Korea, Viet Nam), Democrats tax working people to fund social give-away programs, and Democrats support 'baby killers' by protecting abortion rights. You counter that Republicans have eroded Constitutional freedoms (Patriot Act), blurred the line between church and state, crossed moral lines in office, and are always pushing to repeal socially responsible court decisions (*e.g.* Roe *v.* Wade or Obamacare). Both of you are trying to persuade the other by presenting facts (or at least your perception of them).

Affective persuasion relies predominantly on feelings and emotional issues. It relies on the good will, empathy, and shared emotional experiences of the parties involved. This is often the method of choice for Middle Easterners and Asians.

> Example: Your brother had a serious motorcycle accident, and is at the hospital on life support; your parents are both deceased, and you are his only remaining relative. The doctors have diagnosed severe brain damage; and, if he ever comes out of his coma (which is unlikely), he will probably have the IQ of a zucchini. You want to 'pull the plug'; the hospital wants to continue life support. In court, you appeal to the judge to "have a heart", that your brother would never have wanted to live that way, and ask the judge how he would act if it were his loved one that was a virtual vegetable and that was only alive as a result of a machine. In this instance, you are trying to persuade the court by getting them to share feelings with you – to empathize with your situation.

Ideological persuasion relies on certain axiomatic principles that are "non–negotiable". This does not generally have any 'regional' adherents, but is often the persuasive form utilized by socialist, religious and moral issue (*e.g.* environmental) driven entities.

> Example: The Republic of Malta is one of the most densely populated countries on earth, with well over 3,000 people per square mile. The soil is poor, and Malta traditionally imports virtually all of its food. To pay for this food, they have developed several major industries. Nevertheless, the average annual Maltese income is less than half that of the United States, and is dropping. Clearly, their increasing population is a social time bomb, and population control is a critical social issue. But, 98% of the Maltese are practicing Roman Catholics, and the church forbids both abortion and birth control. Cultur-

ally, nutritionally, and economically, this is equivalent to a gradual, prolonged suicide. But, the Vatican maintains its position on religious and scriptural grounds. These are non-negotiable, ideological, and axiomatic. It is simply not an option to disagree with this type of persuasion.

Confrontation

The 2 most common forms of confrontation are:

- direct, straight–on, "in your face", (often heated); and,
- quiet, polite, reserved, and restrained.

In general, the nature and degree of social relationship shared by the parties may vary widely. These are typically either:

- avoided (after all, confrontation is not meant to be pleasant); or,
- fostered (on the theory that you always get further if you "know your opposition").

Americans have a tendency to most often prefer avoidance in business and interpersonal situations, and open confrontation for civil and criminal situations (*i.e.* "laying it all on the table"). The selection of one form *versus* the other usually depends on whether the parties each believe that there is some advantage to be gained by having established a certain rapport with their adversary, or whether they feel they are totally justified and there is nothing to be gained by establishing that rapport.

> Example: You are arrested and charged with Second Degree Murder. The District Attorney has called a meeting with you and your lawyer. Clearly, this is a confrontational situation. If the DA's case is rock solid (you really did it, and they have your fingerprints, DNA, and an eye-witness), the DA, at the meeting (*i.e.* confrontation), will not allow a relationship or bond to develop with either you or your lawyer. After all, the law is clear, and they're almost certainly going to win.

> If, on the other hand, the DA's case is weak (they think you did it, but there is only minimal circumstantial evidence, no witness, and they can't figure out your motive), the DA will likely try to establish some level of relationship with you. Why? Because the next step is to try to get you to "plead out"; and, that would be facilitated by you treating each other with civility.

Negotiation

Many Asian cultures make extensive use of silence. This often, but not always, indicates a negative response. Americans generally abhor silence, and usually attempt to fill it. The result is a dramatic reduction in most Americans' ability to negotiate in this type of cross-cultural situation – as they frequently interrupt the natural *synchrony* (to use Hall's term) that enables clear communication to exist between the negotiators.

> Example: You represent a major communications company that is considering sourcing development of some of your next generation software to a firm in India. During the negotiations with their people, you propose a flat rate of $22,000 per year for any of their software developers with a BS in Computer Science, and $24,000 per year for designers with advanced degrees. The president of their firm looks pensive, and begins to walk around the room "thinking". For nearly a full minute, not a word is said by anyone. You offer that, if that is too little for them to be able to operate and still make a profit, you would consider going to $24,000 and $27,000. After a few second, he nods and you agree on arrangements. Over the 3-year life of the contract, he provides you with an average of 40 developers and 12 designers. The increase (because you could not tolerate that prolonged silence in the process) cost your company $348,000. In fact, what he had been thinking about was the broadband system he would finally be able to afford to implement in his factory as a result of your generous proposal. If you had waited, he would have agreed to your original offer.

Similarly, extended eye contact and *facial gazing* is often employed by North and South Americans. This happens only rarely with Asians, where extended eye contact is considered overtly aggressive. This becomes a clear case of misreading body language (PAGE) when Americans or Canadians practice this in the presence of Chinese or Japanese clients. This *faux pas* can be deadly to a successful negotiation.

> Example: You participate as the American representative to an international conference on global warming being held in Beijing. While the Chinese representative is making her opening remarks to the delegates, you try to indicate your interest and attention by maintaining constant eye contact with her – demonstrating that you are totally focused on what it is she has to say. For the following three days of the conference, she is

noticeably cool toward you: whatever you propose, she opposes; whenever you speak, she seems distracted; and, socially, at meals and other gatherings, she avoids you as if you were terminally contagious. The problem? She considered your initial eye contact to be a sign not of interest, but an indication that you had come to the conference assuming that there were going to be "sides" – good guys and bad – and, that you and she were clearly not on the same side. To her, the incessant eye contact was blatantly aggressive and hostile.

Opening Gambits

Finally, we need to consider *opening gambits*. Webster defines a *gambit* as either a chess move, "a remark intended to open a conversation", or "a carefully considered strategy". In virtually every form of conflict resolution, it is thus used to describe one's "initial position" – strategically weighed and selected for effect. How we decide what that initial position will be is actually highly culturally sensitive.

Typically, there are three distinct openings available to us:

- ◆ *extreme* – in which you begin by asking for the world, but knowing in advance that you will then be required to negotiate down in order to come to an agreeable resolution;
- ◆ *moderate* – in which you start by "asking for too much" and then "planting your feet", but not doing it so firmly or resolutely that you alienate the other party (knowing that you will, in all likelihood, be forced to compromise somewhat from this initial position); and,
- ◆ *final* – in which you begin by proposing your "best and final" offer, and from which you adamantly refuse to either compromise or waver.

How are these culturally sensitive?

Extreme openings are usually employed – in business, interpersonal situations, or political negotiations – by Africans, Middle Easterners, Central and South Americans, and Asians (*e.g.* Chinese, Russians, Saudis, Nigerians, Mexicans, Brazilians, Tanzanians, Japanese, Guatemalans, Syrians, Thais, and Indians).

Moderate openings most frequently occur amongst North Americans and West Europeans (*e.g.* Canadians, Americans, French, Germans, Swedes, Danes, and Belgians).

> [Note: some of the southern Europeans fall somewhere in the middle between an *extreme opening* and a *moderate opening*. Examples in this group would include the Spanish, Italians, Greeks, and Portuguese.]

Final openings are relatively rare on the international scene, but are not at all uncommon on either a business or interpersonal level (*e.g.* advertising a car, selling a house, setting prices in a clothing store, discussing the construction of a fence with a neighbor, *et cetera*).

> <u>Example</u>: You decide to purchase a new leather coat while you are on vacation. You go out window shopping to see what you can find – planning to spend no more than $150. If you are at home in the United States, you might go to Macy's Department Store® to see what they have. If you find one for $150, great; but, if you find one for $250, you will need to either spend more than you had wanted, or go without, knowing Macy's <u>will</u> let you walk out the door without the coat.
>
> If, however, you were to find the coat listed in a classified ad in the newspaper, or at a shop in one of the many weekend flea markets, you might find it listed at $180; but, the seller would likely accept (or, at the very least, consider) $150.
>
> Finally, however, if you were in Nogales, México, you might wander into one of the many shops that open up onto the main street and find just the coat you want – for $500. You begin by offering them $20, and then negotiate until you reach a price at which they will sell and you are willing to buy (if they started at $500, this point will likely be somewhere between $50 and $100).
>
> The first example is a business illustration of a *final* opening gambit; the middle example is of a *moderate* opening gambit; and, the last example is of an *extreme* opening gambit.

Bottom Line

"All very interesting," you say, "but what good is all this?" It may, in fact, be of little value to you; but, it could save you time, money, or even a fist to the face. The key point is, whenever you find yourself in a conflict or negotiation, to *know your opponent*, and make sure that you know what it is that they are doing. Only a fool would agree to an initial offer from either an Arab or Japanese; paying full price at a flea market is wasteful; but, trying to cut an initial French proposal by 90% would be just as foolish.

So, what should you do?

- Start by categorizing your differences as severe, serious, or minor.

- Know who it is with whom you are negotiating, debating, or disagreeing.
    - Are they French, Mexican, Chinese, or what?
    - Are they older (*i.e.* steeped in their culture), or younger (*i.e.* more flexible)?
    - Is their interest in the matter personal, commercial, or political?

- Determine which forms of resolution are most likely to be acceptable to everyone.
    - Do you need to step back and let the courts resolve it?
    - Do you need an impartial third party?
    - Should you employ counsel?

- Assess whether your relationship with them is simplex or multiplex.

- Decide if the issue is primarily subjective or objective.
    - Is reaching a "win-win" solution even possible?
    - If you win, will they correspondingly lose?

- Based on culture, decide which of the persuasive arguments is most likely to succeed.
    - Are they fact based (*i.e.* rational argument)?
    - Are they emotionally based (*i.e.* affective argument)?
    - Are they ideologically based (*i.e.* none will work)?

- Again based on culture, decide what type of *opening gambit* you should employ.
    - Ask for the moon and see what you can get?
    - Be reasonable, but leave yourself "wiggle room"?
    - Ask for exactly what you are willing to accept?

- ■ Know how the prevalent culture employs Dr. Hall's communication forms.
  - Do you understand their spatial requirements?
  - Do you know enough about them to work within their context limits?
  - Do you understand their body language?
  - Can you establish a working synchrony with them?
  - Work with this rather than try to overwhelm it.

- ■ Know where the culture falls on Dr. Hofstede's five cultural aspect continua.
  - How individualistic (collectivist) are they?
  - How masculine (feminine) are they?
  - How rooted in time are they?
  - How do they respond to different levels of authority?
  - How comfortable (uncomfortable) are they with the unknown?
  - Again, know what to expect of your adversary, their community, their culture, their social conventions, and use this knowledge to reach a resolution of the issues.

It really doesn't matter whether the issue is interpersonal (*e.g.* a minor "fender bender"), financial (*e.g.* buying a piece of clothing), organizational (*e.g.* enforcing homeowner association rules), or political (*e.g.* settling a border dispute). Knowing how different cultures relate to each of these conflict considerations can make all the difference in the world between a successful resolution and a violent outbreak.

Chapter 27
Commercial Applied Anthropology

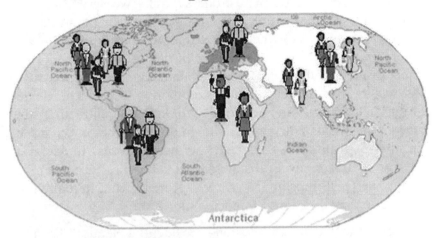

What is *Globalization*?

Many Cultural Anthropology textbooks offer definitions of *globalization* that go something like this:

> "the merger of diverse national markets resulting from international trade agreements and the removal of artificial barriers to the international transport of goods"

or

> "the apperception and bridging of divergent cultural practices to enable transnational business, coöperation, and exchange"

Although these are both true, they are also very "academic" definitions of the term. But, as stated earlier, the role of *applied anthropology* is to make the various sub-fields of anthropology (cultural, archæological, physical and linguistic) *practical* (*i.e.* useful in the real world). It doesn't appear that either of those definitions helps us do that. So, even though they may be correct, it appears that we would benefit from a more user friendly definition for the term. To that end, consider the following definition as an alternative:

> "*Globalization* describes what is happening when we do something – anything – in an environment in which racial, ethnic, national and regional cultural anomalies are set aside for the

'greater good' that can be accomplished by functioning on a global basis."

If you were hoping for a definition that would employ no more than twelve words, each of just one syllable, we apologize; but, the concept isn't that simple. It only gets simpler (as in the first definition given above) when we restrict our consideration to what is more properly known as *commercial globalization*; and, many textbooks do just that. To them, globalization is a synonym for *outsourcing*. It is the relocation of automotive factories to México, the outsourcing of computer jobs to India, the contracting of income tax form data entry by the IRS to the Philippines, the production of American appliances (*e.g.* microwave ovens) in Malaysia, and cost reduction by utilizing foreign labor (*e.g.* producing the majority of The Simpsons TV show in Korea). But, in reality, it is much more than that – much, much, much more.

During the debates for the 2004 presidential election, President George W. Bush took the position that economic globalization was ultimately "good for America"; Senator John F. Kerry took the opposite position that these were practices that needed to be stopped. Surprise; they were both wrong! Unfortunately for politicians, the issue is not that simple; but, politicians generally need to be able to portray the world as being in black and white in order to persuade voters to support them. When it isn't (as in the case of globalization), they are forced to over simplify. So, let's broaden the field (by considering examples of both *commercial globalization* and *non-commercial globalization*) to see what it really includes.

Commercial Globalization

This is essentially what you have when the first definition given above is used: it is the bridging of cultural and national boundaries for the purpose of commercial exploitation. It is extremely broad, but includes such examples as:

Software Development   A recent published statistic stated that over 70% of major US businesses were "outsourcing software work" to other countries (most often India, but also large amounts to Ireland and México). At the same time, it seems that nearly everyone either is, or knows someone, in that field who is looking for work.

Data Entry   Many of the large financial and accounting firms use overseas offices to perform data entry (transferring information from paper forms to data files on computers). Perhaps one of the most surprising instances of this to many is when IRS tax forms are shipped and/or faxed to the Philippines so that Filipino data entry clerks can input the data to files that are then shipped back to the US electronically. Although the author has never seen this acknowledged by the IRS, he personally witnessed the practice at a facility on the outskirts of Manila in the late 1990s. The US classifies this type of work as a semi-skilled job – one for which it would require only minimal training to get an unemployed American qualified.

Manufacturing and Assembly   Automotive and appliance factories have often moved to México and other countries with the finished products shipped back to the United States for sale. At the same time, American manufacturers have closed plants, laid off workers, and made virtual ghost towns out of former industrial areas. Opponents use these facts in an attempt to bring political pressure on companies to stop the practice; but, the fact is that it works in both directions:

- Honda™ builds the Accord® in Marysville, Ohio;

- Toyota™ builds the Camry® in Kentucky;

- Hyundai™ inaugurated a new Sonata® assembly plant in 2005 in Montgomery, Alabama;

- there is a large Mercedes-Benz™ facility in Tuscaloosa, Alabama;

- Mitsubishi™ built an assembly plant in Normal, Illinois;

- Nissan™ recently shipped its seven millionth vehicle from its plant in Smyrna, Tennessee;

- BMW™ builds its Z4 Roadster® and X5® SUV in Spartanburg, South Carolina;

- Toyota™ currently has the production capacity to build well over 1½ million vehicles in the US annually;

- foreign-owned auto plants account for 26% of goods shipped from the state of Alabama;

- there are nearly 25 Japanese, German, and Korean auto factories in the United States; and,

- Toyota™ has a pickup truck factory in Princeton, Indiana, and operates the largest pickup truck assembly facility in the world in San Antonio, Texas.

Decision Factors

What goes into making the decision on whether or not to out-source (commercially globalize)? And, what are the potential consequences for the ultimate decision once it is made? There are many, and it would be impractical to try and list all of them. Some factors are only factors in certain industries, for certain regions, or at certain times; but, even without these, there are a lot of possibilities. Potential decision factors include:

1) **Cost.** Although this is admittedly an important factor, it is certainly not the only factor (although many Americans seem to think that outsourcing is driven solely by greed). In general, it is a fact that non-American laborers, as well as non-American physical resources, usually (not always) cost less than their American counterpart.

2) **Resource Availability.** The outsourcing recipient must possess the necessary resources. It would be foolish to try to outsource IT jobs (*i.e.* information technology) to a tribe in Papua-New Guinea; moving oil production to Switzerland would be idiotic (they don't have any); and, it would likely be inefficient for Hyundai™ to outsource the English translation of their owner's manuals to Paraguay.

3) **Infrastructure.** Manufacturing and Assembly plants need to have a solid road structure, as well as water, sewerage, electricity, *etc.* IT facilities need computers, high-tech conferencing, broad-band network access, *etc.*

4) **Quality.** Sourcing work to someone who will perform the needed tasks at an inferior quality level will ultimately damage the reliability, reputation, marketability, and – inevitably – profits of the company.

5) **Integration.** The new source must be able to integrate seamlessly into the corporate structure. If they remain a disjointed supplier, they will likely require oversight, supervision, and quality checks that cost more than they will save.

6) **Domestic Availability.** Is a comparable resource available domestically? With IT jobs, what is the availability of skilled programmers and designers? What is the prognosis for future availability? Industry experts maintain that the American IT job market expands each year faster than the resource pool (new grads + immigrants – death, retirement, change of careers, emigration, *etc*) by approximately 60,000 people. By contrast, a few regions appear to be increasing their resource pool faster than domestic demand (*e.g.* India).

7) **Developmental Ability.** How difficult would it be to develop the necessary resources? If a 2 week training program would qualify the average unskilled worker to do the task, it may make sense to do that rather than engage in all of the problems typically encountered when outsourcing it. If, however, the required resource is a PhD in biomedical technology with specialization

in the human autoimmune system, it will almost certainly be necessary to go wherever the resource is to get it. For example: we outsource diamond mining to where the diamonds are. As an absurd example: local jewelers couldn't simply decide to mine diamonds in Brevard to keep domestic jobs, for there aren't any to be mined. The mine would produce nothing but sand and coquina, and be an exercise in futility. That resource market could not be developed. successfully

8) **Flexibility**. America is big, and not all resources (physical or human) are readily mobile. Studies have shown that New Englanders are less likely to be willing to relocate to other parts of the country than people from other regions; but, the New England area has a higher concentration of colleges and universities than any other comparable area in the country (including some highly respected institutions, such as Harvard, Yale, MIT, Dartmouth, *etc*). As a result, unemployment among college grads is usually higher in Massachusetts than it is in Texas; and, many grads take what appear to be lesser positions rather than relocate. As a result, having unemployed engineers in Boston may not influence the decision on whether or not to outsource engineering jobs by a company needing engineers in Dallas (a lot of Bostonians would choose flipping burgers over relocation to Texas).

9) **Tax Laws**. Despite efforts of groups such as the WTO (World Trade Organization) to remove barriers to international trade, tax laws around the world generally favor domestic operations. This is the reason it is more than likely that the Toyota or Honda you might buy was manufactured in the United States – these Japanese companies outsourced their manufacturing and assembly to the US primarily to improve their tax situation.

10) **Environmental Laws**. Most of the more industrialized nations have stricter environmental laws than the less developed nations. Companies that worry more about their continued survival than about global environmental impact may decide to move operations rather than to invest heavily in financially non-recoverable, but environmentally friendlier, processes.

11) **Benefits**. Some countries provide significant government assistance in providing health and other benefits, reducing the demand for employers to provide them. This can be a major cost factor for companies in these nations. Examples: the Canadian socialized health care system; the Scandinavian retirement system; and, many of the European public transit systems.

12) **Work Laws**. Child labor laws differ from country to country; so do rules that govern overtime, safety, and other factors. Companies can leverage areas where these are less stringent (*i.e.* where it costs less to comply with them) by moving certain operations to these areas.

So, let's look at one of the examples offered above (the others would be similar).

Software Development

The cost for software engineers in the largest English-speaking country in the world (India) have climbed dramatically in recent years, but are still about half what they are in the United States. So, there are potential cost savings that can be significant if IT work is *globalized* by being outsourced to India.

India currently graduates more IT professionals with 4 year college degrees than any other country on earth; and, Indian technical education is conducted in English, so there is no language barrier. To a much lesser degree, Ireland is in a similar situation.

The Indian infrastructure has essentially all been built since the 1990s; so, it is modern, sophisticated, and technologically superior in many respects to the much older American infrastructure. The Irish infrastructure is more comparable to that in the United States.

As for quality, the first software firm in the world to reach the top level of quality certification under ISO standards was in India (so were the second and third). Typically, Indian software company quality certifications are at a higher level than the American firms that contract with them.

Foreign investment rules were significantly relaxed in India under the Indian administrations of the 1990s. As a result, it is relatively easy for American firms to establish subsidiaries, partnerships or divisions in India – allowing for easy integration into the corporate structure. Ireland has always been this way.

The United States (as mentioned above) does not graduate enough new IT professionals each year to meet the demands of the growing market and retiring workers. India and Ireland, on the other hand, graduate more than they need domestically, so they are looking for work. Assuming you can find employees who <u>want</u> to be retrained, it takes from 3 to 8 years to train unskilled workers to do this type of computer work.

Ford has much of its operation in the so-called *rust belt* (Michigan, Ohio, Illinois, *et cetera*); so does GE, GM, ITT, MicroSoft, and so on. Many American IT professionals, if they are not from these areas, are reluctant to relocate there. The one enticement that might get them to go (money) raises the cost of the product, making it is even less competitive with foreign products than it already is.

IBM wants to sell computers in India; GE wants to sell jet engines in China; Ford wants to sell cars in Thailand; and so on. But, each of these countries is also trying to protect their workers; so, they often take note of the percentage of the production in their country compared to the volume of sales made to their country. In some countries, they legally require that a certain *offset level* be maintained if a company wants to have access to their markets. The US didn't invent the *Buy Domestic* concept. The European Community has a *Buy Euro-*

pean goal that is every bit as strong; and, this is a serious disadvantage to companies such as Oracle™ when they try to compete with the German SAP™ for sales to European customers. In addressing this, GE™ went so far as to form a 50-50 partnership with the French aircraft engine firm SNECMA™ in the 1970s (a company called CFM International™).

On shared products (mostly engines for the Boeing™ 737), SNECMA™ makes roughly half the parts, and GE™ makes the other half. About 20% of the revenue stream goes to cover the cost of assembly and test; and, *Assembly and Test* is done by whoever makes the sale. Under this arrangement, SNECMA™ markets engines to European airlines as predominantly European (because, if they sell it, they do the assembly and test – giving them 60% of the sale); meanwhile, GE™ is marketing to airlines in the US as predominantly American (because if they sell it, GE™ gets the 60%). And, they're both telling the truth! Buried within these costs (at both companies) is the cost of outsourcing software to firms in India [photo: an office for Tata Consultancy Services™, the largest of the software firms in India.]

A number of companies have established *maquilladoras* – companies located in México along the US border. Governed by Mexican laws, the environmental laws are more lax than those in the US. Some of these companies (not all) have taken advantage of this by being ecologically irresponsible.

Canadian companies have successfully marketed software services to the US while offering much less expensive health benefits packages to their employees than their US clients – essentially because the Canadian government has a socialized medical structure where much of the cost of coverage comes out of the government's tax receipts rather than off the companies' bottom line.

Albeit uneducated nine to twelve year old children are generally not qualified to do software development, many companies in the so-called *third world countries* (since the break-up of the Soviet Union, also known as *southern countries*) use these children in unskilled support roles: sweeping floors, making tea, cleaning restrooms, *etc.* Although avoided by the more responsible American companies, it is not uncommon to find children working in support of engineers who are doing outsourced work for American and European firms – thus reducing costs and making their firms more competitive in the US market.

Decision Consequences

Recognizing the consequences – the effects – of economic globalization is often difficult; but, there are some results that occur often enough to be noticeable. A few of these are:

1) **Ecological Impact.** Moving work to an area with less stringent environmental restrictions often leads to decisions or processes that cause significant ecological impact (*e.g.* air pollution, water pollution, land contamination, ozone depletion, global warming, rain forest reduction, natural habitat destruction, *et cetera*).

2) **Unemployment.** When work is moved, the associated jobs (*i.e.* second tier functions) are also no longer available. For example, the foreign-owned auto facilities in the United States employ about 20,000 Americans; but, these plants require parts, resources, services, *et cetera* that account for numerous other jobs. In round numbers, each auto plant job spawns 5-6 other "direct" jobs (typically, suppliers) and 10-12 "indirect" jobs (such as service personnel). So, 20,000 auto plant workers means there are more than 100,000 other American workers who owe their jobs directly to these plants, and about ¼ million who do so indirectly.

   By contrast, not moving the work could also contribute unemployment to the area to which it wasn't moved. For example, if nobody outsourced IT work to India, roughly 750,000 people in India would get laid off (plus all of the ancillary jobs). Although Americans might say "that isn't my problem", it quickly would be if India solved its unemployment problem by expanding Telco™ production and shipping the excess product to the United States for sale. Telco™ (also called *Tata Motors*) is India's largest auto manufacturer, and a Telco™ vehicle would probably sell for roughly half that of a comparable Ford™ or Chevrolet™. Today, they don't sell in Europe or North America; but, that is because they decided it would cost too much to set up the support network. To save several million jobs, however, they might rethink that decision, and perhaps even get government help to do it.

3) **Reduced Exports.** Not only do less developed regions need the work to be able to purchase American goods, many of their governments won't allow the American company to try and sell their goods if they aren't willing to also share in some of the production related tasks. For example, General Electric™ (the world's largest manufacturer of aircraft engines) makes more than half of their sales outside the United States, and has a net trade *surplus*!

4) **Loss of National Technical Hegemony.** Whether or not this is actually a concern, it is often a fear of those opposed to any form of globalization. Basically, it is a fancy way of saying that the US would need to expose other nations to our technical knowledge and secrets in order to be able to get them to do work for us. Ethnic bigotry often cites Japan: assuming that there was no way that Japan could have developed their auto industry if the technology hadn't been stolen from the United States (similar to the theory of the Soviet theft of American nuclear technology). To put this bias into perspective, realize that:

   ♦ India and Pakistan both developed nuclear technology without even a hint of having stolen technology, and North Korea and Iran aren't far behind;

♦ the telephone and television were invented at virtually the same time in both the United States and Russia;

♦ Nazi Germany was, by most estimates, only a few months from completing development of the nuclear bomb when World War II ended in the European theatre; and,

♦ the automobile wasn't invented in the United States, but in Germany – essentially, <u>we</u> stole it.

To be fair, not everyone in the field agrees with this assessment. So, as a counterpoint to this perspective, I recommend the *International Forum on Globalization*, which maintains an excellent collection of reports, essays, statistics and opinions at their web site at http://www.ifg.org. They are an activist organization that opposes economic globalization.

Case Study

If anti-globalization forces were to gain control of our national government, what might happen? First, it is unlikely they could actually do anything. We have come to rely on our government to manage, or control, economic actions of national consequence. But, "the nation-state, it seems, is eroding, or perhaps 'withering away'. The eroding forces are transnational."* So, the government might very well be unable to do much of anything to stop it. Typically, they might try to control outsourcing through tax incentives and disincentives; and, if this failed, they could simply make it illegal by legislatively banning it by US companies. The problem is that it is likely that many of these large companies would just reincorporate outside the United States. At that point, what little influence the government did have would entirely disappear.

In addition, either approach (tax disincentives or legislation banning it) would likely have extreme repercussions for the US, since both approaches would run afoul of the WTO agreements we have signed. But, we could try it if we wanted. Even if the WTO allowed us to go this route (which is extremely improbable), what might happen? Consider a hypothetical situation:

---

* Von Wright, Georg Henrik. "The crisis of social science and the withering away of the nation-state"; *Associations* (1997).

- As was mentioned, General Electric™ has a division that designs and makes Aircraft Engines.
- This division sells nearly 60% of its products outside the United States.
- Perhaps 90% of its customers are in nations with off-sets expecting the purchase of their goods or services before they permit the sale of your goods.
- GE Aviation (this division of GE™) has an annual revenue stream of about $20 billion.
- They have a profit margin of approximately 15%.
- Their cost structure is roughly half fixed (you pay it even if you don't sell anything – buildings, heat, taxes, *etc*) and half variable (which go up and down with sales – labor, materials, *etc*).

What would happen if the US government made it so that GE Aviation could no longer buy software, engineering and materials from other countries (either because it was made illegal or because it was taxed into oblivion)?

- GE Aviation could lose up tp 90% of their foreign sales (60% of their total) – with a resultant net loss of ~54% of division sales and revenue.
- In other words, their $20B business would become a $9.2B business.
- 54% of the employees would be cut (about 20,400 jobs).
- Although the variable costs to GE Aviation would drop by the same ratio, the fixed costs wouldn't change. The result being that costs would drop from $17B per year to $12.4B per year.
- The annual profit to GE™ of $3 billion would become an annual loss of $3.2 billion.
- GE™ would logically decide they could no longer afford to make and service jet engines, and would close the business – dropping another 17,400 jobs.
- The US Department of Defense would now only have a single domestic supplier for military aircraft engines: Pratt & Whitney™. But, P&W™ would be facing the exact same restrictions and United Technologies™ (their parent company) would likely make the same decision. So, there would be no domestic suppliers.
- But, US law requires military suppliers be domestic.

What would be the net effect in the aircraft engine business? A net loss of perhaps 60,000 jobs (between GE™ and P&W™); a loss of foreign income of more than $10 billion dollars annually; a drop in foreign expenditures of perhaps $2 billion annually (what is currently spent off-shore); and, a net increase in the US trade deficit of several billion – from this one business! And, this does not even consider the domestic losses from direct and indirect pro-viders to this industry which, as we saw in the automotive industry, can combine to amount to as much as 15 to 18 times the principal's employment.

This does not mean that all globalization or outsourcing is "good for America". But, it does show one area where it certainly is. The bottom line is that every situation must be evaluated on an individual basis; and, any government intervention (if it worked at all) would likely be damaging. The problem is that this still does-n't answer the question of how to prevent those cases where it is "bad for America", and there really is no simple answer to that. Nobody has a foolproof answer to how we prevent bad decisions without also destroying those that are good for America. Evident-ly, neither do the politicians.

Footnote on Economic Globalization

The example was mentioned of the IRS shipping US tax forms to the Philippines to be entered into electronic files through data entry. Although the author has admittedly never seen this either discussed or documented anyplace, it was during a visit to the Phi-lippines in the late 1990s that a tour of a data entry facility reveal-ed boxes and boxes of paper US tax forms (1040s, *et cetera*). The room held about 16 eight-foot tables in two rows of 8. On each table there were 4 computer keyboards and screens. Data entry clerks were furiously typing these paper forms into their computers to be stored as electronic files so that they could be shipped back to the US (where the IRS could process the now electronic forms). These clerks were being paid *by the keystroke*. Automatic equip-ment measured the number of keystrokes they entered, deducted any backspaces and corrections they had to make, and then calcu-lated their day's pay based on what they did. It was stated that a typical ten hour day for a good clerk could produce a salary of five to six dollars (per day, not per hour). This wasn't some business getting greedy; it was the United States government trying to get work done as inexpensively as possible – under working condi-tions that few Americans would have tolerated (no air condition-ing, and a workroom about 95°F). If you don't approve, e-file!

The author has no way of knowing if this is still an on-going practice, as the IRS has never publicly acknowledged the practice to the best of my knowledge; but, it was in the 1990s, and may very well be continuing to the present.

Chapter 28
Non-commercial Applied Anthropology

NGOs and SGOs

These are both acronyms for things that are actually fairly recent historical developments. NGO stands for *non-governmental organization*, while SGO stands for *supra-governmental organization*. Let's consider, and look at some examples of each.

NGO

A *Non-Governmental Organization* (NGO) is one which is not dependent on, or tied in any way to, a national, state, regional, or local government. Typically, these organizations perform functions which governments either choose not to do, or have some politically vested interest in the outcome which would bias their participation. There are a lot of these organizations, and you can undoubtedly think of examples other than those provided here. However, a few examples may help to clarify what is meant by providing some definition to the term.

- *C.A.R.E.* is an NGO that provides food, shelter and the 'necessities of life' to those in need – regardless of who, or where, they are.

- *The Child Fund* (formerly the *Christian Children's Fund*) specifically targets children in need.

- *International Red Cross* (and its affiliate, *International Red Crescent*) offer medical and physical assistance wherever they see it is needed.

- *Salvation Army* is a largely philanthropic group (although technically a Protestant Christian denomination) that provides human services at little or no cost to those who can least afford to pay for them at times of crisis or emergency.

- *American Friends Service Committee* (an activity of the Religious Society of Friends, or Quakers) is frequently active domestically and internationally in providing needed relief assistance.

- *Greenpeace* is primarily an activist environmental group that frequently takes radical action in an attempt to prevent activities they consider damaging to the environment.

♦ *PETA* is the infamous *animal liberation* group that often resorts to what are generally considered to be extreme actions to protect animals.

♦ *The Great Ape Project* is an international group of academics pursuing a UN declaration defining the great apes (Gorillas, Chimps, Bonobos and Orangutans) as "persons" rather than things, which would provide the apes with protection against captivity, experimentation or torture.

These groups (NGOs) often find themselves at odds with the responsible governing body; but, to their credit, they usually see their mission as morally justified, and tied to the needs of the individual, regardless of political consequences.

♦ *C.A.R.E.* has had problems in Africa where the distribution of food and water has been seen as an aid to rebels or unwanted minority populations in areas of civil unrest. Their convoys have been blocked, attacked, and bombed.

♦ *The Child Fund* has occasionally been an irritant in Indonesia, parts of the Philippines, and other areas where the Christian in their name was equated with the European colonial powers that enslaved them for generations (which prompted their name change).

♦ *International Red Cross* was extremely offensive, and barred from entry, in many parts of the world as a covert evangelical effort – until their Muslim affiliate, the *International Red Crescent*, was established.

♦ *Salvation Army* occasionally finds itself at odds with local governments when they attempt to establish homeless shelters, used needle exchanges, soup kitchens, and the like in neighborhoods where the politically powerful would rather not have them (*e.g.* those in which they reside).

♦ *American Friends Service Committee* was constantly criticized (and threatened) by the American government during the Viet Nam war as being a communist front organization – because they provided drugs, medical supplies and even medical aid to the Viet Cong. Although they offered this assistance to both sides of the conflict, the US typically had all the supplies they needed and declined their assistance. The Viet Cong, however, did not, and readily accepted the help. The US Military thought that allowing a Viet Cong fighter to die slowly in pain from infection would demoralize their troops and hasten their defeat. AFSC aid clearly obstructed that result. At the same time, the Viet Cong thought that using the crosses on Medical Service Corps helmets as targets would demoralize the Americans and make them go home sooner. Bottom line: war is hell; nobody fights nice; and, the combatants in this war (both sides) were especially nasty. The AFSC refused to take sides in what they perceived as a humane crisis, and helped anyone in need. That got them in trouble with the US government.

♦ *Greenpeace* often protests things in ways that irritate national governments – such as oceanic nuclear testing by France (who used frogmen to blow up the Greenpeace ship), Arctic seal cub slaughter in Canada (where they were arrested and detained for 'disturbing the peace'), oil drilling on national park land in the US (which tried to fine the organization into bankruptcy), whale hunting by Japan (which rammed their ship and shot harpoon guns at their inflatable boats), *et cetera*.

♦ *PETA* has raided laboratories of companies that conduct unnecessary animal testing (such as Gillette™, and Proctor and Gamble™), thrown paint at actresses wearing furs, sponsored legislation protecting farm animals from abuse, *et cetera.*.

♦ *The Great Ape Project* has had some success (such as in Spain), and this has only heightened resistance to their efforts by leading pharmaceutical firms and doctors on their payrolls. Their objection is their claim that giving apes terminal illnesses may be the only way to avert some unknown future pandemic,

SGO

By contrast, a *Supra-Governmental Organization* (SGO) is typically one into which multiple governmental bodies have voluntarily entered. Although the best known examples tend to be national governments, there are also state and local examples. Consider the following examples.

♦ *United Nations* is the ultimate SGO, and nearly every national government in the world has applied for membership. In addition to peace keeping efforts, the UN has also spawned numerous subsidiary SGOs for specific concerns: *UNESCO* (education, science, and culture), *UNICEF* (children), *UNRRA* (relief and restoration), *UNHCR* (refugees), *et cetera*.

♦ *World Trade Organization (WTO)* is a voluntary collective of nations that have banded together to establish globally equitable trade practices. They have worked toward the elimination of government market subsidies, oppressive border taxes, import quotas, *et cetera*.

♦ *North Atlantic Treaty Organization (NATO)*, although primarily a mutual defense military alliance, has also become involved in peace keeping missions, cultural exchange programs, and economic disputes.

♦ *European Union (EU)* is the financial and (to a much lesser degree) political union of numerous European states – originally similar in many ways to NAFTA – to leverage their proximity to mutual advantage by allowing for the free movement of people and goods across national borders. Their ultimate goal is a sort of "United States of Europe" (although all members don't share the same enthusiasm for this).

- ◆ *New England College Consortium* is a collective of the public universities in the 6 New England states that allows (among other initiatives) "in-state tuition" at any of their schools for students from any of their states when their home state does not offer their field of study. This allows the member states to avoid redundancy and reduce costs.

Despite the fact that these groups are formed through the voluntary affiliation of member states, they often find themselves at odds with their member governments. Their voluntary participation does not rule out the possibility that the collective association will make decisions, or start programs, to which some members may object (unanimity is rare in SGOs). For example:

- ◆ *United Nations* has had member states temporarily leave the SGO rather than submit to their decisions (*e.g.* when the Soviet Union withdrew over the UN decision to intervene in the conflict which became known as the *Korean War*).

- ◆ *WTO* and other groups have had members who have strongly objected to decisions they felt either disadvantaged their home state, or that appeared to require their relinquishing sovereign rights to this multinational group.

- ◆ *NATO* agreed with the United States regarding Slobodan Milosevic and the Bosnia-Herzegovina phase of the war in Yugoslavia (sending troops and supplies), but disagreed with the US regarding Saddam Hussein and the second Gulf war (war in Iraq) and declined to send either troops or supplies (although a few states broke with the majority and provided limited support to the United States).

- ◆ *European Union (EU)* managed to sort out all of the internal conflicts over finances to achieve monetary union (creating the Euro-based currency system), but has run into major problems in achieving the more difficult political union envisioned through a common European Constitution.

- ◆ *New England College Consortium* has been relatively conflict free, with the exception of budgetary disagreements when smaller states (such as New Hampshire and Vermont) have expected larger states (*e.g.* Massachusetts and Connecticut) to bear more of the burden for certain expensive disciplines.

Consequences of NGOs and SGOs

Although governments enter SGOs voluntarily (almost always because they believe, at least initially, that it is in their best interests), there is a definite relinquishing of independent decision making when that happens. This makes it more likely that the group will introduce and support group cultural norms within the individual states. In many cases, these may displace traditional cultural standards; and, that may become part of a general disintegration of local traditions and practices. NGOs also introduce non-native cultural norms, and this also can lead to a dilution or disintegration of those native, indigenous norms.

Opponents of SGOs usually adopt one of several arguments as their primary objection:

♦ The apparent loss of sovereign rights to a multi-national organization. This is based on a strong sense of nationalism, and the fear that, by agreeing in advance to abide by the SGO's decisions, they are ceding control over their own national interests. To a degree, this is true; but, the question that all nations must address when entering into an SGO is whether the international benefits derived from membership outweigh whatever areas of national sovereignty are, in fact, ceded.

♦ SGOs are essentially multinational committees, and committees of all types are renowned for their ineffectiveness and slowness to act. There is often a concern that those issues of significant concern to one of the member states can be more quickly and effectively addressed by that member state than by an international committee which may have little collective concern over that specific issue.

♦ Many of the national governments around the world (including that of the United States) have significant ties to the commercial sector. If this is a deliberate result (as it appears to be in countries such as Singapore and Switzerland), or if it is unintentional and indirect (*e.g.* as a result of obligations often tied to financial contributions, as often appears to be the case in countries such as the United States, France, and the United Kingdom), these commercial interests (*i.e.* business) appear to exert significant influence. When this gets brought to the international arena through national participation in SGOs, the result could be regional, national, or environmental concessions for the sole benefit of these industries. This is the concern of some groups (*e.g.* the IFG, the *International Forum on Globalization*) with SGOs such as the WTO – which is what led to teach-ins, demonstrations and protests against the WTO's ministerial meetings in Seattle, Washington in late 1999 [right].

♦ Many of the opponents perceive a significant difference in influence between the large, industrialized nations and the small, less developed nations. They fear that these differences only perpetuate the inequities that already exist between these *north* and *south* nations, and that this inevitably reinforces the destitute poverty of the poorest nations.

Sustainability

Sustainability is that state where an entity is able to sustain a certain level of activity indefinitely. For instance, economically, you may personally be able to spend twice your salary next month by simply putting the excess costs on your credit cards; but, this is not a sustainable practice, because you couldn't spend twice your salary every month without going bankrupt. This is just as true for governments as it is for individuals (forget all of the political hype that goes along with it – the United States can not maintain the current annual budget deficit indefinitely; the question is not "can we?", but "how long can we?"; it is ultimately a non-sustainable practice). But, these are both economic activities; and, sustainability applies to all aspects of life – economics, politics, resources, culture, *et cetera*.

Examples of some of these areas of activity include:

♦ ***Economics*** At a cost of six to eight million dollars for each occurrence, Brevard County, Florida can not afford to replenish its beaches every year. The county would go bankrupt. It must either:

- hope that erosion will be less severe in most years than it was in 2004 (with three, major, east-coast hurricanes);

- acquire supplemental external funding sources (such as from the federal government) to off-set local costs;

- learn to accept that a certain level of annual erosion is unfortunate, but unavoidable; or,

- find ways to institute some alternative to preclude future erosion (such as a massive breakwater, or creation of a submerged, artificial reef just off shore).

♦ ***Politics*** The United States can not indefinitely assume the role of the world policeman. The cost to the US is too great in dollars, resources, and human suffering; and, in addition, it tends to alienate traditional friends when we insist that they do things our way rather than us ever doing things their way. This is neither a judgment nor a criticism of recent political decisions, but merely an attempt to show that always demanding that other nations do things our way is ultimately a non-sustainable political position.

♦ ***Resources*** Nobody really has any idea exactly how much petroleum is beneath the world's surface, nor how long it will last at current world consumption rates. But, it is unquestionably a finite amount (since it is the liquefied remains of prehistoric animal and plant products), and the world can not continue to draw from that resource pool indefinitely. Actually, any petroleum usage level is nonsustainable; it is simply a matter of usage level *versus* time of availability. The question is not "will it run out?", but "when will it run out?". If we were to discover that the entire earth is a hollow sphere with a crust 20 miles thick, and completely filled with crude oil (ridiculous, but bear with me), the earth would hold ~5.1 sextillion barrels of oil. At current consumption rates, that would last about 163 billion years. The point is: that's a really big number, but it is still finite. The greater the annual consumption level and the lower the actual amount of oil, the sooner it will no longer be available (or will cost so much to find and recover that it will be virtually unavailable); the lower the annual consumption level, the longer it will last.

♦ ***Culture*** This is primarily where this book gets involved. For that reason, this topic needs to be covered in more depth.

Cultural Sustainability

If you have any interest whatsoever in the beauty and uniqueness of the world's cultures, one of the most depressing parts of traveling the world is this field of *cultural sustainability*. Do you know what is either at, or close by (*i.e.* visible from):
- the entrance gate to the grounds of the *Taj Mahal* in India;
- the observation deck of the *Eiffel Tower* in Paris;
- the *Hermitage Museum* in St. Petersburg, Russia;
- the *Pyramid of the Sun* at Teotihuacán, México City, México;
- the base of a trail up the *Matterhorn* in Zermatt, Switzerland;
- the *Tower of London* in London, England; and,
- *Il Duomo* in Florence, Italy?

Do you know? No? *McDonald's*™ Golden Arches and a *Coca-Cola*™ billboard! Economically, you may simply consider this to be an example of American marketing and know-how; but, culturally, many people consider this to be a travesty. Why? Because it also has a direct (and permanent) impact on the local culture; and, that impact is not usually a positive one.

The first satellite television channel to be beamed into India wasn't *CNN*™, *NBC*™, or the *BBC*™ – it was *MTV*™. This was during the early 1990s. In 1992, traditions were almost always followed in the very conservative culture of India: women going to work or the local temple wearing a sari [left]; men having their lunch sent from home to their work by a complex, but effective, delivery system; *et cetera*. Between 1992 and 1996 was when *McDonald's*™ entered the Indian market with a vengeance, *MTV*™ became available throughout the country, *Coca-Cola*™ purchased the domestic cola company (*Thums Up*®) and then effectively discontinued it in favor of their own product line, and the hottest new store in the country was *Levi Strauss*™. By 1996, common sites in Mumbai included young Indian women in blue jeans riding motorbikes on their way to work, men stopping by local fast food places for lunch, young girls in short, tight dresses heading to the local discotheque (the hottest new night clubs), *et cetera*. To many people, however, the most noticeable (and detrimental) change had to be music: in the mid 1990s, it was announced that tickets would be going on sale for the Mumbai appearance of an American musical group on their world tour. They were going to appear at the local stadium (seating tens of thousands of patrons). The newspaper reported the next day that the concert was a complete sell-out in less than 3 hours! The performers? *The Village People*®.

This may all seem cute or amusing to you; but, to those people who place as much value on their traditional culture as most Indians do, this is catastrophic. They see the problems of the United States (crime, poverty, war, divorce, ...) and are desperately trying to avoid the same things from happening to them; and, they see this mass intrusion of western culture as a severe threat – one that might make that result inevitable.

Believe it or not, one of the most successful recruiting tools for terrorist groups (*e.g.* *al Qaeda*) is the threat of western hegemony. They equate the intrusion of western culture with a deliberate destruction of their local culture, beliefs and families; in other words, they perceive a *Coca-Cola*™ billboard as an act of aggression.

So What Can Be Done ?

What has to happen first is a determination of the cultural sustainability level. In other words, it must be determined just how much that is different can be absorbed and tolerated without destroying that which one already has. A practical reality of what this means can be seen in one very poignant example.

Ossama bin Laden convinced foreign leaders of his Afghani *MAK* to stay with him even after the Soviets had been driven out of Afghanistan by the *mujahideen*. He explained that they needed to remain to fight an even greater enemy – western culture (and the societies that spread it). His reason? He maintained that it was western ideas, western commercialization and western culture that were slowly, inexorably destroying the Islamic world. In other words, western culture was being introduced to the Muslim world at a rate greater than the cultural sustainability level (although it is highly probable that he didn't use those words).

So, one role for cultural anthropologists is to aid:

◆ *businesses* when they intend to implement a level of commercial globalization;

◆ *NGOs* when they act to gain entrance to a particular society (whatever purpose, no matter how noble); and,

◆ *governments* and *government entities* when they join SGOs with any stated objectives (again, regardless of how illustrious or moralistic their motives may be).

Their task is to determine if these goals can be accomplished, and still remain below the cultural sustainability level. Geologists, economists, *et cetera* will help them determine the sustainability level for their fields of expertise; but, the cultural anthropologist is needed to determine the cultural sustainability level. Otherwise, we can be assured that we will be forced to fight this battle again – perhaps at another time, in another place, in another way, with another enemy – but; most assuredly, again.

Appendix A
Reading List

The following books are suggested for students interested in following up on this survey course with more detailed treatments of the subjects covered.

Cows, Pigs, Wars, and Witches Marvin Harris (1989; NewYork: Vintage Books)

Our Kind Marvin Harris (1990; New York: HarperPerennial)

The Third Chimpanzee Jared Diamond (1992; New York: HarperCollins)

Guns, Germs, and Steel Jared Diamond (1997; New York: WW Norton & Company)

The Human Zoo Desmond Morris (1996; New York: Kodansha America)

The Dance of Life Edward T. Hall (1983; New York: Anchor Books)

The Hidden Dimension Edward T. Hall (1966; New York: Anchor Books)

Culture's Consequences Geert Hofstede (1984; Newbury Park, California: Sage Publications)

Race and Culture: A World View Thomas Sowell (1994; New York: BasicBooks)

On Human Nature Edward O. Wilson (1978; Cambridge, Massachusetts: Harvard University Press)

Multicultural Manners Norine Dresser (1996; New York: John Wiley and Sons)

Class Paul Fussell (1983; New York: Touchstone Books, a division of Simon and Schuster)

The Art of Crossing Cultures Craig Storti (1990; Yarmouth, Maine: Intercultural Press)

Culture Shock! – a series of nearly 40 books published originally in the 1990s, each focusing on a different regional or national culture (Portland, Oregon: Graphic Arts Center Publishing Company)

Appendix B
Photo Credits

All photographs not otherwise credited were taken on location by the author.

Cover collage [clockwise, from top left]:

Taj Mahal (Agra, India) – an uncharacteristic Islamic mausoleum; Scandinavian 'sod roof' – developed to conserve energy and withstand the extremes of Norwegian weather – typically "trimmed" by putting a goat on the roof; St. Peter's Basilica (Vatican City); Mayan ruins (Tulum, Quintana Roo, México); Dragör Village, Amager Island, Denmark.

Page 16 – Photo of Joseph Henry in the collection of the Smithsonian [public domain]; portrait of Charles Robert Darwin painted in the 1870s [public domain]

Page 17 – 19th century photo of Auguste Comte [copyright expired]

Page 18 – Photo of Herbert Spencer [died 1903] taken *circa* 1880, and is thus in the public domain; photo of William Graham Sumner [died 1910] is in the public domain.

Page 19 – Photo of Franz Boas is from the Canadian Museum of Civilization, who holds the provenance of the photo, and has determined that it is in the public domain; photo of Bronislaw Kasper Malinowski is in the public domain.

Page 21 – Photo of David Émile Durkheim is in the public domain.

Page 33 – African savanna (with the Umbrella Thorn Acacia tree) is property of the University of Tartu, Estonia (a publicly funded entity), and is thus in the public domain.

Page 35 – Photos of spider, snake, and girl at edge of building are all in the public domain.

Page 41 – Winona LaDuke (Promotional photo; no source identified).

Page 68 – Edward Sapir & Benjamin Lee Whorf – public domain (source unknown; if either was ever copyrighted, all rights have expired); Lera Boroditsky photo from Stanford University (public domain).

Page 69 – Dog butcher photo published by Republic of China government agency (public domain).

Page 73 – Dishdasha photo is from Middle East clothing supplier and claims no copyright.

Page 74 – Lederhosen, and Aymara bowler appear in mass advertising with no source credited or copyright claimed.

Page 76 – Dashiki appears in mass advertising with no source credited or copyright claimed.

Page 78 – Photo of Dr Wallace is from the collection of the American Philosophical Society (Philadelphia), and is used in compliance with Fair Use standards.

Page 83 – Hawai'ian hula dancer performing for tourists on Kauai is public domain (property of the governmental Hawai'ian Tourist Bureau)

Page 84 – Photo of Pope Francis I is in the public domain.

Page 88 – These photos are of pieces of Shipibo-Conibo pottery on sale at the *Faith / Works Global Gallery* in Flintstone, Georgia. This gallery, which supports endangered indigenous cultures, adheres to Fair Trade organizational network (FINE) standards. Samples of their offerings can be seen on line at http://faithworksglobalgallery.com

Page 92 – Caricatures of Obama and Hitler are public domain.

Page 93 – This *Three Stooges* image has served as the corporate logo for their work since 1994, and is used in compliance with the Fair Use Standards under US Copyright law; promotional photo of Jerry Lewis (b.1926) is in the public domain.

Page 107 – !Kung hunters (UK public domain].

Page 108 – Métis party [public domain; copyright lapsed]; Kwakiutl fisher [public domain; copyright lapsed].

Page 109 – Mayan homestead, México [photo taken by author]; Amish farm [public domain: State of Indiana]; large American agribusiness [use permitted by license, © 1997 The Learning Company, inc]

Page 110 – Weaver in India [Indian government photo].

Page 115 – George Ripley & Nathaniel Hawthorne [public domain; all copyrights lapsed]

Page 132 – Koko & Kali copyrighted by *MarryYourPet* web site (Fair Use).

Page 135 – Both logos (the *Chicken Ranch Brothel* and *The Resort at Sheri's Ranch*) are commonly used in both advertising and the media, and are thus within the public domain for informational purposes.

Page 153 – Map of Montana by Montana State Gov. (*i.e.* public domain).

Page 162 – Eugene Victor Debs copyright info on page 163.

Page 163 – All presidential candidate photos from US Library of Congress collection (public domain); their photo of Eugene V Debs is credited to a 1912 Presidential campaign pamphlet.

Page 170 – Yakima Elder — photogravure by Edward S. Curtis; originally published by John Andrew & Son (Boston; 1910). Copyright expired; Navaho shaman — photogravure by Edward S. Curtis; originally published by John Andrew & Son (Boston; 1904). Copyright expired.

Page 171 – Hamasaka, a Kwakiutl big man from the turn of the nineteenth century — photogravure by Edward S. Curtis, and originally published by John Andrew & Son (Boston; 1914). Copyright expired.

Page 172 – Chief Joseph of the Nez Perce — photogravure by Edward S. Curtis, and originally published by John Andrew & Son (Boston; 1903).

Page 173 – President Fidel Castro of Cuba. Official government photograph used in compliance with the requirements set forth by the Cuban government; General Secretary Xi Jinping and former Chairman Mao Zedong of China. Official government photographs used in compliance with the requirements set forth by the Chinese government.

Page 174 – President Ronald W. Reagan of the United States. Library of Congress portrait used in compliance with the requirements set forth by the American government.

Page 175 – Queen Elizabeth II of the United Kingdom. Official British government photograph used in compliance with the requirements set forth by the British government.

Page 176 – Photo is public domain photo of a Town Meeting gathering in Plymouth, Massachusetts.

Page 185 – Promotional photo [Public Broadcasting Service]. Public domain.

Page 195 – Photo of WEB DuBois (photographer unidentified) from 1903. Copyright lapsed; Louisiana state photo (public domain) of David Duke from his unsuccessful run for governor.

Page 212 – Both photos are TV promotional photos of respective television programs.

Page 227 – Photos of desk (and mirror image) used under license from *The Learning Company, inc.* (© 1993 21st Century Media).

Page 239 – Photo of Dr Hall by US State Department [public domain].

Pp 243-261 All drawings and pictures on these pages are from licensed Micro-Soft® Clip Art. The graphs are all original to this work.

Page 265 – Dr. Hofstede image published by European Union. Public domain.

Pp 280-288 All of the photos of professors/psychologists on these pages are owned by their respective public institutions, and are thus in the public domain.

Pp 294-295 Photos of George & Barbara Bush, Jacques Chirac, and Mahmoud Ahmadinejad are widely published without provenance or attribution. Photo of Ronald Reagan is a US Library of Congress portrait used in compliance with requirements set forth by the US government. President Obama & Senator McCain public domain. Photo of Bill Clinton unattributed

Pp 296-298 Afghan photo owned by American Services Press Office, and thus public domain. Nixon photo from US Library of Congress, and used in compliance with requirements set forth by the US government. Photo of Kim Young Sam, General Davis & President Clinton property of US State Dept.

Page 300 – Pueblo crew and Bucher photos property of US Defense Dept.

Page 315 – World map is from licensed MicroSoft® Clip Art.

Page 331 – Photo of the WTO Seattle meetings (1999) attributed to Al Crespo, and copyrighted by the University of Washington — use permitted by UWa when credited.

CPSIA information can be obtained at www.ICGtesting.com
Printed in the USA
LVOW12s1838290813

350227LV00016BB/922/P